God, the Teacher of Mankind

A Plain & Comprehensive Explanation of Christian Doctrine

Fr. Michael Muller, C.SS.R.

TO OUR HOLY FATHER, PIUS IX:

WHO defined the dogma of the Immaculate Conception of theVirgin Mother.

Who convened the Ecumenical Council of the Vatican anddefined the dogma of Papal Infallibility.

Who is the Successor of St. Peter, the Supreme Head of theimmortal Church of Christ, the Infallible Teacher and Guardian of the Faith,the Sovereign Judge of Councils, enjoying the Primacy both of honor and ofjurisdiction, the Centre of Christian faith and Unity; the Corner-stone uponwhich the City of God on earth reposes, the Prince of priests, the Pastor ofpastors, the Guide of guides, the cardinal Joint of all Churches, the Keystoneof the Catholic Arch, the impregnable Citadel of the communion of the childrenof God.

Who lives in the hearts of more than two hundred millions ofChristians, and in whose heart the whole world lives:

This work is most reverently dedicated by his unworthypriest and devoted Son in Christ.

~The Author

imprimatur:
THOMAS FOLEY,

FR. MICHAEL MULLER, C.SS.R.

Bishop Administrator of Chicago.

CONTENTS

INTRODUCTORY

OUR Lord and Savior, Jesus Christ, has declared that he was sent by his heavenly Father "to preach the Gospel to the poor." (Luke iv, 18.) "Let us go," said he to his apostles, "into the neighboring towns and cities, that I may preach there also, for to this purpose am I come?' (Mark i, 38.) This mission of Jesus Christ was and is to be continued by his priests: "As the Father hath sent me, I also send you." Immediately before ascending to heaven, he again laid and impressed upon all pastors of souls that most important duty of preaching. His last solemn word to those whom he charged to continue his work is: "All power is given to me in heaven and on earth." The universe belongs to me by the title of heritage. Already heaven is acquired by my labors and sufferings. The earth remains to be conquered, and I rely on you, my apostles, my priests, to subdue it to the empire of my grace: "Go, then, and teach all nations, and preach my Gospel to every creature."

In compliance with this obligation, "the apostles went forth and preached everywhere" (Mark xvi, 20), in the face of all kinds of opposition. "They obeyed God rather than men." (Acts v, 29.) St. Paul would not even allow anyone to regard as a merit his zeal to announce the Gospel. To preach was for him, as he tells us, a necessity. He uttered against himself a kind of anathema if ever he neglected so sacred a duty: "Woe to me if I do not preach the Gospel!" What he most emphatically insisted on, in his Epistles to Timothy and Titus, was the duty of preaching the word of God. He adjures his two disciples, and all pastors of souls, by all that is most holy and awful; he adjures them by the presence of God and of Jesus Christ, by his future coming, by his eternal reign, to preach the word of God, to preach it in season and out of season—to use all persuasive means which the most ardent charity inspires: "I charge thee, before God and Jesus Christ, who shall judge the living and the dead, by his coming and his kingdom, preach the word; be instant in it in season and out of season; reprove, entreat, rebuke in all patience and doctrine." (2 Timothy iv, 1, 2.)

Hence the Church has never ceased to exhort her pastor to discharge most faithfully their duty of preaching the word of God. In one of her canons she ordains that, if a priest having charge of souls should fail to give them the bread of the word of God, he should be himself deprived of the Eucharistic Bread; and if he continue in his criminal silence, he should be suspended. The preaching of the word of God has, indeed, always been the great object of the solicitude of the Church. The Council of Trent arms the bishops with her thunders, and charges them to inflict her censures upon those mute pastors whom the Holy Ghost has branded as "dumb dogs, not able to bark." (Isaiah lvi, 10.) The all-important duty of giving religious instruction was never more binding, and more necessary to be complied with, than it is in our age. What the Fathers of the Council of Trent say on this duty applies more emphatically to our age and country:

"As the preaching of the divine word," they say, "should never be interrupted in the Church of God, so in these our days it becomes necessary to labor, with more than ordinary zeal and piety, to nurture and strengthen the faithful with sound and wholesome doctrine, as with the food of life: for false prophets have gone forth into the world

(1 John iv, 1), with various and strange doctrines (Hebrews xiii, 9), to corrupt the minds of the faithful, of whom the Lord has said: I sent them not, and they ran; I spoke not to them, yet they prophesied. (Jeremiah xxiii, 21.)

"In this unholy work their impiety, versed as it is in all the arts of Satan, has been carried to such extremes, that it would seem almost impossible to confine it within bounds; and did we not rely on the splendid promises of the Savior, who declared that he had built his Church on so solid a foundation that the gates of hell should never prevail against it (Matthew xvi, 18), we should be filled with most alarming apprehensions, lest, beset on every side by such a host of enemies, assailed by so many and such formidable engines, the Church of God should, in these days, fall beneath their combined efforts. Not to mention those illustrious states which heretofore professed, in piety and holiness, the Catholic faith, transmitted to them by their ancestors, but are now gone astray, wandering from the paths of truth, and openly declaring that their best claims of piety are founded on a total abandonment of the faith of their fathers,—there is no region however remote, no place however securely guarded, no corner of the Christian republic, into which this pestilence has not sought secretly to insinuate itself. Those who proposed to themselves to corrupt the minds of the faithful, aware that they could not hold immediate personal intercourse with all, and thus pour into their ears their poisoned doctrines, by adopting a different plan, disseminated error and impiety more easily and extensively. Besides those voluminous works by which they sought the subversion of the Catholic faith, they also composed innumerable smaller books, which, veiling their errors under the semblance of piety, deceived with incredible facility the simple and the incautious?' (Preface to the Catechism of the Council of Trent.) "It is, indeed, incumbent upon the ministers of the altar," says our Holy Father, Pius IX, in his address of 1877 to the Lenten preachers, "to lift up their voices as loudly as possible, to save society from the abyss?' "Cry," says the Lord to the pastor, "cease not, lift up thy voice like a trumpet, and show my people their wicked doings." (Isaiah lviii, 1.) "If thou dost not speak to warn the wicked man from his way, that wicked man shall die in his iniquity, but I will require his blood at thy hand." (Ezechiel xxxiii, 8.)

Now, if we see such perverse zeal in the ministers of Satan to spread, by all possible means, their doctrines, with what zeal should not Christians, and especially Christian pastors, be moved to make known the Gospel truths, and repeat them in season and out of season, regardless of fastidious minds which are displeased when a priest repeats a thing, and goes over old but necessary ground again! "What!" exclaims St. Francis de Sales, "what! is it not necessary, in working iron, to heat it over and over again, and in painting, to touch and retouch the canvas repeatedly? How much more necessary, then, is it to repeat the same thing again and again, to imprint eternal truths on hardened intellects, and on hearts confirmed in evil! St. John the Baptist and the Apostle St. Paul spoke from out their prison walls; St. Peter spoke freely and forcibly before the ancients, saying that it is better to obey God than men; and the Apostle St. Andrew spoke from the wood of the cross."

When in Japan, St. Francis Xavier climbed mountains, and exposed himself to innumerable dangers, to seek out those wretched barbarians in the caverns where they dwelt like wild beasts, and to instruct them in the truths of salvation. St. Francis de Sales, in the hope of converting the heretics of the province of Chablais, risked his life by crossing a river everyday for a year, on his hands and knees, upon a frozen beam, that he might reach, and preach to, those stubborn men. St. Fidelis, to bring the heretics of a certain place back to God, cheerfully offered up his life for their salvation.

Being desirous to contribute my mite to meet and withstand the mischievous activity of the emissaries of Satan, to rear the edifice of Christian knowledge on its own secure and solid basis,—the true teaching of its divinely commissioned teachers,—to afford the great mass of the faithful a fixed standard of Christian belief, easily accessible to their understanding, and to pastors a practical form of religious instruction; to supply a pure and ever-flowing fountain of living waters, to refresh and strengthen at once the pastor and the flock, I have, to the best of my ability, arranged in order, expounded, I trust with clearness, and sustained by argument, the entire economy of religion, comprehending, as it does, the whole substance of doctrinal and practical religion. As, in imparting instruction of any sort, the method and manner of communicating it are of considerable importance, so, in conveying instruction to the people, the method and manner should be deemed of the greatest moment. As to the method, I have been guided by St. Augustine, who says in his treatise, "Manner of Teaching the Ignorant:" "The true method of teaching religion is to begin our account of religion from the creation of all things in a state of perfection, and develop the whole history of Christianity down to the existing period of the Church, and, through the Church, down to our own time;" in other words, to show how Almighty God, from the beginning of the world, has always been the teacher of mankind through those whom he first taught in person, and then commanded to teach others in his name and by his authority. This method I have followed in my series of Catechisms as the one which appeared to me the most natural, the most sensible, the easiest to be understood, the best calculated to establish faith, and the most necessary in our age of unbelief and corruption. What is more natural than to speak first of the divine teacher, and afterward of what he teaches? What more sensible than to rear the sublime edifice of all Christian knowledge on its own secure and solid foundation,—the authority of God in the Church? What is easier to understand than the foundation of our religion, if historically developed? What can be better calculated to inspire faith than the method which shows how God teaches us through those whom he has appointed to teach in his name and by his authority? What, above all, more necessary in these days than to give Catholics and non-Catholics a correct idea of the spirit and essence of our religion, in order to make them love and embrace it with a steadfast faith?

A large portion of the Catholic laity are insufficiently instructed in the principles and reasons of their religion, and need a fuller instruction, to detect and resist the wiles of their Protestant and infidel enemies, who lie in wait for their souls. They need the fullest instruction, not only in Catholic dogmas and practices, but in the great underlying principles which show that the Church is inherent in the divine order of creation and represents it, and that whatever is incompatible with her teaching is incompatible with her divine order, nay, with the Divine Being himself. They need it, to detect and avoid the poisonous breath of the world. The Church is not the one religious body among many; it is the only religious body. As without God there is nothing, so without the Church, or outside of her, there is no religion, no spiritual life. All the pretended religions outside of her are shams, at best have no basis, stand on nothing, and are nothing, and can give no life or support to the soul, but leave it out of the divine order to drop into hell. Catholics need to know this, and to understand well how their religion is based on divine revelation, and its guardianship on earth invested in a body of men presided over by an infallible guide, divinely commissioned to teach all men, authoritatively and infallibly, all its sacred and immutable truths,—truths which we are consequently bound in conscience to receive without hesitation. This is the fixed standard of Christian belief; it is the basis upon which all dogmas rest. If this all-important truth is well understood by Catholics, they will not easily be caught in the snares of infidelity.

Nor can a discussion of doctrinal points be of any great use for one who is not thoroughly convinced of the divine authority of the Church. This being once accepted, everything else follows logically, as a matter of course. Hence, f no one should be admitted to the fold of Christ who does not firmly hold and declare that the Roman Catholic Church ruled by the successor of St. Peter is God's sole appointed teacher of the Gospel on earth. However familiar persons outside the fold may be with Catholic doctrines, or however much they may believe in Catholic dogmas, without holding this the fundamental truth of Catholic faith, they should never be allowed to join the Church. The moment it is well understood and firmly believed, there need be but little delay about their abjuration.

As to the manner of presenting the truths of the Catholic religion, it should be, says St. Francis de Sales in his happy way, very charitable. "Mildness," said he, "has more influence over men than severity. We catch more flies with a spoonful of honey than with a barrel of vinegar. Pride is so natural to man, especially to religious sectarians, because they have no infallible authority for their doctrine. Hence every harsh word imbitters their hearts, rather than instructs them. Every time I have made use of cutting language, of reproachful or fault-finding words, I had cause to regret it. If it has been my fortune to win over some heretics" (he is said to have converted seventy-two thousand), "it is to be attributed to the power of gentleness. Charity and sincere affection have more influence over the heart, I will not say than severity, but even more than the force and solidity of argument. Jesus Christ, who might have thought severity necessary toward the stiff-necked Jews, nevertheless taught his divine doctrine with unparalleled amiability and affection. Those who allow their zeal to get the better of their temper when conversing with sinners and non-Catholics, make their cause suspicious. The light of truth, even when presented by a cautious hand, often injures the weak eyes of dissenters; but when it is rash, and regardless of feelings and dispositions, thrust full into the face, it entirely blinds them. Never will truth make its way forward without charity. It is quite different with impiety; for, if we take from the works of Luther, Calvin, Zwinglius, and Beza, all calumnies, abusive language, invectives, mockeries against the pope and the Church, there will be very little left to engage attention?' When attacked by heretics with insolent language, he answered them calmly and mildly, without the least appearance of contention, in accordance with the doctrine of St. Paul: "If any man seems to be contentious, we have no such custom, nor hath the Church of God." (1 Corinthians xi, 16.) He listened most kindly to the objections of heretics or infidels. When it was his turn to speak, instead of wasting his time in disputing with them, he showed them the beauty of the Catholic faith in general; then depicted the impiety of those who had defamed it and showed the deadly effect of Protestantism on the soul, on the heart, on the intellect, on the morals and manners, on politics and society itself. Each truth of the faith, in particular, he presented in its genuine simplicity, and extolled the grace and beauty peculiar to it in such a natural manner, that all hearts were irresistibly won for it. He was most careful never to allow a single word of controversy to fall from his lips. Then he passed on to such pious reflections and thoughts as the subject naturally suggested, and it was in this that his hopes principally rested: "For," said he, "my experience of thirty years' ministry has taught me that man is converted only when his heart is touched, his conscience awakened from its slumbers, convicted of sin, startled with a fearful looking forward to judgment to come, and made to cry out, 'Men, brethren, what shall we do to be saved?' When we present moral truths with piety and zeal, they are like so many burning coals thrown into the faces of our hearers, who are edified by this manner of speaking, for they have a conscience, though it may have long slept, and in the interior of their souls a witness for the truth of what we tell them, though they may have long smothered his voice. When, assisted by the grace of God, we have awakened conscience from its slumbers, and made the voice of reason, which has been silenced, as it was amid pagan abominations, audible in the depths of the soul, and the man has become alarmed for his safety, he becomes more tractable, and is more easily induced to receive private instruction, in which we may easily brush away the cobweb theories, negations, sophistries and falsehoods of Protestantism, and instruct the neophyte in the glorious and life-giving truths of the Gospel."

As I have endeavored to follow St. Augustine's method, and St. Francis de Sales' manner, of conveying instruction, it is hoped that this work may prove to all a treasure of knowledge, a source of comfort, a monitor of conscience, an arsenal of defense, an antidote to neutralize the poison of false doctrines and principles, a minister to do away with prejudice, remove ignorance, promote piety, and confirm belief.

Should some answers be thought rather long for catechetical instruction, it should be borne in mind that the work is intended not only for the ignorant who are to be catechized, but also for all persons who desire information and instruction; and principally for priests, school-brothers and school-sisters, Sunday-school teachers, and for all those who have charge of the religious training of the young. It is left to the discretion of the teachers to select such portions of the answers as suit best the capacity of those whom they are to instruct.

The "Intermediate No. III Catechism, for High Schools and Academies," published in 1877, forms the text of the work; and the order of questions and answers there observed is preserved throughout.

I have only to add that I submit this, and whatever else I have published, to the better judgment of our bishops, but especially to the Holy See, as I am most desirous to think nothing, to say nothing, to teach nothing, but what is approved of by those to whose charge the sacred deposit of faith has been committed,—those who watch over us, and are to render an account to God for our souls."

THE VALUE AND NECESSITY OF CHRISTIAN DOCTRINE

IF we wish to go to a certain city, the first thing we do is to ask the way that leads to it. If we do not know the way, we can never arrive at that city. So, too, if we wish to go to heaven, we must know the way that leads to it. Now, the way that leads to heaven is the knowing and doing of God's will. But it is God alone who can teach us his will; that is, what he requires us to believe and to do, to be happy with him in heaven. And God himself came and taught us the truths which we must believe, the commandments which we must keep, and the means of grace which we must use to work out our salvation. To know God's will is to know the true religion. This knowledge is, indeed, the greatest of all treasures. Hence the Lord says to all men, through the great prophet Jeremias: "Let not the wise man glory in his wisdom, nor the strong man in his strength, nor the rich man in the abundance of his wealth; but let him that does glory, glory in his knowledge of me," that is, of my will. (Jeremiah ix, 23). It is for the same reason that Jesus

Christ, the Son of God, exhorts all men to "seek first the kingdom of God and his justice" (Matthew iv, 33), and calls those "blessed who hunger and thirst after justice," that is, after the knowledge of God's holy will. "Martha, Martha," he said, "thou art solicitous about, many things. Mary," who is sitting at my feet, to listen to my words, has "chosen the better part."

As the Christian Doctrine, or the way to heaven, has been revealed by God himself, it is clear that all those who do not know the Christian Doctrine, who never attend to its explanation, but remain ignorant of their religious duties during life, cannot know the way to heaven, and, not knowing it, can never reach heaven. They are continually going astray, and taking the wrong road that leads to hell. There is no middle way. If we are not on the road to heaven, we are on the road to hell. We must walk either one way or the other.

How necessary it is, then, to learn the Christian Doctrine! What will become of us, or what sort of life shall we lead hereafter, if we are careless about being instructed in the religion upon which the happiness not only of the present, but also of the future life, depends. Not knowing God, not knowing how to love and serve him, man is like the beasts of the field, nay, inferior to those beasts; for the life of a man without religion is a daily outrage against God, who created man to know him, love him, and serve him in this world. Instead of this, the man without religion becomes the servant of the devil; when he dies, God will not receive him he will cast him off, and the miserable man will fall into the hands of the devil, whom he has served all his life, and who will repay that service by tormenting him forever in hell.

A person who knows and speaks many languages, — French, Latin, German, Italian,—is admired for his learning. But to be fully instructed in our religion is a thousand times more beautiful, and a thousand times more necessary and more useful. It is the knowledge of knowledge, the service of services. It is for this reason that our dear Savior said: "Blessed are they that hear the word of God;" and again: "Blessed are the ears that hear what you hear," i.e., the Christian Doctrine.

If pastors of souls are obliged, under pain of mortal sin, to preach the word of God, the faithful, too, are bound in conscience to go and listen to the word of God.

Does a child not listen to the word of his father? Does a servant not listen to the word of his master? Does a senseless beast not hear the voice of its keeper? And shall a Christian not listen to the word which God, his Creator, speaks to him in sermons and instructions? The Gospel tells us that Jesus Christ went to the temple in Jerusalem, and there listened attentively to the explanation which the Jewish priests gave of the law of God. It was our Lord himself who had given the law, and he knew its meaning. There was, then, no necessity at all for him to listen to the explanation of the law. Yet he went and listened attentively to it, to show us, by his example, the obligation under which we are of listening to the word of God. As, in corporal distempers, a total loss of appetite, which no medicines can restore, forebodes certain decay and death, so, in the spiritual life of the soul, a neglect of, or disrelish for, religious instruction is a most fatal symptom. What hopes can we entertain of a person for whom the science of virtue and of eternal salvation seems to have no interest?

"He who turneth away his ears from hearing the law," says the Holy Ghost,— "his prayers shall be an abomination." (Proverbs xxviii, 9.) St. Paul wrote to the Christians of Rome that "those who did not like to have the knowledge of God, were delivered up by God to a reprobate sense, to do those things that are unbecoming, to become filled with all iniquity, malice, fornication, avarice, wickedness, full of envy, murder, contention, deceit, malignity, hateful to God, proud, haughty, inventors of evil things, disobedient to parents, foolish, dissolute, without affection, without fidelity, without mercy." (Romans i, 28-32.) "He, therefore, who is of God," says Jesus Christ, "heareth the word of God; but he who heareth it not, is not of God." (John viii, 47.) But "whosoever shall not receive you, nor hear your words," says our Lord to the apostles, "going forth out of that house or city, shake off the dust from your feet. Amen I say to you, it shall be more tolerable for the land of Sodom and Gomorrha in the day of judgment, than for that city."

Daily experience, indeed, shows that there is no more effectual means for reclaiming sinners to penance, and rousing the just to greater fervor in the service of God, than an assiduous listening to the word of God. David, learned and enlightened as he was, repented of his crime of adultery only after Nathan the prophet had reproved him for it in the name of God. Josaphat would not have given up his sinful alliance with an idolatrous people, had not Jehu, in the name of God, sharply reprimanded him for it. St. Augustine was very learned; his conscience reproached him sharply for his bad life; he felt very unhappy, and yet for all that, he did not abandon his evil ways until he came to Milan, where he was converted by the sermons and instructions of St. Ambrose. Would that we could see the hearts of many before and after a sermon or an instruction! What a sudden change for the better would be noted in many hearers who went to hear the word of God without thinking in the least of changing their manner of life, but who, after the sermon, left the church with deep sorrow for their sins, and a true purpose of amendment!

The devil knows and fears this power of the word of God. Hence, he makes all possible efforts to prevent both the just and sinners from going to listen to sermons and instructions. He suggests to them: You are sufficiently instructed; you know all your Christian duties;

you have already heard so many sermons, you can hear nothing new; you may read in books all that can be said in sermons, and thus save yourself the fatigue of going to church and staying there so long. If he cannot prevent them at all from going, he does all in his power to distract them during the sermon, or make them feel sleepy, or bored in listening to it, in order thus to prevent them from reaping any benefit from the word of God.

We read in the life of St. Anthony of Padua that the devil often caused disturbance during the sermons of this great saint. One day a noble lady was listening with the greatest attention to his preaching. Suddenly a strange messenger stood before her and gave her a letter which stated that her darling child was dead. Alarmed at this sad news, she rose immediately to leave the church. On beholding this, St. Anthony cried out to her: "Stay, for your child is not dead. That strange messenger is but a disguised devil." Something similar happened during a sermon of St. Vincent Ferrer. One day, whilst he was preaching in a public square, in the presence of a large audience, there were seen three wild horses, running toward the people. Now, when St. Vincent saw that every one of his hearers was greatly frightened, and endeavored to save himself by flight, he cried in a loud voice: "Stay, be not afraid, those horses will not hurt you; they are evil spirits, who have come to prevent you from listening to the word of God, and from being converted?" He then made the sign of the cross over the horses, and the evil spirits suddenly disappeared.

If only all men were so well persuaded of the necessity of hearing the word of God, and of its wholesome effects, as the devil is, the Church would be crowded at every sermon and instruction. Whilst we listen to the word of God, Jesus Christ speaks at the same time to our hearts, since he is then present with us, according to his promise; "Where there are two or three gathered together in my name, there am I in the midst of them." (Matthew xviii, 20.) Whence the same happens to us as befell the two disciples on the road to Emmaus: hearing the words of Christ, they felt their hearts bum within them. (Luke xxiv, 32.)

St. Anthony the hermit, while listening to the words of the holy Gospel, felt himself so powerfully moved, that he forsook the world and all that it had, and withdrew into the wilderness, to live alone with God. The like is also related of St. Nicholas of Tolentino. On hearing a sermon on the vanity of earthly things, he conceived such a disgust for them, that he turned his back upon the world, and hastened to hide himself in a cloister.

Every Christian should, then, always bear in mind what our Lord says in the Gospel: "Not in bread alone doth man live, but in every word that proceedeth from the mouth of God." (Matthew iv, 4.)

God is so pleased with those who eagerly listen to the explanation of the Christian Doctrine, that he often manifests his pleasure by miracles.

One day four thousand, and at another time five thousand people followed our Lord into the wilderness to hear him preach; and as they had nothing to eat, he multiplied a few fishes and loaves of bread in so wonderful a manner that all were filled. St. Gregory relates a remarkable circumstance of a visit which St. Benedict paid to his sister, St. Scholastica. After they had taken supper, Scholastica requested her brother Benedict to delay his return to his monastery until the next day, in order that they might entertain themselves until morning on religious subjects, especially on the happiness of the other life. St. Benedict, unwilling to transgress his rule, told her that he could not pass a night out of his monastery. So he begged her not to insist any longer upon the violation of his rule. When Scholastica saw that her brother was resolved on going home, she laid her hands, joined, upon the table, and her head upon them, and with many tears begged of

Almighty God to prevent her brother from returning home, in order that she might have the pleasure to listen to his spiritual discourse. No sooner had she ended her prayer, than a tremendous storm of rain, thunder, and lightning, began to rage. St. Benedict was forced to remain, in spite of himself. He complained to his sister, saying: "God forgive you, sister! what have you done?" She answered: "I asked of you a favor, and you refused it; I asked it of Almighty God, and he granted it. Go now if you can." So, St. Benedict was obliged to stay with his sister Scholastica until next day. They spent the night in conversation upon spiritual subjects, chiefly on the happiness of the blessed, after which bothmost ardently aspired, and which she went to enjoy four days after.

One day Brother Albert, Provincial of the Franciscans, was to preach in the church of the convent in which St. Catharine of Bologna lived. Catharine had just put the bread in the oven when the bell rang for the sermon. Immediately making the sign of the cross, she said to the bread, "I recommend you to the Lord's care," and thereupon she left the bakehouse, and went into the church. The preacher spoke for five hours: it was more than time enough for the bread to be burned and reduced to cinders; however, when she took it out of the oven, it was of a more beautiful brown than usual. (Life of the Saint, p. 327.)

One day St. Anthony of Padua preached to an immense concourse of people. It was a beautiful summer's day. But scarcely had he began his sermon, when the sky clouded over, and showed every symptom of a very severe storm. The saint went on quietly, notwithstanding the peals of thunder and the flashes of lightning that played among the clouds. The people were frightened, and prepared to seek shelter from the drenching rain that threatened them. When St. Anthony noticed the uneasiness and fright of his auditors, he recollected himself for a moment, and then cried out, in a loud and clear voice: "Christians, fear nothing; do not leave your places, remain where you are, and I promise you, in the name of God, that not one drop of rain shall fall upon you." At these words the people felt easy: no one moved from his place. Wonderful to relate, the rain fell in torrents, the hail devastated the surrounding fields, but the sky above the auditory of St. Anthony remained clear and serene. (Life of St. Anthony of Padua.)

If God, on the one hand, has, by miracles, shown the great pleasure which he takes in those who are eager to hear his word, he also, on the other, has, by frightful punishments, shown his great displeasure with those who do not care for the Christian Doctrine.

St. Francis Regis once gave a great mission in the city of Naples. Several nights before the mission began, he went through the streets to every house. He knocked at each door, as he went along, and when it was opened, he said: "Please, for the love of God, to come to the sermons of the mission. "In a certain house there was living a very wicked woman: her name was Catharine. St. Francis knocked at the door of Catharine's house. When it was opened, he said: "Please, for the love of God, to come and listen to the word of God during the mission." Catharine answered and said: "No, I will not go to the mission." St. Francis left the house and went on his way. The next evening St. Francis came again to Catharine's house and knocked at the door. The door was opened. "How is Catharine?" said St. Francis. "Catharine!" a voice answered, "Catharine is dead!" "Then," said St. Francis, "let us go upstairs, and see the dead body." They all went up to a room where a dead body was laid on a bed. It was the dead body of the wicked Catharine, who only the night before had said, "I will not go to the mission." They stood round the dead body. St. Francis stood in front of it, and looked at the pale, lifeless face. Then he said, with a loud voice, "O Catharine! Catharine! you that would not come to the sermon! tell me,—in the name of God, I command you to tell me,—where are you? where is your soul?" A moment passed, and the corpse opened its mouth. That dead tongue moved, and answered in a frightful voice, "I am in hell."

Catharine had lived many years and committed many dreadful mortal sins. Still our dear Lord did not send her to hell. Then St. Francis came to her from God. He asked her to listen to him and be converted. She answered: "No, I will not listen."

Another terrible example of divine justice occurred in 1745, when St. Alphonsus and his missionary priests were preaching at Foggia. One of the priests went through the public places, to call the people to the church. Happening to pass before a tavern, he invited the drinkers to listen to the word of God and take part in the other exercises of the mission. A tipsy fellow, holding up his glass, called out, "My father, would you like to see what my mission is?" and putting the glass to his lips, he instantly dropped down dead. (Life of St. Alphonsus.)

When we hear the Christian Doctrine explained, we should listen with the intention to profit by it. Our dinner, says Father Furniss, C.SS.R., does us very little good, unless we have an appetite for it. So hearing God's word in a sermon, instruction, or Catechism, or when we read a good book, will do us very little good, unless we have an appetite for it, and a desire to hear it. If we do not feel this desire, we should at least wish for it, and pray for it, and it will be given to us. It is one of the seven gifts of the Holy Ghost, called the gift of "understanding."

Moreover, we must not go to an instruction or sermon through mere curiosity, for example: to hear how somebody preaches, nor only because we are obliged to go, and would be scolded if we were absent. We must go to hear the word of God, because it is able to save our souls. (James i, 21.)

In almost every instruction we hear something recommended which we feel in our hearts just suits us. This is a particular light which God sends from heaven into our hearts. We must then say to ourselves, Now I will begin this very day to do that very thing: "Be ye doers of the word of God, and not hearers only." (James i, 6.)

When we have eaten our dinner, we keep the food in our stomach, to feed our body. So, when we have heard an instruction, we should keep some of it in our mind, to think about afterward, and feed our souls with it. In the stable of Bethlehem there were the infant Jesus, Mary his mother, and Joseph, and the shepherds. When the shepherds were gone away, Mary, who was full of divine wisdom, kept the words of the poor ignorant shepherds in her heart, and thought of them, and meditated on them. (Luke ii.)

Again, when we go to an instruction, we should listen to it with attention. The sin of Adam has made our minds very weak, and we cannot always keep our attention fixed. But we should not be willfully distracted. Sometimes people will listen to any little trifle, instead of listening to an instruction. There was a great city called Athens. The soldiers were on their way to this city to destroy it. The people of the city were in great fear. They met together to think what should be done to save the town. Amongst them was one very wise man, called Demosthenes, who stood up and began to speak to them.The people would not listen to him. They talked and made a great noise, so that he could not be heard. Demosthenes, therefore, gave over speaking, and was silent for a few minutes. Then he cried out to the people that he had a story to tell them. When they heard that he was going to tell them a story, they became very quiet, silent, and attentive. He began his story: "There were two men," he said, "travelling together. One of them had hired an ass from the other. In the middle of the day they stopped. He who had hired the ass got off it. As the sun was very hot, he sat down in the shadow of the ass. 'No,' said the other, 'you shall not sit down in the shadow of my ass. You hired my ass, but you did not hire its shadow.'" When Demosthenes said this, he gave over speaking. The people called out to him to go on. Then he said to them: "My good people, when I speak to you about the shadow of an ass, you listen to me; but when I speak to you about the safety of this town, you do not listen." So, many people will let themselves be distracted by the shadow of a fly, or any little trifle, instead of listening to the word of God. Hear what the fishes did: —

You may have heard how God made an ass speak to Balaam, to tell him that he was doing wrong. (Numbers xii.) He was angry with the ass, and beat its side with a stick, and the Lord opened the mouth of the ass, and it said: "What have I done to thee? Why dost thou strike me?" Something like this happened in times of old: —One day St. Anthony was preaching in a town called Rimini. The people would not listen to him. So he came down from the pulpit, went out of the church, and walked till he came to the sea. He stood on the sand of the sea-shore, and cried out to the fishes in these words: "Fishes of the sea and of the rivers! listen to me. I wanted to preach to the people, but they would not listen to me. So I am going to preach to you." When he had said these words, an immense number of fishes of all sizes came round him, covering all the sea; The little fishes came first. Behind them were the middle-sized fishes, and then the great fishes. They were in good order, and very quiet, with their heads out of the water, turned toward the preacher. Then St. Anthony spoke to them in these words: "Fishes, my little brethren! you ought to thank your Creator for all the good things he has given you. First, there is the beautiful water in which you live,—the sea water as well as the fresh water, whichever you like best. Then there are the holes and caves in the rocks, where you can go when a storm troubles the water. God has made you able to swim, and given you all that you eat, to preserve your lives. In the great Deluge, when it rained on the earth for forty days and forty nights, all the other animals were drowned, and you only were kept alive. When the prophet Jonas was thrown into the sea, God gave him to you, to keep him alive for three days. When the people came to Jesus, and asked him to pay the tribute, you helped him to pay it. You were the food of Jesus Christ, the Son of God, before and after his resurrection! Now, when you remember all these great favors you have received from God, you ought to bless him and thank him, even more than other creatures." When the fishes heard these words, they opened their mouths, and bowed their heads, and showed how great was their desire to thank God. Then St. Anthony, full of joy, cried out: "Blessed be the great God, because the fishes praise him when men refuse to praise him." And now, when the people heard what a wonderful thing had happened to the fishes, they all went out to see it. They knelt down before St. Anthony, and asked him to pardon them, which he did. Then the saint turned round, gave his blessing to the fishes, and sent them all away. So Almighty God worked a miracle, to let us see how much he desires that we should listen to his holy word, which is full of power.(Eccles, viii.)

Let us be at least as good as the fishes and listen to the words of life which Almighty God speaks to us. What we hear in an instruction is not the word of a man, but the word of God. "You received my word," says St. Paul, "not as the word of man, but as it is indeed, the word of God." (1 Thessalonians ii, 13.) We should always have a great love for the Christian Doctrine, and especially for the book which briefly contains the Christian Doctrine in question and answer,—the Catechism. One day St. Teresa was asked by her sisters in religion what book they should often read and study. The great saint answered: "The Catechism; for this is the book which contains and explains the law of God;" that is, it treats, 1, of all the truths we must believe; 2, of the commandments we must keep; and, 3, of the means of grace we must use,—that is, the sacraments and prayer,—in order to be happy with God forever in heaven.

AN EXHORTATION TO SPREAD THE TRUTH

KENELM DIGBY, author of the "Ages of Faith," who did so much to awaken what was afterward the "Oxford Movement," was led to the Catholic faith by means of the barber who used to shave him when he was a member of the university. The barber began to instruct him in the broken conversations occurring from day to day. Then he lent Mr. Digby books, and the barber thus became the teacher of the university man. Let us rest assured that God has given to every good Catholic his vocation, his sphere of action, and holy influence, wherein he can proclaim to those around him that faith which maketh wise unto salvation. Let no one be a coward; let everyone show as much determination and courage for the propagation of the truth as its enemies evince for the spreading of error.

Our women are doing what they can; and if not always as well as we could wish, they deserve our gratitude for their good intentions, and their efforts in a right direction. But our educated laymen are doing comparatively nothing. They seem to be too much engrossed in the business world, in the world of politics, in making or in spending their fortunes, to have time or thought for the interests of their religion. If they had the proper spirit, and were animated by an ardent zeal for religion, they might, working in submission to, and under the direction of, the pastors of the Church, do incalculable good. It is a shame for them that they should allow their proper work to be done by women, or not be done at all.

The motives which should induce us to be zealous in spreading the truth, especially in instructing in it the little ones, are: first, the great interest which Jesus Christ takes in children; second, the more abundant fruits reaped from the care bestowed upon the young, and the great merit which is derived from giving religious instruction.

Children are the most noble part of the flock of Christ. For them he has always shown a particular love and affection. It was to children that he gave the special honor of being the first to shed their blood for his, name's sake. He has held them up to us as a model of humility, which we should imitate: "Unless you become like little children, you shall not enter the kingdom of heaven." He wishes that everyone should hold them in great honor: "See that you despise not one of these little ones." Why not? "For I say to you, that their angels always see the face of my Father who is in heaven." (Matthew xviii, 10.)

He wishes everyone to be on his guard, lest he should scandalize a little child: "He that shall scandalize one of these little ones that believe in me, it were better for him that a millstone should be hanged about his neck, and that he should be drowned in the depth of the sea."(Matthew xviii, 6.) He says the love, attention, and respect paid to a child, is paid to himself: "And Jesus took a child, and said to them: Whosoever shall receive this child in my name, receiveth me." (Luke ix, 48.)

He rebuked those who tried to prevent little children from being presented to him that he might bless them: "And they brought to him young children, that he might touch them. And the disciples rebuked those who brought them; whom, when Jesus saw, he was much displeased, and saith to them: Suffer the little ones to come unto me, and forbid them not: for of such is the kingdom of God. Amen I say to you, whosoever shall not receive the kingdom of God as a little child, shall not enter into it. And embracing them, and laying his hands upon them, he blessed them." (Matthew x, 13-16.)

The Son of God came into the world to redeem all who were lost. But do children profit by his abundant redemption? Do they draw from the source of graces that are open to all? Will they be marked with the seal of divine adoption, and be nourished with his own flesh, in the sacrament of his love? Will they be counted, in the course of their career, among the number of his faithful disciples, or among the enemies of his law? Will they one day be admitted into his kingdom? Will they be excluded? Is heaven or hell to be their lot for all eternity? The fate of children is in the hands of their natural guardians, and of those set over them. If the zeal of those to whom their training and education are confided be not active for their salvation, Jesus will lose in them the fruit of his sufferings and death. How many are deprived forever of the knowledge, sight, and possession of God, because they have not received right religious instruction! And who is answerable to God and humanity for the loss of those souls, unless those whose plain duty it was to impart such instruction?

If the first years of life are pure, they often sanctify all the afterlife; but if the roots of the tree are rotten and dead, the branches will not be healthier. Man will become, in his old age, what religious education made him in his youth: "A young man, according to his way, even when he is old, he will not depart from it." (Proverbs xxii, 6.) All is a snare and seduction for youth. If the fear of God, the horror of evil, the maxims of religion, are not profoundly engraven in the soul, what

is to protect young people from their passions? What can be expected
of a young man who has but seldom heard of the happiness of virtue,
the hopes of the future life, and the blessings or the woes of eternity?
Can we, knowing, as we do, how much Jesus Christ loves children,
resign ourselves to leaving them in their misery? "The kings of the
earth have their favorites," said St. Augustine. The favorites of Jesus
Christ are innocent souls. What is more innocent than the heart of a
child whom baptism has purified from original stain, and who has not,
as yet contracted the stain of actual sin? This heart is the sanctuary of
the Holy Ghost. Who can tell with what delight he makes of his abode!
"My delicts are to be with the children of men." Look at the mothers
who penetrated the crowd that surrounded the Savior, to beg him to
bless their children. They are at first repulsed; but soon after, what is
their joy when they hear the good Master approve their desires, and
justify what a zeal, little enlightened, taxed with indiscretion! Ah, let
us understand the desires of the Son of God. "Suffer," says he to us,
—"suffer little children to come to me." What! You banish those who
are dearest to me? They who resemble them belong to the kingdom
of heaven. If you love me, take care of my sheep, but neglect not my
lambs. "Feed my lambs." "Despise not one of my little ones." "See that
ye condemn not one of these little ones." (Matthew xviii, 10.) I regard,
as done to myself, all that is done to them. O Savior of the world! the
desire to be beloved by thee, and to prove my love for thee, urges me
to devote myself to the thorough instruction of children.

How great and consoling are not the fruits of zeal, when it has
youth for its object! What difficulties do we not encounter, when we
undertake to bring back to God persons advanced in age! Children, on
the contrary, oppose but one obstacle to our zeal, —levity. All we need
with them is patience. Their souls are like a new earth, which waits
only culture to produce four-fold. They are flexible plants, which take

the form and direction given to them. Their hearts, pure as they are from criminal affections, are susceptible of happy impressions and tendencies. They believe in authority. A religious instinct leads them to the priest and the good teacher. They adopt with confidence the faith and the sentiments of those who instruct them. Oh, how easy to soften that age, in speaking of a God who has made himself a child, and who died for us—to awaken the fear of the Lord, compassion for those who suffer, gratitude, divine love, in souls predisposed, by the grace of baptism, to all the Christian virtues! Ask the most zealous pastors, and all will tell you that no part of their ministry is more consoling than that which is exercised for youth, because the fruits are incomparably more abundant. Although all our efforts for the sanctification of an old man, ever unfaithful to his duties, should be crowned with success, they could not help his long life being frightfully void of merits, and a permanent revolt against heaven. But, if there be a child in question, our zeal sanctifies his whole life; we deposit in his soul the germ of all the good that he will do, and we shall participate in all the good works with which his career will be filled. All believers have come out of one single Abraham. From one child well brought up a whole generation of true Christians may proceed. In the little flock that surrounds any one of us, God sees, perhaps, elect souls, regarding whom his Providence has formed great designs, —pious instructors, holy priests, who will carry far the knowledge of his name, and aid him in saving millions of souls. Into what astonishment would the first catechists of a St. Vincent de Paul, of a Francis Xavier, be thrown, had they been told what would become of those children, and what they would one day accomplish! But even supposing that all those confided to us follow the common way, we have in them the surest means of renewing parishes. Today they receive the movement, in fifteen years they will give it. They will transmit good principles, happy inclinations to their own children, who will transmit them in their turn. It is thus that holy traditions are established, and a chain of solid virtues perpetuated: ages will reap what we have sown in a few years. It is by these considerations that the greatest saints and the finest geniuses of Christianity became so much attached to the religious instruction of youth. St. Jerome, St. Gregory, St. Augustine, St. Vincent Ferrer, St. Charles Borromeo, St. Francis de Sales, St. Joseph Calasanctius, Gerson, Bellarmine, Bossuet, Fenelon, M. Olier, etc., believed they could never better employ their time and talents than in consecrating them to the religious instruction of the young. "It is considered honorable and useful to educate the son of a monarch, presumptive heir to his crown.... But the child that I form to virtue, —is he not the child of God, inheritor of the kingdom of heaven?" (Gerson.) Have we always comprehended all the good that we can do to children by our humble functions?

There is, indeed, nothing more honorable, nothing more meritorious, nothing which conducts to higher perfection, than to instruct men, especially children, in their religious duties. This instruction is a royal, apostolic, angelic, and divine function. Royal, because the office of a king is to protect his people from danger. Apostolic, because the Lord commissioned apostles to instruct the nations, and, as St. Jerome says, thus made them the saviors of men. Angelic, because the angelical spirits in heaven enlighten, purify, and perfect each other according to their spheres, and their earthly mission is to labor without ceasing for the salvation of man. St. Peter Chrysologus calls those who instruct others in the way of salvation, "the substitutes of angels." Indeed their mission is divine; they carry on the very work of God himself. Everything that Almighty God has done from the creation of the world, and which he will continue to do to the end, has been, and will be, for the salvation of mankind. For this he sent his Son from heaven, who enlightened the world by his doctrine, and who still continues to instruct his people by his chosen disciples. Those, then, who direct children in the paths to heaven, who allure them from vice, who form them to virtue, may fitly be termed apostles, angels, and saviors. Oh, what glory awaits those who perform the office of angels, and even of God himself, in laboring for the salvation of the souls of children! If this employment is honorable, it is also not less meritorious. What is the religious instruction of children, but conferring on a class of our race, the weakest and most helpless, with inconceivable labor and fatigue, the greatest of all blessings? For, while the physical development of the child advances with age, it is not so with the mental: religious instruction alone can develop the noble faculties of the soul. The soul of a child would, so to speak, continue to live enshrouded in pagan darkness, if the teacher did not impart and infuse the light of truth. All the gold in the world is but dross incomparison with true religious knowledge.

Our Savior says: "Whosoever shall give to drink to one of these little ones, even a cup of cold water, shall not lose his reward." (Matthew x, 42.) May we not infer that those who bestow upon children the treasures of divine knowledge will receive an exceedingly great reward? If God denounces so severely those who scandalize little children, "But he that shall scandalize one of these little ones, it were better for him that a millstone were hanged about his neck, and he were drowned in the depth of the sea" (Matthew xviii, 6), what recompense will those receive who instruct and sanctify them?

Those who give their efforts and means to this object, choose the surest way to appease the anger of God, and to insure their own salvation. They choose the best means of attaining a high degree of perfection. Almighty God gives to each one the graces proper to his vocation. Those, therefore, who are devoted to the religious instruction of children, must rest assured that God will give them extraordinary graces to arrive at perfection. "Whoever," says our Lord, "shall receive one such little child in my name, receiveth me." (Matthew xviii, 5.) Whosoever, then, believes that our Savior will not allow himself to be surpassed in liberality, must also believe that he will bestow his choicest blessings on those who instruct children in the knowledge of God and the love of virtue.

What obligations have not the "angels" of children, "who always see the face of the Father who is in heaven " (Matthew xviii, 10), to pray for these teachers, their dear colleagues and charitable substitutes, who perform their office, and hold their place on earth! "Believe me," said St. Francis de Sales, "the angels of little children love with a special love all those who bring them up in the fear of God, and who plant in their tender souls holy devotion." The children will pray for their teachers, and God can refuse nothing to the prayers of children, and their supplications will ascend with the prayers of the angels.

To be destitute of ardent zeal for the spiritual welfare of children, is to see, with indifferent eyes, the blood of Jesus Christ trodden under foot; it is to see the image and likeness of God lie in the mire, and not care for it; it is to despise the Blessed Trinity: the Father, who created them; the Son, who redeemed them; the Holy Ghost, who sanctified them; it is to belong to that class of shepherds, of whom the Lord commanded Ezechiel to prophesy, as follows: "Son of man, prophesy concerning the shepherds of Israel: prophesy and say to the shepherds: Thus saith the Lord God: Wo to the shepherds of Israel. . . . My flock you did not feed. The weak you have not strengthened; and that which was sick, you have not healed; that which was broken, you have not bound up; and that which was driven away, you have not brought again; neither have you sought that which was lost.... And my sheep were scattered, because there was no shepherd: and they became the prey of all the beasts of the field and were scattered. My sheep have wandered in every mountain, and in every high hill: and there was none, I say, that sought them. Therefore, ye shepherds, hear the word of the Lord: Behold, I myself come upon the shepherds. I will require my flock at their hands." (Ezechiel xxxiv, 2-10.) To be destitute of this zeal for the religious instruction of our children, is to hide the five talents which the Lord has given us, instead of gaining other five talents. Surely the Lord will say: "And the unprofitable servant, cast ye out into the exterior darkness. There shall be weeping and gnashing of teeth." (Matthew xxv, 30.).

What a shame for us to know that the devil, in alliance with the wicked, is at work, day and night, for the ruin and destruction of youth, and to be so little concerned about their eternal loss; just as if what the holy fathers say was not true, that the salvation of one soul is worth more than the whole visible world! When has the price of the souls of little children been lessened? Ah! as long as the price of the blood of Jesus Christ remains of an infinite value, so long the price of souls will remain of a like value! Heaven and earth will pass away, but this truth will not. The devil knows and understands it but too well. He delights in us if we are hirelings, because we have no care for the sheep, and see the wolf coming, and leave the sheep and fly. (John x, 12.)

On the day of judgment, those who have neglected this great duty will be confounded by that poor man of whom we read, in the life of St. Francis de Sales, as follows: "One day, this holy and zealous pastor, on a visit of his diocese, had reached the top of one of those dreadful mountains, overwhelmed with fatigue and cold, his hands and feet completely be numbed, tovisit a single parish in that dreary situation. While he was viewing, with astonishment, those immense blocks of ice, of an uncommon thickness, the inhabitants, who had approached to meet him, related that some days before a shepherd, running after a strayed sheep, had fallen into one of these tremendous precipices. They added that his fate would never have been known if his companion, who was in search of him, had not discovered his hat on the edge of the precipice. The poor man, therefore, imagined that the shepherd might be still relieved, or, if he should have perished, that he might be honored with a Christian burial.

"With this view he descended, by the means of ropes, this icy precipice, whence he was drawn up, pierced through with cold, and holding in his arms his companion, who was dead, and almost frozen into a block of ice. Francis, hearing this account, turned to his attendants, who were disheartened with the extreme fatigues which they had every day to encounter, and availing himself of this circumstance to encourage them, he said: "Some persons imagine that we do too much, and we certainly do far less than these poor people. You have heard in what manner one has lost his life in an attempt to find a strayed animal; and how another has exposed himself to the danger of perishing, in order; to procure for his friend a burial, which, under these circumstances, might have been dispensed with. These examples speak to us in forcible language; by this charity we are confounded, we who perform much less for the salvation of souls entrusted to our care, than those poor people do for the security of animals confided to their charge? Then the holy prelate heaved a deep sigh, saying: 'My God, what a beautiful lesson for bishops and pastors! This poor shepherd has sacrificed his life to save a strayed sheep, and I, alas! have so little zeal for the salvation of souls. The least obstacle suffices to deter me, and makes me calculate every step and trouble. Great God, give me true zeal, and the genuine spirit of a good shepherd! Ah, how many shepherds of souls will not this herdsman judge!" Alas! how just and how true is this remark! If we saw our very enemies surrounded by fire, we would think of means to rescue them from the danger; and now we see thousands of little children, redeemed at the price of the blood of Jesus Christ, on the point of losing their faith, and with it their souls; and shall we be less concerned and less active for these images and likenesses of God, than for their frames, their bodies?

We hear a little child weeping, and we at once try to console it; we hear a little dog whining at the door, and we open it; a poor beggar asks for a piece of bread, and we give it; and we hear the mother of our Catholic children, the Catholic Church, cry in lamentable accents, "Let my little ones have the bread of life,—a thorough religious instruction," and shall we not heed her voice? We hear Jesus Christ cry, "Suffer the little ones to come unto me," by means of solid instruction; we see him weep over Jerusalem, over the loss of so many Catholic children, and we hear him say, "Weep not over me, but for your children;" and shall neither his voice nor his tears make any impression? Shall we say with the man in the Gospel: "Trouble me not, the door (of our heart) is now shut: I cannot rise and give thee"? (Luke xi.) If an ass, says our Lord, fall into a pit, you will pull him out, even on the Sabbath-day; and an innocent soul, nay, thousands of innocent children, fall away from me, and pass over to the army of the apostate angels, and become my and your adversaries-—and will you not care? What cruelty, what hardness of heart, what great impiety! Truly the curses and maledictions of all those who led a bad life, and were damned for want of Christian instruction, which we neglected to give them, will fall upon us! What shall we answer? "And he was silent?" (Matthew xxii.)

THE CHURCH

EXPLANATION OF THE INTRODUCTION TO THE CATECHISM

WHY WE ARE IN THIS WORLD

MANY years ago, a strange sight, a singular contrast, might have been witnessed in the great city of Babylon. Throughout the streets and public places of that populous city the inhabitants were feasting, singing, and rejoicing. Wherever the eye turned, it beheld signs of triumph and gladness. But in the midst of this rejoicing there is one spot where sadness reigns. Upon the banks of Babylon's streams, a vast multitude is assembled. There are strongmen borne down by sorrow; there are feeble women pining away with grief; there are old men whose hoary heads are bowed down with sadness; little children languishing in pain. The faces of all are pallid, their eyes filled with tears. They rest their wearied limbs beneath the shade of the mournful cypress. Their harps, their musical instruments, hang sadly upon the branches of the willow. No hand is raised to touch them, no finger evokes sweet music from their chords. They are silent; they are neglected. There naught is heard save the sighs, the moans, the sobs of the multitude, as they blend confusedly with the murmur, the dash of the stream. Naught is seen save the tears that trickle down from their eyelids, and blend with the flood. Let us draw near those poor unhappy creatures and ask them the cause of their tears. They weep, they are heart-broken, because they are exiles; because they are far, far away from their home, their native land. This alone is the cause of their tears.

How mournful are the days of exile! How sweet it is to breathe once more the air of our native land! The bread of the stranger, like the bread of the wicked, is bitter to the heart. The streams of a foreign land may murmur in soothing tones, but they speak an unknown tongue. The birds in foreign lands may sing sweetly, but they want one melodious note: they do not sing to us of home. The scenes in other lands may be wildly fair, but they have not that sweet, that soothing charm, which endears every object in our native land. We are poor exiles here below, far away from heaven, our true home; we, therefore, constantly suffer the pain of exile. We are never satisfied in this world. We always crave for something more, something higher, something better. Whence is this continual restlessness which haunts us through life, and even pursues us to the grave? It is the homesickness of the soul. It is the soul's craving after a good that is better and more excellent than the soul herself is.

King Solomon, in search of happiness, devoted his mind to the gratification of every desire of his heart: "I said in my heart, I will go, and abound with delights and enjoy good things. I made great works,

I built houses, and planted vineyards. I made gardens and orchards, and set them with trees of all kinds, and I made me ponds of water, to water therewith the wood of the young trees. I got me men-servants and maid-servants, and had a great family: and herds of oxen, and great flocks of sheep, above all that were before me in Jerusalem: I heaped together for myself silver and gold, and the wealth of kings and provinces: I made me singing-men and singing-women, and the delights of the sons of men: cups and vessels to serve to pour out wine: and I surpassed in riches all that were before me in Jerusalem: my wisdom also remained with me. And whatsoever my eyes desired, I refused them not: and I withheld not my heart from enjoying every pleasure: and esteemed this my portion, to make use of my own labor."

After such ample enjoyment of all earthly pleasures, might we not think that Solomon was happy indeed? Nevertheless, he tells us that his heart was not satisfied, and that he found himself more miserable than before. "And when I turned myself," he says, "to all the works which my hands had wrought, and to the labors wherein I had labored in vain, I saw in all things vanity and vexation of mind, and that nothing was lasting under the sun." (Eccles, ii, 11.)

What happened to Solomon happens still, in one shape or form, to every man. Give to the man, whose dream, whose waking thought, day and night, is to grow rich, to live in splendor and luxury; whose life is spent in planning, and thinking, and toiling,—give all the kingdoms of the earth, all the gold of the mountains, all the pearls of the ocean. Give him the desire of his heart. Will he be happy? Will his heart be at rest? He will find that riches are like thorns—that they only wound and burn. They seem sweet, when beheld at a distance; but indulge in them, and at once you taste their bitterness. All the goods and pleasures of this world are like a fisher's hook. The fish is glad while it swallows the bait, and spies not the hook; hut no sooner has the fisherman drawn up his line, than it is tormented within, and soon after comes to destruction from the very bait in which it so much rejoiced. So it is with all those who esteem themselves happy in their temporal possessions. In their comforts and honors they have swallowed a hook. But a time will come when they shall experience the greatness of the torment from which they expected unalloyed delight.

Now, why is it that the riches and pleasures of this world cannot make us happy! It is because the soul was not created by and for them, but by God for himself. It is God who made our heart, and he made it for himself. When man first came forth from the hand of God, his heart turned to God naturally, and he loved creatures only as loving keepsakes of God. But sin and death came into the world. The heart of man was defiled and degraded. He turned away from the pure and holy love of God and sought for love and happiness amid creatures. But our heart seeks in vain among creatures. Our heart is small indeed, but its love is infinite. It can find rest only in God. Whatever we love out of God brings only pain and bitter disappointment.

A thing is made better only by that which is better than the thing itself. Inferior beings can never make superior beings better. The soul, being immortal, is superior to all earthly things. Earthly things, then, cannot make the soul better. God alone is the soul's supreme goodness and happiness. He who possesses God is at rest. The more closely we are united with God in this life, the more contentment of mind, and the greater happiness of soul, shall we enjoy. For this reason, St. Francis of Assisi used to exclaim:

"What to me are earthly treasures,
Flashing gems and gleaming gold?
Gems and gold heal not the heartache,
Gleam in vain where love grows cold.
Thou, dear Lord, art my heart's treasure,

Thy pure love, is all I prize;
Thou hast boundless wealth unfailing
In the home beyond the skies."

St. Teresa, too, would often exclaim:

"Earthly joys soon end in sorrow,
Pleasure brings but grief and pain;
Beauty's bloom is frail and fleeting,
Darkness and the grave remain!
Thy sweet smile, dear Lord, brings gladness,
Thy love's sweetness ne'er can cloy;
Thy immortal, dazzling beauty
Fills all heaven with endless joy."

Certainly, true contentment is that which is found in the Creator, and not that which is found in the creature, — a contentment which no man can take from the soul, and in comparison with which all other joy is sadness, all pleasure sorrow, all sweetness bitter, all beauty ugliness, all delight affliction. Hence it is that St. Augustine, who had tasted all pleasure, exclaimed:

"Earthly fame dies with its echo,
Earthly love but half reveals
Life's dread meaning, man's deep blindness,
And the fate that death conceals.
Thou, dear Lord, art all my glory—
Praised by thee, I shall be blest:
In thy wisdom's cloudless splendors
Shall my yearning soul find rest."

Ah, we are poor exiles here below. God created us, and he created us for himself; and until we can enjoy God, and see him face to face, we can never find true rest. There is always a void in our heart, —a void which cannot be filled by father or mother, by brother or sister, or our dearest friend: it can be filled by God alone. Hence the first and most important question in the Catechism is:

1. What is most necessary for us to know and to believe?

And the answer is: It is most necessary for us to know and to believe that there is a God, who rewards the good and punishes the wicked.

Our future and true home is heaven. To go to heaven, we must know the way that leads to it. Now, the beginning of the way to heaven is the knowledge of God. "For he that cometh to God must believe that he is and is a rewarder of those that seek him." (Hebrews xi, 6.) "And this is life everlasting," says our Savior, "that they may know thee, the only true God, and Jesus Christ, whom thou hast sent." (John xvii, 3.) "Without this faith it is impossible to please God." (Hebrews xi, 6.) But as without this faith man cannot please God and be saved, his Creator has made faith easy for him.

Man is born a believing creature, and cannot, if he would, destroy altogether this noble attribute of his nature. If he is not taught, and will not accept, a belief in the living and uncreated God, he will create and worship some other god in his stead. He cannot rest on mere negation. There never has been a real, absolute unbeliever. All the Gentile nations of the past have been religious people; all the pagan powers of the present are also believers. There never has been a nation without faith, without an altar, without a sacrifice. When Columbus discovered America, he found that the Indians had their creed, though of a vague and simple nature.

They believed in one supreme being inhabiting the sky, who was immortal, almighty, and invisible. Every family had a house set apart, as a temple to this deity. The natives had an idea of a place of reward, to which the spirits of good men repaired after death, where they were reunited to the spirits of those whom they had most loved during life, and to all their ancestors. Here they enjoyed, uninterruptedly and in perfection, those pleasures which constituted their felicity on earth. (Irving's "Columbus," vol.i.) "It is only the fool, the impious man, that says in his heart, there is no God." (Psalm xiii, 1.) He says so "in his heart," says Holy Writ; he says not so in his head, because he knows better. There are moments when, in spite of himself, he returns to better sentiments. Let him be in imminent danger of death, or of a considerable loss of fortune, and how quickly, on such occasions, he lays aside the mask of infidelity! He straightway makes his profession of faith in an Almighty God; he cries out: "Lord! save me; I am perishing; Lord! have mercy on me!" The famous Volney was once on a voyage with some of his friends off the coast of Maryland. All at once a great storm arose, and the little bark, which bore the flower of the unbelievers of both hemispheres, appeared twenty times on the point of being lost. In this imminent danger, everyone began to pray. M. de Volney himself snatched a rosary from a good woman near him, and began to recite Hail Marys with edifying fervor, nor ceased till the danger was over. When the storm had passed, someone said to him, in a tone of good-natured raillery: "My dear sir, it seems to me that you were praying just now. To whom did you address yourself, since you maintain that there is no God?" "Ah, My Friend," replied the philosopher, all ashamed, "one can he a sceptic in his study, but not at sea in a storm." (Noel, "Catech. de Rodez" i, 73.)

A certain innkeeper had learned, in bad company, all sorts of impiety. In his wickedness he even went so far as to say that he did not believe in God. One night he was roused by the cry of "Fire! fire!" His house was on fire. No sooner had he perceived the dreadful havoc going on than he cried, with clasped hands: "My God! O my God! God Almighty! God of grace and mercy! have pity on me and help me!" Here he was suddenly stopped by one of his neighbors: "How! wretch, you have been denying and blaspheming God all the evening, and you would have him come now to your assistance!" (Schmid and Belet, "Cat. Hist.," i, 43.)

From these examples it is clear that the mouth of the infidel belies his own heart. That there is one God, who made all things, and who rewards the good and punishes the wicked, is the first and most necessary truth for us to know and to believe,—a truth to which no reflecting man can shut his mind: it is so deeply impressed on the mind of man, that to banish it altogether is impossible. Hence the Vatican Council says: "Therefore, if anyone shall deny one true God, Creator and Lord of things visible and invisible, or who shall not be ashamed to affirm that, except matter, nothing exists, or shall say that the substance and essence of God and of all things is one and the same, let him be accursed." (Vatic. Coun. I, Canons 1, 2, 3.)

2. Who is good before God?

Those only are good before God who do his holy will.

This God gave us to understand, in express terms, when he said to Adam: "And of the tree of knowledge of good and evil, thou shalt not eat. For, in what day soever thou shalt eat of it, thou shalt die the death."(Genesis ii, 17.)

By this commandment man was clearly given to understand that the continuation of his happiness, for time and eternity, depended upon his obedience to the will of God. To be free from irregular affections and disorderly passions, and to transmit his happiness to his posterity, was entirely his power. If he made a right use of his liberty, by always following the jaw of God; if he preserved unsullied the image and likeness of his Creator and heavenly Father; if, in fine, he made a proper use of the creatures confided to his care, he would receive the crown of life everlasting, as a reward for his fidelity. But if he swerved, even for a moment, from this loving will of God, he would subject himself to the law of God's justice, which would not fail to execute the threatened punishment.

But did God, perhaps, afterward, in consideration of the Redemption, lay down other and easier conditions for man's happiness and salvation? No. He did not change these conditions in the least. Man's happiness still depended on his obedience to the divine will. "Now if thou wilt hear the voice of the Lord thy God, to do and keep all his commandments, the Lord thy God will make thee higher than all the nations of the earth, and all these blessings shall come unto thee, and overtake thee: yet so if thou hear his precepts." (Deuteronomy xxviii, 1, 2.) And our divine Savior says: "You are my friends, if you do the things that I command you." (John xv, 15.) He himself gave the example, having been obedient even unto the death of the cross; thereby teaching all men that their happiness and salvation depend on their constant obedience to the will of their heavenly Father, All men, without exception, were made by God to be happy with him forever in heaven, on this one condition: "He that doth the will of my Father who is in heaven, he shall enter the kingdom of heaven." (Matthew vii, 21.)

3. What will be the reward of the good?

The reward of the good will be to enjoy God forever in heaven, God says: "I am thy reward exceeding great." (Genesis xv, 1.) Even in this life, the reward of those who do the will of God is very great. It was for his obedience to the will of God that Abel obtained from the Lord the testimony that he was just; that Henoch was translated by God, in order that he should not see death. On account of his obedience to the will of God, Noe and his family were saved from the deluge; Abraham became the father of many nations; Joseph was, raised to the highest dignity at the court of the King of Egypt. For the same reason Moses became the great servant, prophet, and lawgiver of the land, and the great worker of miracles with the people of God. Obedience to the will of God was, for the Jews, at all times, an impregnable rampart against all their enemies; it turned a Saul, a persecutor of the Church, into a Paul, the apostle of the Gentiles; it turned the early Christians into martyrs—for martyrdom does not consist in suffering and dying for the faith; it consists, rather, in the conformity of the martyr's will to the divine will, which requires such a kind of death, and not another. Nay, Jesus Christ has declared that it is by obedience to the will of his heavenly Father that everyone becomes his brother, his sister, and even his mother; "Whosoever," he says,"shall do the will of my Father who is in heaven, he is my brother, and sister, and mother." (Matthew xii, 50.)

But in the world to come, in heaven, God is the reward of the obedient, in a manner altogether incomprehensible. He is an infinite ocean of happiness. In this ocean of happiness, the saints live forever and ever. They are penetrated with God's own happiness more than iron can be penetrated with fire; and therefore, "Eye hath not seen, nor ear heard, neither hath it entered into the heart of man, what things God hath prepared for them that love him." (1 Corinthians ii, 9.)

4. What will be the punishment of the wicked?

The wicked will suffer the eternal torments of hell.

Man, when leading a life contrary to God's will, is altogether out of his place. A tool that no longer corresponds to the end for which it was made, is cast away; a wheel that prevents others from working, is taken out and replaced by another; a limb in the body which becomes burdensome, and endangers the functions and life of the others, is cut off and thrown away; a servant whono longer does his master's will, is discharged; a rebellious citizen, violating the laws of the state, is put into prison; a child in unreasonable opposition to his parents is disinherited. Thus, men naturally hate and reject what is unreasonable or useless, or opposed to, and destructive of, good order, whether natural or moral. What is more natural, then, than that the Lord of heaven and earth, the author of good sense and of good order, should bear an implacable hatred to disobedience to his holy will?

The man in opposition to the will of God suffers as many pangs as a limb which has been dislocated; he is continually tormented by evil spirits, who have power over a soul that is out of its proper sphere of action; he is no longer under the protection of God, since he has withdrawn from his will the rule for man's guidance and has voluntarily left his watchful providence. God sent Jonas the prophet to Ninive, and he wished to go to Tarsus. He was buffeted by the tempest, cast into the sea, and swallowed by a monster of the deep! Behold what shall come upon those who abandon God's will, to follow their own passions and inclinations! They shall be tossed, like Jonas, by continual tempests; they will remain like one in a lethargy, in the hold of their vessels, unconscious of sickness or danger, until they perish in the stormy sea, and are swallowed up in hell: "Know thou and see that it is a bitter and fearful thing for thee to have left the Lord thy God, when he desired to lead thee in the way of salvation, and that my fear is not with thee, saith the Lord God of hosts."

God grants to the devil great power over the disobedient. As the Lord permitted a lion to kill a prophet in Juda, in punishment for his disobedience to the voice of the Lord, so he permits the infernal lion to assail the proud and the disobedient everywhere with the vilest temptations, which they feel themselves too weak to resist, and thus fall a prey to his rage. Unless they repent soon, like Jonas, of their sin of idolatry, as it were, they will not be saved, as was the prophet, but will perish in the waves of temptations, and sink into the fathomless abyss of hell. And even in this world sin becomes its own punishment. It destroys health, peace of mind, good-will to men, ruins the body, and tortures the soul; in a word, makes life, that God certainly did not will to be unhappy, the greatest misery to its possessor.

Disobedience to God's will turned the rebellious angels out of heaven; it turned our first patents out of paradise; it made Cain a vagabond and a fugitive on earth; it drowned the human race in the waters of the Deluge; it brought destruction upon the inhabitants of Sodom and Gomorrah. Disobedience to the will of God led the Jews often into captivity; it drowned Pharao and all his host in the Red Sea; it turned Nabuchodonosor into a wild beast; it laid the city of Jerusalem in ashes; it has ruined, and will still ruin, whole nations, empires, and kingdoms; it will finally put an end to the world, when all those who always rebelled against the will of God will, in an instant, be hurled into the everlasting flames of hell by these irresistible words of the Almighty: "Depart from me, ye cursed, into everlasting fire, which was prepared for the devil and his angels," there to obey the laws of God's justice forever.

5. What, then, should be our greatest care in this world?

Our greatest care in this world should be to know and to do the holy will of God.

To serve God according to his will is the principal end of life. To regulate all the affairs of the universe, to be always successful in our undertakings, to heap up the riches of this world, obtain great honors and dignities, extend our possessions beyond bounds, without having rendered our Creator the service, which is due him, is, in the judgment of heaven, to have done nothing, to have lived on earth in vain. On the other hand, to have done nothing for the world, to have always languished on a sick-bed, to have been despised by all our fellow-men, to have lived in some obscure abode, but to have served God throughout, would be enough, because we should have conducted to its last end the only thing for which this present life was given us.

The remembrance of this truth has more than once rendered the wisdom of children superior to that of old men. In a tender age St. Teresa retired into a solitary place, and spoke to herself thus: "Teresa, you will be either eternally happy or eternally unhappy! Choose which you please." Young Stanislas de Kostka gave all to God, and nothing to the world. Being asked why he acted so strangely: "I am not made for this world," he replied, "but for the world to come." Let the world cry out against this truth; let the flesh revolt against it; let all the demons deny and oppose it,—it is and remains an immortal truth, that we were created by God to serve him in this world according to his will, and, as a reward for this service, to possess him forever in the next, or to be punished in hell forever for having refused to obey the Lord. Who but an atheist would dare deny this truth?

GOD THE TEACHER OF MANKIND

§1.—GOD THE FATHER OUR TEACHER

1. Who can teach us how to serve God according to his will?

God alone can teach us his holy will, either by himself, or by those to whom he has made his will known.

Man was created by God for a state of perfection. But man cannot learn even in what that perfection consists, without being taught. This is a plain fact. Everyone bears witness to it. Each one has had a mother who taught him the first elements of instruction. The mother watches over the gradual dawning of reason. She teaches the child how to think, how to reason, by teaching it words and language. She teaches it how to distinguish between right and wrong, to love virtue, and to hate sin, to pray to God. Thus, she implanted in the child's heart the first lessons of religion.

The means, then, by which all of us began to acquireknowledge, and to advance in the way of perfection, was instruction; and the means by which we continue to acquire knowledge and to approach perfection, is also instruction. The powers of reasoning, in a full-grown man, are but the fruit of instruction. He is still the child of men, the child of parents, the child of those who surround him.

Instruction is necessary, to acquire the knowledge of natural truths; but instruction is still more necessary to learn those truths which are supernatural. and lead us to heaven. For, "hardly do we guess aright at things that are upon earth," says Holy Scripture, "and with labor do we find the things that are before us: but the things that are in heaven, who shall search?" (Wisdom ix, 16.) For this reason, St. Paul says: "No man knows what is in man, except the spirit of man; and in like manner no one knows what is of God, unless the spirit of God." (1 Corinthians ii, 11.) The end for which man was created, his everlasting union with God, says the Vatican Council, is far above the human understanding. It was, therefore, necessary that God should make himself known to man, and teach him the end for which he was created, and what he must believe and do, to become worthy of everlasting happiness.

2. How does God make himself known?

God makes himself known: 1, by the visible world; 2, by our conscience; 3, by his word.

Never, from the very beginning of the world, has God the Father, who is most merciful and kind, been wanting to his own. Having created men to know him, he did not leave them in the dark, but on many occasions, and in various ways, manifested himself to them, and pointed out, in a manner suited to the times and circumstances, a sure and direct path to the happiness of heaven. He revealed himself to man by creation. Although hidden in creation, he constantly speaks to man through his great works. An architect speaks to us through a beautiful building, a painter through a painting, a writer through a book. God the Father speaks to men in like manner: "He hath manifested his power and divinity in the creation of the world." (Romans i, 19.) He shows his power in the storm, in the cataract, in the earthquake: "For the invisible things of him are understood by the things that are made." (Romans i, 20.) He makes known his wisdom in the laws by which he governs the boundless universe: "The wisdom of God reaches from end to end mightily and orders all things sweetly." (Wisdom viii, 1.) God the Father shows his beauty in the flower, in the sunbeam, in the many-tinted rainbow; his justice in the punishments which he has inflicted, and continues to inflict, on the wicked; he displays his goodness and liberality in the heavens, which give us light and rain; in the fire, which gives us warmth; in the air, which preserves our life; in the earth, which furnishes us with various kinds of fruit; in the sea, which gives us fish; in the animals, which give us food and clothing: "He left not himself without testimony, doing good from heaven, giving rains and fruitful seasons." (Acts xiv, 16.) Hence: "All men are vain in whom there is not the knowledge of God; and who, by these good things that are seen, could not understand him that is, neither, by attending to the works, have acknowledged who was the workman.... For, if they were able to know so much as to make a judgment of the world, how did they not more easily find the Lord thereof?" (Wisdom xiii, 1, 9; Romans i, 20; Acts xiv, 16.) Therefore, "if anyone shall say that the one true God, our Creator and Lord, cannot be certainly known by the natural light of human reason, through created things, let him be accursed." (Vatic. Counc. II, 1.)

3. How does God make himself known by our conscience?

By our conscience, God reminds us of his justice in rewarding the good and punishing the wicked.

God speaks to man, not only through the visible works of his creation, but also through an inner voice in the soul of man, which is called conscience. For instance, a wicked man wishes to gratify his evil desires, without shame, without remorse. To do this, he tries to get rid of religion. So he says: "There is no God, there is no hell, there is no hereafter; there is only this present life, and all in it is good." But a secret voice and monitor within him speaks, and will not be silenced, and tells him: "There is a just God who will punish you for your crimes in hell; there is a strict and terrible judgment that awaits you after death." This is conscience, that never deserts a man, that cannot be stifled or killed. In the silence of the night, when others are sleeping around him, he cannot sleep. His conscience tortures him. It asks him: "Were you to die in this state this night, what would become of you? It is a terrible thing to fall unprepared into the hands of the living God! Think of eternity! eternity! eternity! Think of the worm that never dies, and the fire that never quenches!" No wonder that men sometimes commit suicide. They cannot bear the remorse of conscience, and so they try to find rest in death. The hell of the wicked begins even in this world, and it continues throughout all eternity in the next. For this reason, St. Paul says: "Tribulation and anguish upon every soul of man that worketh evil." (Romans ii, 9.) Witness Adam, who, after his fall, hid himself from the face of the Lord amidst the trees of paradise." (Genesis iii, 8.) Cain, who, after the murder of his brother Abel, said: "My iniquity is greater than that I may deserve pardon... I shall be a vagabond and a fugitive on the earth. Everyone that find me shall kill me." (Genesis iv, 13, 14.) Henry VIII, King of England, when on his deathbed, took those who stood around his bed for so many monks whom he had cruelly treated. This vision was but his bad conscience tormenting him for his evil deeds.

Another man was a great sinner; but he went to make a good confession. See him after confession: his countenance is radiant with beauty; his step has become again light and elastic, his soul reflects upon his features the holy joy with which it is inebriated; he smiles upon those whom he meets, and everyone sees that he is happy. He trembles now no more when he lifts his eyes to heaven; he hopes, he loves; a supernatural strength vivifies and animates him; he feels himself burning with zeal and energy to do good; a new sun has risen upon his life, and everything in him puts on the freshness of youth. And why? Because his conscience has thrown off a load that bent him to the earth; it tells him that now he is once more the companion of angels; that he has again entered that sweet alliance with God, whom he can now justly call his Father; that he is reinstated in his dignity of a child of God. He is no longer afraid of God's justice, of death and hell. Now this voice of conscience, which fills the souls of the just with peace and happiness, and strikes terror into the souls of the wicked, does not come from ourselves, for it punishes us, and admonishes us to dread an invisible avenger of sin, and to hope in a rewarder of virtue; nor does it come from education, for it is found even in the untutored savage. When Columbus discovered America, the chieftain of an Indian tribe one day said to him: "I am told that thou hast lately come to these lands with a mighty force, and subdued many countries, spreading great fear among the people; but be not, therefore, vainglorious. Know that, according to our belief, the souls of men have two journeys to perform after they have departed from the body: one, to a place dismal and foul, and covered with darkness, prepared for those who have been unjust and cruel to their fellow men; the other, pleasant and full of delight, for such as have promoted peace on earth. If, then, thou art mortal and dost expect to die, and dost believe that each one shall be rewarded according to his deeds, beware that thou wrongfully hurt no man, nor do harm to those who have done no harm to thee." (Irving's "Columbus," chap, v, p. 483.) From this short oration of a heathen it is evident that there is a voice of conscience even in the savage, telling him what is right and wrong, praiseworthy and blameworthy.

Therefore, St. Paul says: "When the Gentiles, who have not the law, do by nature those things that are of the law: these having not the law are a law to themselves, who show the work of the law written in their hearts, their conscience bearing witness to them, and their thoughts between themselves accusing, or also defending one another." (Romans ii, 14, 15.) The voice of conscience is, then, from God, from that holy and just Being who made our heart, and from the beginning stamped upon the soul of man the conception of right and wrong. Therefore, it is said: "In every work of thine regard thy soul in faith;" that is, follow the voice of thy conscience in every work of thine, "for this is the keeping of the commandments." (Ecclesiasticus xxxii, 27.)

4. When did God make himself known by his word?

God made himself known by his word when he spoke to men; 1, in his own person; 2, by the patriarchs and prophets; 3, by his only Son.

God speaks to man by his works; he speaks to him through his conscience. But, to leave man no possible excuse for not arriving at the knowledge of God, he revealed himself to man by his own word. If a friend visits us at night, and finds us sitting in the dark, he speaks, he makes use of words, to show that he is really present. In like manner God, wishing to reveal himself to man sitting in the darkness of this life, addressed words to him. This is the very first article of faith. God spoke to our first parents in the garden of paradise. After God had made man, he appeared to him, and, like a good father, told him who he is, why he had made him, and what he must believe and do to be happy with him in heaven, and escape the everlasting pains of hell. God gave man the light of the Holy Ghost, so that man knew God, knew his holiness and perfections. And he knew himself, and the nature in which God had created him; he knew the law of God, the reward attached to its observance, and the punishment incurred for its transgression.

And how intimate was the intercourse between God and man, even after the fall! Though cast out of Eden, man had not entirely lost one of his greatest privileges: that of hearing the voice of God and receiving direct communication from him. God promised Adam a Redeemer; he taught him to offer sacrifice: that is, the way in which he wished to be worshipped; for the sake of the Redeemer, he promised him, and all his descendants, pardon and grace to merit heaven, by obeying his law.

The familiarity between God and Cain and Abel was quite as close as it was between God and Adam: "The Lord had respect to Abel and his offerings, but to Cain and his offerings he had no respect." (Genesis iv, 4, 5.) The fall did not entirely break that communion. What broke it was the subsequent wickedness of mankind. As in the case of Cain, a willful crime lost him the privilege of that near presence of God which original sin had not. But as yet man had very close and constant intercourse with God, —so constant, that it seems nothing could be done in the way of religious observance without God's direction. Immediately, too, on sacrifice being offered, there was a sensible sign of God's acceptance or otherwise; and a voice from God was so usual that no surprise or change in ordinary feeling was caused by it.

5. Who were the patriarchs?

The patriarchs were those holy men who lived from the time of Adam to that of Moses; as Noe, Abraham, Isaac, Jacob, etc.

The world in which we live is the temple of God. The earth, with its flowers and verdure, forms the carpeted floor. The sky above, with its sun and moon and stars, is the vaulted dome. God created this temple, in order that man might worship him therein, lead a holy life, and gain an eternal reward. But God foresaw, from all eternity, that man would not always live up to this sublime end. God, then, would have been frustrated in his design in creating the world, had he not decreed, from all eternity, to send a Redeemer, through whom he was to be reconciled to man. It was, therefore, principally for the sake of the Redeemer that the world was created, for he was to come into this world for the justification and glorification of man: "Ordo enim natures creatus est et institutus propter ordinem gratia," says St. Thomas Aquinas.

The principal end of the creation of the universe is Christ, that through him man might receive the grace of God here below, and everlasting glory in the world to come. Although it be true that the Redeemer, so to speak, is a certain part of this world, which is prior to him in material existence, yet, if considered in his final end, he is prior to the world. For this reason St. Paul calls our blessed Redeemer, Jesus

Christ, the beginning, the first-born from the dead, that in all things he may hold primacy: "Because in him it hath pleased the Father that all fulness should dwell, and through him to reconcile all things unto himself, making peace through the blood of the cross, both as to things on earth, and the things that are in heaven."(Colossians i, 18-20.)

As God created the world principally for the sake of the Redeemer and his religion, so also for his sake he has preserved the world. To create the world, God used no effort. He simply said, "Be it done," and all was done. But, to redeem the world, God the Father willed that his well-beloved Son should become man, sacrifice wealth, honors, pleasure, and everything that man holds dear; that he should suffer poverty, contempt, persecution, and at last die upon the cross, and pour out every drop of his heart's blood. Now, if God preserves the universe, — the material temple,—for the sake of religion, he must, of course, watch with still greater care over the preservation of his religion. Wishing, then, that the religion revealed to Adam should be handed down uncorrupted to his descendants, and foreseeing, at the same time, that this religion would be abandoned or misinterpreted by many, he provided, from the beginning, a set of holy men called patriarchs, to whom he spoke, and who, in his name, should proclaim the revealed truths, and teach the way of salvation to their fellow-men.

The first who abandoned the truth was Cain, Adam's son. He had sinned in the choice of his offering. God reproached him for it. Instead of being sorry for his sin, he added to it the sin of murder. Soon after, God appeared to him, saying: "Cain, where is thy brother Abel?" "I know nothing of him: am I my brother's keeper?" he impudently replied. "What hast thou done with thy brother?" said the Lord. "Thou hast killed him, thou hast shed his blood upon the ground, and that blood cries to heaven for vengeance. Cursed shalt thou be, a wanderer and a vagabond on the earth." This terrible threat was fulfilled to the letter, and for several hundred years that Cain lived after, he was made to suffer the frightful consequences of his crime.

Cain was now banished from the "face of the Lord," and was condemned to live separate from the members of Adam's family, who feared God. He became the father of a numerous family, who were brought up by him without any fear or knowledge of God. Cain had now become what is called an open infidel or unbeliever and had ceased to teach and practice any religious duty. God, however, provided a believer and faithful bearer of truth in Seth, the next son of Adam, born after the murder of Abel. The whole family of Cain were unbelievers, who never troubled themselves in any way at all about prayer or sacrifice, or the worship of God; while Seth was a just man, who taught all his household to fear God, and to offer the sacrifices which God had commanded. Enos, the son of Seth, was particularly remarkable for having exerted himself to assemble the people for the public worship of God; and so strong was the feeling on the part of the different families of Seth and Cain, that they remained for some centuries separated from one another; the religious families looking upon the impious race as quite unfit company for themselves, and the unbelievers having just the same scorn and contempt for those who feared God as the same kind of persons have still at the present day. Then began the distinctive term, "sons of God," or "people of God." in contradistinction to the term, "sons of men," the descendants of Cain.

In this state of things Almighty God showed mercy to the unbelieving race. He sent Enoch, a very holy man, to warn them that God would come surrounded with all his holy angels, "to execute a judgment against all the blasphemers of his name, for all the hard things they had spoken against him." (Jude xv.) God, however, gave them still a trial of one hundred and twenty years; but seeing that, instead of profiting by his repeated warnings, they grew more wicked, he destroyed them all in the Deluge.

All men, except the pious Noe, with his, family, had perished in the Deluge. Noe taught his children the religion which God had taught man from the beginning. From him all nations carried away with them, into the lands in which they settled, the knowledge of a just God, who rewards the good and punishes the wicked; the hope in a Redeemer to come; the consciousness of right and wrong; the duty of prayer, and of observing the Sabbath with sacrifices. Such was the simple religion which Noe taught his sons; and this would have continued if the nations had preserved what they had learned from Noe. Unhappily, however, they did not preserve it. Though they were too frightened at the memory of the terrible judgment of the Deluge to become infidels like the people before the Deluge, they began to wish for objects of worship which they might be able to see. So they gave themselves up to their evil inclinations, and became, at last, so wicked and foolish, that, instead of worshipping the true God, they worshipped the sun and the moon, certain men and animals, and even idols of gold and silver, and of stone and wood.

At this time, about three hundred and fifty years after the Deluge, God appeared to Abraham, and commanded him to leave his country, his family, his home, in order that he might not be exposed to the society of the wicked, and to induce him to consider the earth as a place of exile, and heaven his true home: to make him the father of a people who were to be different, in manners and religion, from all the other peoples of the earth. Abraham believed and obeyed God, who rewarded him for his submission. By a solemn alliance which he made with him, God promised to take him and his posterity under his protection, to make him the father of a great people, to give him a land that was rich and abundant, called Chanaan, for himself and his posterity. God also promised that the Redeemer, or Messiah, should be born of the race of Abraham. (Genesis xviii.) God swore by himself to the fulfilment of these promises, and appointed circumcision as a mark to distinguish Abraham and his posterity from all the other peoples of the earth. (Genesis xvii, 14; xxii, 16; Hebrews vi. 13; xvi, 17.)

Jacob, the grandson of Abraham, and heir to the promise, went into Egypt, where the covenant, and the warning threats against those who forgot God, began to be fulfilled. The descendants of Abraham became very numerous, but they entirely lost his singleness of mind and purity of heart. God, ever faithful to his warnings, to center in himself the hopes and aspirations of this ungrateful people, caused them to feel the bitterness and ignominy of the degrading bondage of the Egyptians, but at the same time raised up Moses to be among them the representative of the God of Abraham, Isaac and Jacob. Holy Scripture tells us that God also appeared and spoke to many other holy and illustrious men. All these were teachers from God, and therefore infallible in their teaching, "whether men would hear, or whether they would forbear." That patriarchal body, simply because it was God's ordinance, was a guide, sure and infallible, to the extent of the revelation of God, as then made known.

6. How did the patriarchs serve God?

The patriarchs served God: 1, by faith, hope, and charity; 2, by prayer and sacrifice; 3, by doing what they knew to be the will of God.

During their lives the patriarchs gave abundant proofs of their implicit faith in the one living God of their firm hope in the faithfulness of his promises, and of their charity toward God, by scrupulously keeping his commandments, and walking reverently in his sight. Holy Scripture tells us of Henoch: "Henoch walked with God, and was seen no more, because God took him." (Genesis v, 24.)

This "walking with God" is, of course, walking by God's rule or law, leading a practical, highly religious life, and consequently enjoying close communion with God on earth, especially when at prayer, and in the act of offering sacrifice to the Lord. The patriarchs had their places of worship. They did not merely worship God under the vault of heaven; they had places set apart for divine worship. The phrase, "before the Lord," frequently occurs, and in a local sense. Cain and Abel, for instance, brought their offerings to a certain spot; and when Cain was banished, he "went out from the face of the Lord" (Genesis iv, 16), which, in regard to God's omnipresence, would, of course, have been impossible. The reference, therefore, is to a local presence, to a place in which God met his worshippers, and made himself known to them, either by showing his glory, or by an answer to prayer, or by some other sensible means. So, also, in the case of Abraham (Ibid, xviii, 22), after the angel had left him, and gone toward Sodom, "Abraham as yet stood before the Lord."

The patriarchs clearly believed that in certain places, especially consecrated to his service, God would be best propitiated and served.

Then, again, besides places of worship, there were ministers: special persons appointed to officiate, and to offer sacrifice. The instance of Melchizedek shows this: "He was priest of the most high God." And Abraham must have been quite familiar with the character of the priestly office, from the respect which he showed Melchizedek, and his receiving a blessing from him: "Without all contradiction, that which is less is blessed by the greater." (Hebrews vii, 7)

The patriarchs had also their religious ceremonies and customs. There was the consecration ceremonial, by which places were set apart for worship, by anointing them with oil, as at Bethel, when Jacob anointed the pillar, and poured a drink-offering on it.

There was the ceremony of baring the feet on entering consecrated places, which is still observed in the East.

There was also a posture for worship, viz., the bowing down to the ground in prayer before the Lord.

There was a special day for the performance of religious duties: the Sabbath, the institution of which dates from the creation, appearing in the book of Genesis by the mention of weeks. Noe, we are told, "waited yet seven other days," and "sent forth the dove out of the ark," and "he stayed yet other seven days, and he sent forth the dove, which returned not any more unto him." (Genesis viii, 12.) "And before the giving of the ten commandments, it is spoken of as a Sabbath; "And he said to them, this is what the Lord has spoken: Tomorrow is the rest of the Sabbath, sanctified to the Lord." (Exodus xvi, 23.) And in the 27th verse of the same chapter we have that Sabbath spoken of as the seventh day: "And the seventh day came, and some of the people going forth to gather (the manna) found none."

From all this it is clear that the patriarchs were men of a lively and definite faith; men of constant prayer, and models of scrupulous exactitude in complying with all the precepts of the Lord. The God of Abraham, Isaac and Jacob, lives among us Christians with a far more tender love. What a shame and confusion for us, if, on the day of judgment, we shall see that the patriarchs have surpassed us in faith, hope and charity!

7. Who were the prophets?

The prophets were holy men, sent by God to teach especially the Jewish people to observe God's law given through Moses.

About the time of Moses the grossest darkness of understanding, and the most lamentable depravity of the will, prevailed almost over the entire world. All mankind, with the exception of the Jews, had lost the knowledge of God, and the hope in the Redeemer to come; they worshipped creatures, even the very demons, as gods, and the most shameful vices were praised as virtues. From the corrupt mass of mankind, however, God had chosen the Jews, or Israelites, as his people; over them he watched with special care, in order that, through them, all those truths of religion which he had made known to mankind from the beginning, should be preserved, and that from them, at last, should be born one holy enough to be the mother of the Redeemer. God appeared to Moses, his faithful servant, and made him his great lawgiver, prophet, and performer of miracles. Through him he led the Jews out of Egypt, gave them the ten commandments, and instituted the priesthood of Aaron, whose duty it was to preserve and to teach all that God had commanded the Jews to observe in their religion.

From time to time, God sent other prophets for the salvation of his people. These men led holy lives, often secluded from the world, in poverty and hardship. They left their retreats only by the order of God, and to perform the duties of their ministry; they did not flatter kings or princes; they denounced all evildoers, regardless of their smiles or frowns; they sought only God and his holy religion. Good kings honored the prophets as men of God, the wicked persecuted them, and sometimes put them to death, because these holy men freely denounced their evil passions, and reproached them with their crimes. The very celebrated prophets were Elias, Eliseus, Isaias, Jeremias, Ezechiel and Daniel.

8. How did the prophets prove their divine mission?

The prophets proved their divine mission by miracles and prophecies.

When God sent a prophet to his people, he would speak to him in this or a similar manner: "I sanctified thee and made thee a prophet unto the nations ... thou shalt go to all that I shall send thee: and whatsoever I shall command thee, thou shalt speak." (Jeremiah i, 57.) Now, in order to make the people believe the prophets, God wrought through them great miracles.

9. What is a miracle?

A miracle is an extraordinary work, which cannot be done by natural powers, but by the power of God alone.

A miracle is an effect produced contrary to the laws of nature, and which can be performed by the power of God alone. He has established the order of nature. He also can change and suspend that order. He alone can derogate from the laws which he has established for the government of the world, so that, when a miracle takes place, God acts and makes known his power. When a man, then, declares himself to be a messenger from God, and at the same time, in support of the truth of his assertions, performs true miracles, his assertion must certainly be believed. His declaration is confirmed by the power of God, who cannot allow the performance of a miracle in support of deception or lying. Miracles are, as it were, credentials signed by the hand of God himself; and not to believe an assertion so confirmed, is to resist the voice of God, who speaks through miracles. Miracles were, then, the strongest and most striking proofs which God could furnish, to make the people believe the prophets. Elias, for instance, prevented rain for three years, exterminated four hundred and fifty idolatrous priests, raised to life the son of a widow, made fire descend from heaven, divided the river Jordan with his mantle, and passed through it on dry land, confronted kings, was fed by a raven and an angel, foretold that Jesabel, an idolatrous queen, would be devoured by dogs; he was carried in a chariot of fire to heaven, and he will return to the earth at the end of the world, to labor for the conversion of the Jews. (3 Kings xvii; 4 Kings, i; Ecclesiasticus xlviii; Malachi iv, 5; Matthew xi, 14, xvii, 10; James v, 17.)

Eliseus, like Elias, made a dry path through the waters of the Jordan, multiplied oil for a widow, raised a dead child to life again, cured Naaman of leprosy, foretold the victory of the kings of Juda, Israel, and Idumea, over the Moabites; also the miraculous victories of the Israelites over the Syrians; and lastly, by the touch of his body, he raised a dead man to life. (4 Kings xvii; Ecclesiasticus xlviii, 13; Luke iv, 27.)

10. To whom does God grant the gift of miracles?

God grants the gift of miracles to such only as hola or teach the truth.

God is true. He can neither deceive nor be deceived, and therefore he can reveal nothing but the truth. To convince men of the truth, he has wrought miracles in confirmation of the truth. "In order that the obedience of our faith," says the Vatican Council (c. iii), "might be in harmony with reason, God willed that to the interior help of the Holy Spirit there should be joined exterior proofs of his revelation, to wit: divine facts, and especially miracles and prophecies, which, as they manifestly display the omnipotence and infinite knowledge of God, are most certain proofs of his divine revelation, adapted to the intelligence of all men. Wherefore, Moses and the prophets ...showed forth many and most evident miracles and prophecies." If God, then, performs miracles through certain men, it is evident that they hold and teach the truth, for it would be blasphemous to think that God would grant the gift of miracles to such as neither hold nor teach the truth.

There were false prophets before and after the coming of the Redeemer. They pretended to be sent by God; and to prove their divine mission, they tried to perform miracles. But they never succeeded. In some instances they succeeded, with the help of the devil, whose ministers they were, inperforming certain wonderful things, or false miracles. When Moses performed great miracles before Pharao in Egypt, the magicians of the king tried to imitate the miracles of the great servant of God. They cast their rods before the king, and, by devilish enchantments, their rods seemed to be changed into serpents. But, when Moses continued to perform miracles, the magicians were constrained to confess that they were unable to do what Moses did, saying to the king, "This is the finger of God."

One day the prophet Elias "came to all the people of Israel and said: How long do you halt between two sides? If the Lord be God, follow him; but if Baal, then follow him. And the people did not answer him a word. And Elias said again to the people: I only remain a prophet of the Lord: but the prophets of Baal are four hundred and fifty men. Let two bullocks be given us, and let them choose one bullock for themselves, and cut it in pieces and lay it upon wood but put no fire under; and I will dress the other bullock and lay it on wood, and put no fire under. Call ye on the names of your gods, and I will call on the name of my Lord: and the god that shall answer by fire, let him be God. And all the people answering said: A very good proposal. Then Elias said to the prophets of Baal: Choose you one bullock, and dress it first, because you are many: and call on the names of your gods but put no fire under. And they took the bullock which he gave them and dressed it: and they called or the name of Baal from morning even till noon, saying. O Baal, hear us. But there was no voice, nor any that answered. And when it was now noon, Elias jested at them, saying: Cry with a louder voice, for he is a god, and perhaps he is talking, or is in an inn, or on a journey, or perhaps he is asleep and must be waked. So they cried with a loud voice ... but there was no voice heard, nor did anyone answer, nor regard them as they prayed. Elias said to all the people: Come ye unto me. And the people coming near unto him, he repaired the altar of the Lord, that was broken down. And he built with twelve stones an altar to the name of the Lord, and he made a trench for water of the breadth of two furrows round about the altar. And he laid the wood in order, and cut the bullock in pieces, and laid it upon the wood, and he said: Fill four buckets with water, and pour it upon the burnt-offering, and upon the wood. And he said, Do the same the second and the third time, And the water ran round about the altar, and the trench was filled with water. And when it was now time to offer the holocaust, Elias the prophet came near and said: O Lord God of Abraham, and Isaac and Israel, show this day that thou art the God of Israel, and I thy servant, and that according to thy commandments I have done all these things. Hear me O Lord, hear me, that thy people may learn that thou art the Lord God. Then the fire of the Lord fell and consumed the holocaust, and the wood, and the stones, and the dust, and licked up the water that was in the trench. And when all the people saw this they fell on their faces, and they said: The Lord he is God, the Lord he is God." (3 Kings xviii.)

When Simon the Magician, by the aid of the devil, raised himself in the air, to make the people of Rome believe that he was sent by God, St. Peter and St. Paul prayed that God might confound this false prophet; and suddenly Simon fell from on high, broke his legs, and was killed.

At the time of Martin Luther, a certain man named William was drowned. Luther was requested to raise him to life again. He commanded him repeatedly to rise from the dead. It was all in vain. (Bredenbach. 1. vii, c.1.)

A certain Lutheran preacher begged a man named Matthew to feign death and have himself carried as a corpse to the church, and then to rise at his bidding, so that the people might believe he had been raised to life again by the prayer of a Protestant preacher. Matthew complied with the request. He was carried to the church, apparently dead. The preacher approached the coffin and said in a loud voice: "Matthew, I command you to rise in the name of Christ, whose Gospel I preach." But Matthew never rose. He was dead; God had punished him. (Franc. Torrianus, 1. i, "De Dogmatibus.")

Frederick Staphil relates that Luther once endeavored to cast out the devil from a possessed girl in Wirtemberg, but he was so terrified that he tried to escape, both by the door and the window, which, to his great consternation, were both made fast. Finally, one of his companions broke open the door with a hatchet, and they escaped. (Reap, contra Jac. Smidelin, p.404.) Moses, Elias, and other true prophets, proved by real miracles that they were sent by Almighty God, and spoke what God inspired them to speak. Hence, they were readily believed when they reminded the people of keeping the law ofGod, exhorted them to repentance, and extolled the tender mercies of the Lord. "If, then," says the Vatican Council, "any one shall say that divine revelation cannot be made credible by outward signs, and therefore that men ought to bemoved to faith solely by the internal experience of each, or by private inspiration;" or, "if any one shall say that miracles are impossible, and therefore that all the accounts regarding them, even those contained in Holy Scripture are to be dismissed as fabulous or mystical, or that miracles can never be known with certainty, and that the divine origin of Christianity cannot be proved by them, let him be accursed." (Vatic. Counc. Ill, can. 3 and 4.)

11. What is a prophecy?

A prophecy is the foretelling of some future event, known to him only to whom God revealed it.

Through the prophets God also made known to the Jews what should happen to them, and in connection with them, what should happen to other nations; but he especially foretold, through them, the Messiah, whom the Jews expected, and by whom all nations were to be saved.

As to the Jews, the prophets foretold the general ruin of the kingdom of Israel: that the city and temple would be destroyed, and restored for a time; that the Jews would be captives in Babylon, and that they would again return; that they would reject the Messiah, and put him to death; that God would abandon them, and disperse them over the whole earth; that he would make an eternal covenant with another people, and that the Jews would be converted at the end of the world.

As to the prophecies concerning the Messiah, the prophet Daniel foretold the precise time of the Messiahs coming. While the Jews were captives in Babylon, God sent his angel Gabriel to the prophet Daniel to inform him: 1, that the city and the temple of Jerusalem would be rebuilt; and, 2, that seventy weeks would elapse from the publication of the edict for the rebuilding of the city and temple to the coming of Christ; 3, that in the middle of the seventieth week the Messiah would be put to death; 4, that he would be rejected by his own people, and consequently would cease to regard them as his; 5, that, after this, the city and the temple would be entirely destroyed; 6, that, before the demolition of the temple, the abomination of desolation would be seen in that holy place; and, 7, that, immediately after, the Jews would suffer a desolation which would endure to the end of time.(Daniel ix, 24, 25, 27.)

The prophet's weeks are understood, by all interpreters of the Holy Scriptures, to mean years for days, so that sixty-nine weeks of years amount to 483 years. The edict for rebuilding the walls of Jerusalem was made by Artaxerxes Longimanus, in the twentieth year of his reign, which was the year of the world 3548. Now, if to 3548 we add Daniel's weeks of years, 483, the number will be 4031, which is the year of Christ's baptism by St. John, and the commencement of his public life, lasting about three years and three months,—the middle of the last seventieth week, in which Christ was put to death. The Jews abandoned and denied Jesus; they were rejected by him as reprobates, and then the Romans destroyed their city and temple: the abominations committed in the temple, as described by Josephus, were horrible. Since that time the Jews have been dispersed over the whole earth, and, though even aided in their attempts to rebuild Jerusalem by idolatrous emperors who hated Christianity, they failed in every effort.

Isaias foretold that the Messiah should be born of a virgin: "Behold a virgin shall conceive and bear a son, and his name shall be called Emmanuel." (Isaiah vii, 15) "And Christ was conceived by the power of the Holy Ghost and born of the Blessed Virgin Mary." (Matthew i, 23.)

Micheas foretold that the Redeemer should be born in the city of Bethlehem, as even the Jews declared to the Magi, in the presence of Herod. (Mich, v, 2: Matthew ii, 5, 6.) And Christ chose to be born in a stable of Bethlehem.

Isaias and David foretold all the pains, sorrows, and insults, which the Savior was to endure, and that, in a manner so precise and accurate, as to lead one to suppose that they had been eye-witnesses of the sufferings of the Redeemer: "I have given my body to the strikers, and my cheeks to them that plucked them; I have not turned away my face from them that rebuked me, and spit upon me." (Isaiah 1, 6.) "I am reproach of men, and the outcast of the people." (Psalm xxi, 7.) "There is no beauty in him, nor comeliness: despised and the most abject of men, a man of sorrows, and acquainted with infirmity: surely he hath borne our infirmities, and carried our sorrows, and we have thought him as it were a leper, and as one struck by God, and afflicted." (Isaiah liii.) "And they gave me gall for my food, and in my thirst, they gave me vinegar to drink." (Psalm lxviii, 22.) "Many dogs have encompassed me: the council of the malignant hath besieged me. They have dug my hands and feet, they have numbered all my bones. They parted my garments amongst them, and upon my vesture they cast lots." (Psalm xxi, 17-19.)

David foretold the resurrection and ascension of the Redeemer, saying, "Thou hast ascended on high, hast led captivity captive." (Psalm lxvii, 19.) "Sing ye to God, who mounteth above the heavens." (Psalm lxvii, 34.)

The prophet Joel foretold that the Redeemer would send down the Holy Ghost: "I will pour out my spirit upon all flesh, and your sons and your daughters shall prophesy." (Chapter ii, 28.)

The Savior's everlasting priesthood was also foretold in these words: "He shall be a priest upon his throne" (Zachariah vi, 13); "Thou art a priest forever, according to the order of Melchizedek." (Psalm cix, 4.)

The prophets also foretold the conversion of the Gentiles, and the foundation, spread and duration of Christ's Church, saying that the Messiah shall be the light of the Gentiles, and that all nations of the earth shall be blessed in him; that he shall establish a new sacrifice, and a new priesthood, and found a kingdom of God, reaching from sea to sea, to the end of the earth, which shall never be destroyed, but shall stand forever. (Malachi i, 11; Isaiah lxvi, 21; Jeremiah iii, 15; Zachariah ix, 10; Daniel ii, 44, and vii, 14.)

12. Why were all those prophecies made?

They were made: 1, to keep alive man's hope in the Redeemer to come; 2, to prepare him to receive the Redeemer.

When God intends to do something very extraordinary, he generally prepares men for it by revealing to them, beforehand, what he is about to do. When he intended to destroy the world by the Deluge, he made it known through Noe, a hundred years before the event took place. God acts thus with men because he does not wish to overwhelm them by his strange and mysterious dealings. Now the most wonderful thing that God ever decreed is the sending of the Redeemer, —the Incarnation of his well-beloved Son,—for the salvation of mankind. From the beginning he made the provision that, by the holy patriarchs, the hope in the Redeemer should be carefully preserved among the people. But the nearer the time approached for his coming, the more did God the Father reveal, through his prophets, portions of the Jewish history, as well as what regarded the religion to be established by the Redeemer, in order that the Jews, seeing in their own immediate history these prophecies verified by the event, might find in them an evident proof of the prophecies regarding the Messiah and his religion, know him thereby, and receive him with great joy and gratitude. These prophecies were made, long before the coming of the Redeemer, for Malachias, the last of the prophets, prophesied four hundred and fifty years before Christ. They were carefully preserved and read by the Jews as divine oracles; they also were translated into different languages and spread among the pagan nations. Now if it is asked:

13. In whom were all those prophecies fulfilled?

The answer is: In Jesus Christ, the Son of God; and in Christ were also fulfilled all those figures which related to or typified his life, as will be seen in the next instruction.

14. In what condition was mankind at the coming of the Redeemer?

With the exception of the Jews, all mankind had fallen into idolatry and all kinds of vices.

God the Father had promised a Redeemer to our first parents, but he did not send him immediately after their fall. He waited about four thousand years before sending him, in order that men might feel their weakness and misery, and the need they had of a Redeemer, sigh for his coming, and appreciate the great blessings which they were to receive through him. When Christ came at length, the grossest ignorance and immorality prevailed everywhere. The true God was hardly known, save in one single corner of the earth, in Judea: and even there, how very few knew and loved him! As to the rest of the world, some worshipped the sun, some the brutes, some the very stones, and others again even viler creatures still; nay, many even worshipped the very demons as gods.

Everywhere there reigned the night of sin which blinds souls, and hides from them the sight of the miserable state in which they are living as enemies of God, condemned to hell. The most degrading vices were extolled even as virtues. The world cried for light. Men could no longer see their way. Why are we here? Who made us? Whither are we going? Whence the evil in the world? Why have we a desire for immortality? Why does nothing on earth satisfy us? Why our yearning for perpetual happiness? Such were the questions that resounded everywhere—in the schools of philosophy, in the forum, in the marketplace, in the temple, at the fireside. No one could answer; and yet the social, domestic and religious happiness of the world was at stake on these questions then, as it is now. What remedy could be applied to heal such inveterate evils of the mind and the will? Pagan philosophers, poets and orators, had tried their best to elevate mankind; but they had tried in vain. It had become evident to all that no human means were adequate to remedy the evils of the world, and make mankind truly happy. "God himself," exclaimed the great Plato, "must come down and be our master and our guide." (De Legib. 1,4.) "Yes," say the fathers of the Vatican Council, "if anyone shall say that it is impossible or inexpedient that man should be taught by divine revelation, concerning God and the worship to be paid to him, let him be accursed." (Vatic. Counc. II, can. 2.)

God had tried, in many ways, to make the pagans return to him, and do penance for their sins. He sent the terrible disaster of the universal deluge; he sent fire upon the cities of Sodom and Gomorrah; he chastised Egypt, Chanaan, and many other places, in a most frightful manner. He made prophets and other holy men live among them, as Daniel, Jonas, Job, to teach them by word and example how to worship the true God and be saved: "He scattered the Israelites among the Gentiles, in order that they might declare to them his wonderful works, and that there is no other Almighty God besides him." (Tobit xiii. 4.) He instructed King Nabuchodonosor by dreams, Baltassar by a mysterious handwriting on the wall; he also spoke to the pagans by the inner voice of their conscience, and by natural blessings, "doing good to them from heaven, giving rains and fruitful seasons." (Acts xiv, 16.) But all was in vain with the greater part of them. They plunged themselves deeper and deeper in the abyss of idolatry and immorality. Nothing could draw them from their evil ways and stop the universal corruption.

But mankind, though without God, and estranged from him, everywhere looked anxiously forward to the coming of "The desired of nations," foretold by the prophets,--a season annually commemorated by the Catholic Church in her service during Advent, when she sings again the anthem of the prophet: "Drop down dew, ye heavens, from above, and let the clouds rain the Just; let the earth be opened, and bud forth a Savior." (Isaiah xiv, 8.) The "fullness of time" came at last. "The light shone into the darkness:" Jesus Christ, the Son of God, came and was this light by his holy doctrine, divine example, and the means which he gave us to obtain the grace of God, and lead holy lives.

§ 2.—GOD THE SON OUR TEACHER

1. Through whom did God reveal himself most clearly?

Through his only Son, Jesus Christ, whom he sent to teach us: 1, what we must believe; 2, what we must do; 3, what means of grace we must use to be saved.

There is in the human heart a craving, a necessity, to have God for teacher, and God himself satisfied this craving which he implanted in the human heart. God the Father spoke to our first parents in paradise; he spoke to the patriarchs and prophets, and finally, as St. Paul assures us, he has spoken, for the last time, by his only-begotten Son.

But merely to hear the voice of a friend is not enough, the heart longs for something more: the eyes yearn to look upon him. God knows this want of the human heart, and he has satisfied it. The prophets besought him, again and again, to show himself: "Show us thy face, O Lord, and we shall be saved." This, too, was the ardent prayer of Moses: "O Lord! show me thy glory." (Exodus xxxiii, 13.)

In the Old Law God satisfied this desire, by manifesting his presence to the Israelites, under the form of a cloud and a pillar of fire. He next commanded an ark or tabernacle to be made, and there he manifested his presence by a peculiar, supernatural light, called the Shekinah. But all this satisfied neither man's heart, nor God's unbounded love. If we love a person dearly, it is not enough for us to hear his voice, or to see him in disguise: we wish to behold him face to face. God gratified even this desire. He had commanded a tabernacle of wood to be made by the hand of man, and that tabernacle he chose for his dwelling-place. But now, when the fulness of time was come, when God had decreed to send his Son into the world that we might be redeemed and adopted as children; then, with his own divine hands, he made a living tabernacle, holy and spotless, the Immaculate Virgin Mary, and in that tabernacle he took up his abode. There he formed for himself a human body and soul: "Thence he came forth and appeared," as St. Augustine says, "to men, to a world in the decline of old age, and in the throes of death, in order that, while everything about them was rapidly going to decay, he might, by his presence, infuse into all new life and fresh vigor." In becoming man, God revealed himself most clearly. Men saw God, heard God, even touched God.

2. How do we know that Jesus Christ is the promised Redeemer, and the Son of God?

We learn it: 1, from the mouths of the prophets; 2, from the declarations of the angels; 3, from the testimony of his heavenly Father; and, 4, from his own testimony.

The prophets had foretold the coming of a great king, but not a king of this world; otherwise they would not have described him as the "reproach of men, and the outcast of the people" (Psalm xxi, 7), nor called him "a man of sorrows." (Isaiah liii, 3, 4.) They promised a king of a spiritual and supernatural kingdom which was to begin and spread over the earth, to be consummated duly in heaven. Now, what the prophets had foretold of the Redeemer, was all visibly and historically fulfilled in Christ, the son of God; and to deny this true and real fulfillment of prophecy in the person, the life and the death of Christ, and the effect of his life, death, and teaching, on the world, is to deny the value of all testimony, and the truth of all history. Jesus Christ came at the time foretold by the prophets; he lived, suffered and died, in the manner foretold by the prophets; he rose from the dead, ascended into heaven, and founded an everlasting kingdom,—the Church,—as was foretold by the prophets. And not only do we see fulfilled in Christ the prophecies regarding the Redeemer, but we see also fulfilled in him all the figures by which the deeds and sufferings of the Redeemer were indicated many centuries before. The principal types or figures of Jesus Christ are, Abel, Noe, Isaac, Joseph, and Jonas. Abel is a figure of the Messiah, because he offered sacrifice, was killed by his own brother, and because his blood cried aloud to heaven for vengeance. Our Lord offered sacrifice, was put to death by the Jews, his brethren, and his blood cried to heaven for mercy, Abel's murderer became a vagabond on the face of the earth; the murderers of our Lord are condemned to wander over the earth without priest, without king, without sacrifice. Noe is a figure of Jesus Christ. "Noe" signifies consoler: "Jesus" signifies savior. Noe alone finds grace before God; our Lord alone finds grace before his Father. Noe built an ark, which saved him and his family from the Deluge; our Lord built a Church, to save from eternal death all who are willing to enter it. Isaac is a figure of Jesus Christ. Isaac is the well-beloved son of his father; our Lord is the well-beloved son of the Eternal. Isaac, though innocent, is condemned to death, is to be sacrificed by his father, and must himself carry the wood; Jesus Christ is innocently condemned to death; is immolated by his Father, through the hands of the Jews, and carries on his shoulders the wood of the cross. When Isaac was tied to the pile, he did not a murmur and when our Savior was tied to a pillar, he did not complain. Joseph, too, is a figure of the Redeemer. Joseph, the well-beloved son of his father, is sold by his brethren to strange merchants, is condemned for a crime of which he is innocent, is found in a prison with two criminals, to one of whom he announces pardon, to the other punishment. Our Lord, the beloved son of his Father, is maltreated by his brethren, the Jews; is sold by Judas, and given up to the Romans; is condemned for crimes of which he is innocent; is placed on a cross between two criminals; promises heaven to one and leaves the other to his perdition. And as Joseph passed from a prison to a throne, so our Lord passed from the cross to the throne of God. Jonas, who remained three days in the whale, and was delivered from it, is a figure of Jesus remaining three days in the grave, and then arising from it.

From the writings of their own prophets Christ proved to the Jews that he was the Redeemer promised and expected from the beginning of the world: "Search the Scriptures," said he to the Jews, "and the same are they that give testimony of me." (John v, 39.) He also convinced the unbelieving disciples from the writings of the prophets, saying to them: "O foolish and slow of heart to believe in all things which the prophets have spoken. Ought not Christ to have suffered these things, and so to enter into his glory? And beginning at Moses and all the prophets, he expounded to them in all the Scriptures the things concerning him." (Luke xxiv, 25-28.)

From the same writings of the prophets Christ proved also that he was God; for the prophets call the Redeemer: "God, God with us, the Wonderful, the Father of the world to come the Lord, Jehovah, our Just One," etc. (Isaiah 14; ix, 6; xxxv, 4; Daniel ix, 24; Jeremiah xxiii, 6.)

The angels, too, bore witness that Christ was God and the Savior of the world. The angel Gabriel said to the Blessed Virgin: "The Holy Ghost shall come upon thee, and the power of the Most High shall overshadow thee. And therefore, also, the Holy which shall be born of thee, shall be called the Son of God." (Luke i, 35.) "Thou shalt call his name Jesus," said the angel to St. Joseph, "for he shall save his people from their sins." (Matthew i, xxi.)

When Christ was born, an angel appeared to the shepherds, saying: "Fear not; for, behold, I bring you good tidings of great joy, that shall be to all the people. For this day is born to you a Savior, who is Christ the Lord." (Luke ii, 8-11.)

But Jesus had still a greater witness to prove that he is the Son of God. At his baptism, and on Mount Thabor, God the Father himself, by a voice from heaven, recognized him as his well-beloved Son, whom all were to hear. (Matthew iii, 17; xvii, 5.)

God the Father revealed also to St. Peter that Christ is the Son of God. When Christ asked the apostles, "Who do you say that I am?" Simon Peter answered, "Thou art Christ, the son of the living God." And Jesus said to him: "Blessed art thou, Simon, because flesh and blood hath not revealed it to thee, but my Father who is in heaven." (Matthew xvi, 16-17.)

But Christ had still stronger arguments to prove that he is the Redeemer and the Son of God, and equal to his Father in all things. He confirmed his doctrine by many miracles. Hence Christ said to those who doubted his word: "If you will not believe me (my word), believe my works, that you may know and believe that the Father is in me, and I in the Father." (John x, 38.) The miracles by which Jesus Christ proved that he is God and the promised Redeemer, are clear, palpable, many in number, and of various kinds. Heaven and earth obeyed his voice. He restored sight to the blind, hearing to the deaf, and speech to the dumb. A dumb man, possessed by the devil, is presented to him. By a mere act of his will, Christ casts out the devil, and the dumb man speaks. There is no disease that he does not cure, no evil that he does not remedy. The lepers are made clean, the lame walk, the dead arise at his touch or bidding: "Young man, arise!" said he to the widow's son, and the young man was restored to life. "Lazarus, come forth!" he cried out, and Lazarus, dead for some days, arose from the grave. By his will, water is changed into wine, at the wedding-feast in Cana; the winds and waves become calm; the devils leave the persons they possessed; a few loaves of bread are multiplied so as to feed five thousand persons and fill twelve baskets with the fragments which remained. Whilst he was hanging on the cross, the sun acknowledged him for its Lord and Creator, by withholding its light, and the whole world was enveloped in great darkness; the rocks, by rending asunder; the whole earth, by shaking; death, by letting many persons who had been dead, leave their graves alive, and appear to their friends in Jerusalem; the centurion and his soldiers, by exclaiming, "Indeed this was the Son of God?' (Matthew xxvii, 54.)

Christ, by his own power, rose from the dead, ascended into heaven, whence he wrought many miracles through his apostles and the martyrs, teaching and professing their faith in his divinity. One of these miracles is most remarkable. It happened in Africa, in 484, and is attested by most reliable eye-witnesses: Hurich, king of the Arian vandals, most cruelly persecuted those who believed in the divinity of Jesus Christ: he had the tongues of the Christians of Tipasa cut out; yet they spoke without tongues as distinctly and fluently as before, and proclaimed everywhere that Jesus Christ is true God, and equal to the Father. About sixty of these Christians fled to Constantinople, where all the inhabitants saw them, and heard them speak daily for many years.

But Christ proved himself to be the Messiah and the Son of God, not alone by stupendous miracles. He also proved the truth of his assertions by foretelling such things as God alone can know; for instance: his betrayal by Judas, and his denial by Peter; the manner of his death; his resurrection from the dead; his ascension into heaven, and the spreading of his doctrine over the whole earth. One of the most striking prophecies of Christ which we see accomplished is this: Jesus Christ foretold that the temple of Jerusalem would be so totally destroyed, that not even one stone should be left on another. Julian the Apostate, in order to fix on Jesus Christ the brand of imposture, and thus to bring the Christian religion into disrepute, formed the project of rebuilding the Jewish temple, which, if he could have carried out, would have sufficiently answered his wicked design. He commanded the Jews to repair to Jerusalem to rebuild their ancient temple and reestablish their ancient worship. The news that the temple was to be rebuilt was no sooner spread abroad than contributions came in from all hands. The Jewish women strip themselves of their most costly ornaments, to contribute toward the expense of the building: they even helped to dig the ground, and carry out the rubbish in their aprons and the skirts of their gowns. It is also told that the Jews appointed some pickaxes, spades, and baskets to be made of silver, for the honor of the work. The power of Julian, the exertions of the chief overseer, Alypius, the rage and insolence of the Jews and pagans, plunged the disciples of our Lord into the most profound grief. But the good bishop, St. Cyril, lately returned from exile, consoled them by telling them that the power of God would prostrate Julian as wicked design, that the desolation of the temple should last to the end, and that the Jews would not be able to put one stone upon another. The old foundations, and some ruins of the walls of the temple, were first removed. Then they began to dig the new foundation, on which work many thousands were employed. But what they had thrown up in the day, was, by repeated earthquakes, cast back again the night following into the trench. "And when Alypius the next day," says Ammianus Marcellinus, "earnestly pressed on the work, with the assistance of the governor of the province, there issued such horrible balls of fire out of the earth near the foundations, as rendered the place, from time to time, inaccessible to the scorched and blasted workmen. And the victorious element continuing in this manner, obstinately and resolutely bent, as it were, to drive them to a distance, Alypius thought proper to give over the enterprise." Besides the earthquakes and fiery eruptions, Christian writers make mention of storms, tempests, whirlwinds, lightning, crosses impressed on the bodies and garments of the assistants, and a flaming cross in the heavens, surrounded with a luminous circle. The infidels attempted to wash out the shining crosses that were impressed on the bodies and garments of those assisting at the rebuilding of the temple, and in which there was something that in art and elegance exceeded all painting and embroidery: but it was increased by the fiery eruption, which was frequently renewed, till it overcame the rashness of the most obdurate, for it continued to be repeated as often as the projectors ventured to renew their attempt. Socrates tells us that at sight of the miracles the Jews at first cried out that Christ is God yet returned home as hardened as ever. St. Gregory Nazianzen says that many Gentiles were converted and became Christians.

Christ's doctrine having been confirmed by miracles and prophecies, and accompanied by a sinless life and by works of love and mercy (Matthew iv, 23; Acts x, 38,) was received as the teaching of God the Father himself by those whose hearts were well disposed toward so holy a doctrine. Hence the people exclaimed that Christ taught as one having authority, and not as their Scribes and Pharisees. (Matthew vii, 28.)

3. Whom did Christ appoint to teach his doctrine to all nations?

Christ appointed the apostles and their lawful successors to teach all nations.

It was the will of the heavenly Father that no one should be saved unless through Christ, his well-beloved Son; that is, through faith in his doctrine, through hope in his merits, through charity toward God and all men, through the sacraments and prayer, as means of grace, and through obedience to his orders: "I am the way, and the truth, and the life," says Jesus. "No one comes to the Father, but by me." (John xiv, 6.) But Christ did not wish to live forever in the flesh, in this world, to teach and sanctify all nations. So, from among his followers, he chose twelve men to be the witnesses of what he taught and did. As he intended to send them to teach all nations in his name, he called them apostles, which means messengers, giving them to understand that he had chosen them to preach to all nations what they had seen of, and heard from him. Therefore, he said to them: "You shall be witnesses unto me in Jerusalem, and in all Judea and Samaria, and even to the uttermost part of the earth." (Acts i, 8.)

4. How were the apostles prepared for their divine mission?

1, Christ himself instructed them in his doctrine; 2, he promised them the Holy Ghost; 3, he gave them his own powers.

One day the Lord said to the prophet Jeremias: "Before thou was born, I knew thee and sanctified thee, and made thee a prophet unto the nations." Jeremias, thinking that he was not able to preach to the nations, said: "Ah, ah, ah, Lord! behold I cannot speak, for I am a child." To this excuse the Lord replied: "Say not, I am a child; for thou shalt go to all that I shall send thee, and whatsoever I shall command thee, thou shalt speak. Be, not afraid at their presence, for I am with thee to deliver thee." And then the Lord put forth his hand, and touched the mouth of the prophet, and said to him:" Behold I have given my words in thy mouth. Lo! I have set thee this day over the nations, and over kingdoms, to root up, and to pull down, and to waste, and to destroy, and to build, and to plant." (Jeremiah i, 5-10.) By these words ofthe Lord the prophet Jeremias felt encouraged to go and preach to the nations. The apostles had to be encouraged in the same manner. Like Jeremias, they could say to our Lord, when he wished them to go on this hitherto unheard-of and seemingly impossible mission: "Ah, ah, ah, Lord! behold, we cannot speak;" we are ignorant men, children as it were, having no courage for so awful an office. But Christ consoled and encouraged them. After he had taught them for three years and a half, and during forty days after his resurrection, he could say to them, as was said to Jeremias, viz.: "Behold, I have given my words in thy mouth." "Behold," said Jesus to the apostles, "all things whatsoever I have heard of my Father, I have made known to you." (John xv, 15.) But you may tell me: "We are but a few poor fishermen, without human learning, without wealth, without worldly influence or natural eloquence, without any human qualification whatever for so vast an undertaking; we have but our foolishness to confound the learning and philosophy of Greece and Rome, to silence oracles, to destroy the impure orgies of Paganism, to reclaim all mankind from evil ways, and to plant, on the ruins of a gigantic idolatry which possesses the world, the bright, the glorious, the unsullied banner of the cross. Who will listen to us when we preach to a wicked world thy doctrine, which is so contrary to all human passions and evil inclinations? How can we, a handful of poor, ignorant, unarmed men, withstand and overcome a hostile world? And how shall we be able to remember and rightly comprehend all that thou hast taught us, forgetful and slow of understanding as we are?" But I say to you, fear not, for, "the Comforter, the Holy Ghost, whom the Father will send in my name, he will teach you all things, and bring all things to your mind, whatsoever I shall have said to you." (John xiv 26.) He is the "Comforter;" he will give you such courage and wisdom, and knowledge and strength, as no power on earth can cope with. I send you clothed with the same powers with which I myself have been invested by my heavenly Father: "All power is given to me in heaven and on earth. As the Father hath sent me, I also send you." (Matthew xxviii, 18; John xx, 21.)

5. What were those powers of Christ?

1, His power as teacher; 2, his power as priest; 3, his power as ruler.

We find, in the thirty-first chapter of Deuteronomy, that, when Moses had written the law of God in a book, he gave this book to the Levites, and commanded them to place it in the tabernacle, beside the ark of the covenant, as a testimony against Israel. On another occasion, when many of the Israelites rebelled against Moses and Aaron and wished to claim a share in the priestly authority, God ordered twelve rods, each bearing the name of one of the tribes, to be placed in the tabernacle, together with the rod of Aaron. On the next morning it was found that Aaron's rod alone bloomed and brought forth fruit. This miraculous rod was the emblem of authority. It was a witness that

God had confided the spiritual rule to Aaron and his lawful successors, and to them alone. This rod was also placed in the tabernacle beside the law of God. On another occasion, God ordered a vessel filled with manna, —that miraculous bread from heaven, —to be placed beside the law of God and the rod of Aaron.

These three things, —the book, the rod, and the manna, —signify the three distinct powers which God conferred upon the priests of the Old Law. The book signifies the office of teacher; the rod signifies the office of visible head or ruler; and the manna signifies the grace of God, which was given to the Israelites through the ministry of the priests. The three offices, then, of teacher, of priest, and of ruler, or visible head, existed in the Jewish Church of the Old Law, when our divine Savior came on earth.

Our divine Redeemer confirmed and consecrated these three offices, by uniting them in his own divine person. He was a teacher, he was a priest, and he was a king. He was the teacher of nations, the light of the world. He taught all men what they must believe, what they must do, and what means they must use to obtain and preserve the grace of God. He was a priest forever, according to the order of Melchizedek. He was, as the prophet foretold, and as he himself declared, the king of an everlasting kingdom. As teacher, he taught us that to know and do the will of his heavenly Father was the only way to heaven; as priest, he sacrificed his life upon the cross, and thereby obtained for men the graces necessary for salvation; as ruler, or king of an everlasting kingdom, he declared that all men had to believe and to do what he taught them, if they would be saved.

6. What did Christ call the apostles and those who believed in him?

He called them his Church of which he is the invisible head.

Our dear Savior sowed the seeds of his divine doctrine and watered them with his blood. But he himself made very few converts. He left the conversion of the world mainly to his apostles and to their lawful successors. Nevertheless, he had made a sufficient number of converts to form of them a well-organized society, which he called his Church, or his kingdom on earth. This society consisted of the immaculate Virgin Mary, twelve apostles seventy-two disciples, and some other followers of our divine Savior, with Christ himself as its chief teacher, pontiff and ruler: for, "God the Father," says St. Paul, "hath made Christ the head over all the Church." (Ephesians i, 17-22.) But when the time drew near for our Savior to return to heaven, he appointed one of his apostles to take his place as visible head and chief pastor on earth, he himself continuing to be the invisible head of the Church in heaven.

The community of the apostles and the Aher true believers formed the visible body of the Church of Christ; and a visible body or society must have a visible head. It is in the nature of things that this should be so: there never has been, and never can be, a living, active, organized body without a living head. Reason and experience teach us that there can be no order, no law, no civilization, without some final authority which, of its very nature, must be supreme; in other words, supreme authority is the foundation of order and law. We see the necessity of such authority whithersoever we turn. Every ship must have its captain. Every railroad engine must have its engineer. In every society we find a president. In every government there must be a president or a monarch. Even amongst the brute beasts or the tiny insects we find the principle of authority in practice. We find, for instance, that ants and bees have their queen or supreme ruler. Now the same God who gave so wonderful an order to nature, the same

God who planted in our reason the principle of order and authority, must observe this magnificent and necessary law in the greatest of his works,—the establishment of his Church, or kingdom on earth. Nothing, therefore, can be more natural than to find that our Lord Jesus Christ appointed one of his apostles to be the visible head and chief pastor of his Church.

7. Whom did Christ appoint to take his place?

Christ appointed the apostle St. Peter to be the visible head and chief pastor of his Church.

Christ compared his Church to a house, and made St. Peter its foundation, saying: "Thou art Peter (that is, a rock), and upon this rock I will build my Church." (Matthew xvi, 18.) He compared his Church to a flock, and made Peter its chief shepherd, saying: "Feed my lambs, feed my sheep." (John xxi, 15-17.) By lambs, Christ means the faithful, and by sheep, the pastors. To Peter, therefore, Christ entrusted both the pastors and the faithful, when he said, "Feed my lambs, feed my sheep." Peter, being made the head and chief pastor of the Church, received also from Christ greater powers than the rest of the apostles. To him he gave the power to make laws for all the pastors, as well as for all the faithful, and to enforce those laws, saying: "I will give to thee the keys of the kingdom of heaven, and whatsoever thou shalt bind upon earth, it shall be bound also in heaven: and whatsoever thou shalt loose upon earth, it shall be loosed also in heaven." (Matthew xvi, 18-19.) There is no possibility of mistaking or explaining away the plain, emphatic words of Christ to Peter by which he invested him with the prerogatives of the head of his Church.

By virtue of this supreme power, Peter called the disciples together, and presided over the council which they held in Jerusalem to

elect a new apostle in the place of Judas: and the council readily
recognized this power. It was Peter who first preached Jesus crucified,
and converted, by his sermon, three thousand persons. It was Peter
who first declared that the Gentiles were to be admitted to baptism,
according to a revelation which he had received.

Peter, too, first decided, in an assembly of the apostles at Jerusalem,
that the Christians were no longer to be subjected to the Jewish law of
circumcision; and the assembly bowed to his decision. From all this we
clearly see that Peter was the head of the Church; because on all those
occasions he exercised the office of Supreme Head of the Church of
Christ, and no man questioned it.

The apostles and their lawful successors acknowledged Peter as
the head of the Church. When the evangelists give the names of the
apostles, they always name Peter first: for instance, when St. Matthew
gives us the names of the apostles, he says: "The names of the twelve
apostles: The first, Simon who is called Peter." (Matthew x, 2.) Now
it cannot be said that Peter was always named first, either because
he was the eldest, or because he had been called to the apostleship
before the rest, for St. Andrew was both older than. Peter, and had
become a disciple of Christ before him. The true reason, therefore,
why the evangelists always name Peter first, is because he held the first
or highest office in the Church. Hence the Fathers of the General
Council of Ephesus, A. D. 431, say: "It is known in all ages that Peter
was the prince and the head of the apostles, the foundation-stone of
the Catholic Church. This is a fact which no one doubts."

8. What power had the other apostles as teachers?

*They had the power to preach Christ's doctrine, and to be judges in
matters of faith and morals.*

When Christ said to his apostles, "Go and teach all nations, teaching them to observe all things whatsoever I have commanded you" (Matthew xxviii, 19-20), he empowered the apostles to spread abroad, explain, and preserve his holy doctrines, pure and uncorrupted, and to condemn and reject all false teachings; he empowered them to inveigh against crime and to encourage virtue; to trace out to everyone his individual duties, to monarchs as well as to their subjects, to the learned and to the ignorant, to the rich and to the poor, to the just and to the sinner; he empowered them to offer to all men instruction, counsel, and hope; to encourage the good, to exhort the weak, to convert the sinner, to speak of the sweet consolations of the just, and to describe the fearful state of the impenitent sinner; he empowered them to condemn and reject all false principles, impious writings of every description, wicked societies. In a word, Christ empowered the apostles to proclaim his doctrine, everywhere, one and the same; to defend his rights on earth against every enemy; to resist with all their might the passions and evil tendencies of nations, communities, or individuals; to make constitutions and decrees conducive to the preservation of faith and morals, and even to proscribe such opinions as approach, more or less closely, open heresy.

9. What power had the apostles as priests?

They had the power to offer up the holy sacrifice of the Mass, to administer the sacraments, and to perform other priestly duties.

When Christ said to the apostles at the last supper, "Do this (that is, offer the unbloody sacrifice which I have offered) for a commemoration of me" (Luke xxii, 19), he empowered them to change bread and wine into his body and blood by the words of consecration, and offer him to the heavenly Father, under the appearance of bread and wine. Thus, Christ gave to the apostles power over his own sacred body, power over himself. The eternal, omnipotent God, in whose presence the pillars of heaven tremble; that God before whom the earth, and all that dwell thereon, before whom the boundless universe, with all its countless suns and planets, before whom all created things are but as a drop of water, as a grain of sand, as if they were not,—that God of infinite majesty and glory made himself subject to the apostles when he said, "Do this for a commemoration of me!" The monarchs of the earth have great power, their commands are obeyed, their very name is respected and feared, thousands and thousands of their fellow men are subject to them; but the priestly power of the apostles is far greater. Great was the power of Adam when he came forth from the hands of God, in all the majesty of justice and innocence. He was the king of creation, and all the creatures of the earth obeyed him. Great was the power of Moses when, by a single word, he divided the waters of the Red Sea, and led a vast multitude, dry-shod, through the surging billows. Great was the power of Elias, who caused fire to rain from heaven upon the heads of his enemies. Great was the power of Joshua, who, in the heat of battle, raised his hands to heaven, and commanded the sun: "Move not, O sun!" he cried, "and thou, moon! stand still!" and the sun and the moon obeyed his voice. They stood still in the midst of the heavens, for the space of an entire day. Great, indeed, was the power which God thus gave to man, but the power given by Christ to the apostles was infinitely greater. Whenever they said Mass, they held in their hands, after the words of consecration, Jesus Christ, their Lord and God, to receive him, and to give him to all those who wished to receive him in holy communion. This power which Christ gave to his apostles, surpasses far even the power of creation. By creation, God produces the substance of bread out of nothing, by his word; but by the words of the apostles, in consecration, the substance of bread and wine is changed into the most sacred body and blood of Christ. Ah, when we see the apostles, weak, sinful men as they were, gifted with a power which angels could not and did not dare to claim; when we see them exercising power over God himself, possessing power to carry him, and give him to whom they willed, we cannot help exclaiming, in amazement: "O wondrous miracle! O marvelous power!" A greater power than this God could not give—it was his own infinite power.

But, as Christ could not wish to enter, by holy communion, into souls as long as they were in mortal sin, the great power of the apostles to change bread and wine into Christ's body and blood would have been of little avail to the greater part of mankind, had not Christ given to the apostles another power, viz.: that of forgiving sins by means of the sacraments, especially by the sacraments of baptism and penance. Therefore, he said to the apostles: "Go, baptize mankind in the name of the Father, and of the Son, and of the Holy Ghost;" "Whose sins you shall forgive, they are forgiven them." (Matthew xxviii, 19; John xx, 23.) This power was given to the apostles to free men from their sins and prepare them for the union with Christ in holy communion. This power, too, surpasses that of any created being, either in heaven or on earth. An earthly judge has great power, yet he can only declare one innocent who has been falsely accused; but the apostles received power to restore to innocence even those who were guilty.

The kings of the earth are powerful, yet their power extends only to a few countries, while the power of the apostles embraced the whole earth. Their power reached to the highest heavens; it penetrated even to the very gates of hell. The treasures of kings are silver and gold, —perishable metals; but the treasures of the apostles were the imperishable merits and graces of our Lord Jesus Christ. Kings have power over the bodies of men only; but the apostles had power over men's souls. Kings have power over their subjects only; but kings and emperors themselves were subject to the apostles, because from them they had to expect not Only the light of the true faith, but also the pardon of their sins,—the grace of God. Kings have power to open and to close the prison-gates on earth; but the apostles had power to open and to close the gates of heaven and of hell. The influence of their power was felt in heaven, in giving to it the elect; it was felt in hell, in snatching from it victims; it was felt in purgatory, in consoling efficaciously its great sufferers.

But Christ said to his apostles: "To me is given all power in heaven and on earth. As the Father has sent me, I also send you." He who bestows all power, excludes none. Christ, therefore, gave to his apostles the power to cast out devils from possessed persons, and to prevent the evil spirits from hurting men in their bodies or property: "And calling together the twelve apostles," says St. Luke (ix, 1), "he gave them power and authority over all devils." And the same evangelist tells us, also, that the disciples cast out the devils from possessed persons, at which power they were greatly amazed, and said: "Lord, the devils also are subject to us in thy name." (Luke x, 17.) Christ also gave to his apostles power to bless or consecrate things for the divine service, or for the pious use of the faithful: as altars, chalices, vestments, churches, graveyards, holy water, oil, bread, wine, palms. By the sin of Adam the curse of God had come upon all creatures: "Cursed is the earth in thy work," said God to Adam. (Genesis iii, 17.) But Christ came to take away not only man's sin, but also the curse which had fallen upon all other creatures of the earth. And as Christ gave power to the apostles to drive out sin from the souls of men, by their applying to them the merits of his redemption through the sacraments, in like manner he gave them power to free creatures from the curse of sin, by their applying to them the blessing of redemption, through prayers and blessings, in order to make them work good to those that love God; for "every creature," says St. Paul, "is sanctified by the word and prayer." (1 Timothy iv, 5.)

St. Matthew tells us, in his Gospel (vii, 29), that our Savior was teaching the people as one having power and authority, and not as their Scribes and Pharisees, Christ, who chose the apostles to take his place as teacher and priest, wished also that, like him, they should teach with power and authority. To increase their authority, he gave them another power: the power of ruling and governing those who believed in him and were baptized.

10. What power had the apostles as rulers or pastors of the Church?

They had the power of governing the faithful, under the supreme authority of St. Peter.

Christ said to his apostles: "Amen I say to you, whatsoever you shall bind upon earth, shall be bound also in heaven; and whatsoever you shall loose upon earth, shall be loosed also in heaven." (Matthew xviii, 18.)

In these words Christ gave power to his apostles to govern his Church, to regulate the divine service and the manner of administering the sacraments, to govern nations, kings and peoples, according to his unchangeable doctrine; to make laws for them, and to enforce those laws, by refusing the sacraments to those who transgress them, or by expelling such transgressors from her society, or by imposing upon them such works of penance as were deemed proper for their own spiritual good, and that of others.

Gifted with this threefold power of Christ, the apostles were greater than the patriarchs, —greater, more exalted, than the prophets. A widow of Sarephta fed the prophet Elias for some time. As a reward for her charity, the prophet obtained for her the miracle that her pot of meal wasted not, and her cruse of oil was not diminished, and thus sustained that family in a miraculous manner. The apostles did more: they fed not merely one family, but the nations of the world; they gave not mere material bread, but the living bread from heaven: the body and blood of Jesus Christ; they strengthened the souls of men with the oil of grace, which they administered to them in the holy sacraments.

Elias raised, moreover, the widow's son to life; but the apostles did more: they raised to life the dead souls of hundreds and thousands. In the sacraments of baptism and penance, they raised to the life of grace the souls of those that were dead in mortal sin.

Elias caused fire to rain from heaven upon the heads of the wicked. The apostles caused not simply material fire to fall from heaven, they did far more: they caused the fire of divine love to fall upon the cold hearts of sinners and moved them to contrition; they inflamed them to a new and perfect life.

Again, the apostles were greater than the prophets. The prophets beheld the Redeemer only from afar, in the dim future. The apostles beheld him present before their eyes. They touched the long-wished-for Redeemer with their hands; they offered him up to the heavenly Father; they carried him through the streets: they even fed on the precious blood of this Holy One; they received him into their hearts and united themselves most intimately with him in holy communion.

The prophets foretold that, when the fulness of time should come, God would write his laws, not on stone, but on men's hearts; he would govern men, not by the law of servile fear, but by the sweet bonds of holy love; that God himself would dwell in them and direct them by his grace. Now, this fulness of time for which the prophets sighed, came with Jesus Christ. He gave his grace, his own divine life, to man, and he gave it abundantly; and, as the ministers of that grace, he chose, not the prophets, not his angels, but his apostles.

The apostles had the patriarchal dignity of Abraham. Abraham is called the Father of the Faithful. The apostles were, in reality, the fathers of the faithful, for they made them the children of God, by preaching the Gospel, and especially by administering to them the holy sacraments. They stood at the helm of the Church, —the ark of salvation.—like Noe. They were consecrated forever according to the order of Melchizedek. They were invested with a dignity far higher than that of Aaron.

Aaron offered up only the blood of sheep and oxen, while the apostles offered up the blood of the Lamb of God, our Lord Jesus Christ. They had the authority of Moses. Moses led the people of God, through the desert, to the promised land; the apostles led the children of God, through the desert of this life, to the true land of promise, —their home in heaven.

Great, unutterably great, indeed, were the powers of the apostles. But these powers were not bestowed upon them for their own private benefit. They received them for the spiritual welfare of the people. And as Christ came to save and sanctify all men, it was his will that his power as teacher, as priest, and as ruler, should continue as long as his Church lasts.

11. How long will the Church last?

The Church will last to the end of the world.

From the very beginning the Church of Christ was made up of two classes of men: of teachers and hearers, of priests and people, of rulers and subjects. Thus established, it will continue to the end of time, according to Christ's promise, "The gates of hell shall not prevail against my Church." Christ chills his Church his kingdom on earth, which he has acquired at the cost of so much toil, and labor, and suffering; it is that kingdom which he purchased with his own blood, and which he loves more than his own life. It would be blasphemous to think that any power should ever be able to tear that kingdom from Christ. The Church is the sheepfold of Jesus Christ; he is her divine shepherd. No hellish wolf will ever be able to take entire possession of this sheepfold. The Church is the household of which Christ is the master. No power will succeed in destroying that household. The Church, says St. Paul, is the body of Christ. Christ, then, is inseparably united with his Church. Sooner shall the sun refuse its light; sooner shall the stars fall from the firmament; sooner shall the precious blood of Christ lose its atoning power; sooner shall God cease to be God, than Christ cease to protect and defend his body, —the Church. "Behold," says he to the apostles, "I am with you all days, even to the end of the world." (Matthew xxviii, 20.)

12. How can Christ be with his apostles to the end of the world, since the apostles died?

Christ is with his apostles to the end of the world, in their lawful successors.

It is fitting to remember again what Christ said to his apostles: "All power is given to me in heaven and on earth." Had our Savior, when he uttered these words, considered himself God, he could not have said, "is given to me," because, as God, he had, from the beginning, as much power as his heavenly Father. He spoke as man, then, when he said, "All power is given to me," and as man he could and did receive all power from his heavenly Father; that is, his power as teacher, as priest, and as ruler, together with the power of conferring, as man, this three-fold power on other men—on his apostles. He tells his apostles: "As the Father hath sent me, I also send you;" that is, as the Father hath sent me to confer upon you the powers I have received from him, I also send you to confer upon others the powers you have received from me, and they are to confer again upon others the powers they received from you, and soon to the end of time. I shall die, it is true, but the powers received from my Father will not die or cease with my death; they will continue in you. You, too, will die, but with your death the powers received from me will not cease; they will continue in those upon whom you confer them, and so on to the end of the world. It is thus that I am with you, in your successors, to the last day of the world. I will be, to the end of the world, with you, Peter, as head of my Church, in your successor, and also with you, my other apostles, in those who take your place.

13. Who is the lawful successor of St. Peter?

The Pope, or the Bishop of Pome. (Council of Florence, 1438.)

One thousand eight hundred and forty odd years ago, a poor, meanly-clad wanderer went to the capital of the world,—the wealthy, magnificent city of Rome. He passes its gates, and threads his way, unobserved, through populous streets. On every side he beholds splendid palaces, raised at the expense of downtrodden nationalities; he beholds stately temples, dedicated to as many false gods as nations were represented in Rome; he beholds public baths and amphitheaters, devoted to pleasure and to cruelty; he beholds statues, monuments, and triumphal arches, raised to the memory of blood thirsty tyrants. He passes warriors and senators, beggars and cripples, effeminate men and dissolute women, gladiators and slaves, merchants and statesmen, orators and philosophers—all classes, all ranks, all conditions of men, of every language and color under the sun. Everywhere he sees a maddening race for pleasure, everywhere the impress of luxury, everywhere the full growth of crime, side by side with indescribable suffering, diabolical cruelty and barbarity.

And this poor, meanly clad wanderer was St. Peter, the head of Christ's Church. How the noble heart of the poor fisherman of Galilee must have bled when he observed the empire of Satan so supreme; when he witnessed the shocking licentiousness of the temple and the homestead; when he saw the fearful degradation of woman, groaning under the load of her own infamy; when he saw the heart-rending inhumanity which slew the innocent babes, and threw them into the Tiber; when he saw how prisoners of war, slaves, and soldiers, were trained for bloody fights, and entered the arena of the amphitheater, and strove whole days to slay one another, for the special entertainment of the Roman people!

Here, then, was to be the scene of his labors. Into this foul mass, into this carcass of a rotten society, St. Peter was come to infuse a new life, to lay the foundation of a new Rome,—a Rome, which, instead of paganism and depravity, should convey the truth and the blessing of Christian virtues to the farthermost ends of the earth. When Peter, the first pope, came to Rome, that city was the condensation of all the idolatry, all the oppression, all the injustice, all the immoralities, of the world, for the world was centered in Rome. Peter laid his hand to the plough, and never once looked back. For twenty-five years he struggled, and succeeded in establishing, in the very midst of this center of every excess of which the human mind and the human heart could be guilty, a congregation of Christians to whom St. Paul could address an epistle, and state in it that the fair fame of their faith had already spread over the whole world: "I give thanks to my God, through Jesus Christ, for you all, because your faith is spoken of in the whole world." (Romans i, 8; xvi, 19.)

The foundation of a new world had been laid by St. Peter, the first pope. He established his see in Rome; there he suffered martyrdom fort he faith.

That St. Peter resided and died at Rome is a fact which is attested by unvarying and universal testimony, —a fact which has been transmitted by oral tradition, and is recorded in the writings of the Fathers, St. Cyprian, Tertullian, St. Ambrose, St. Athanasius, and others: it is recorded in the writings of historians, St. Irenaeus, St. Epiphanius, Eusebius, St. Isidore; it is recorded in the writings of sovereign pontiffs, and of the Councils of Ephesus, of Chalcedon, of Lyons, of Florence. This fact is also commemorated every year by festivals, such as that of the Chair of St. Peter at Rome; of the Chains worn by St. Peter at Rome. It is a fact of which we are continually reminded by multitudes of the faithful, who are constantly seen around the tomb of the Prince of the Apostles. This fact is also evident from the preeminence which the See of Rome has always held over all other churches. Peter, then, having ultimately fixed his abode and his see at Rome, Rome was called, by the Fathers of the Church, the See of Peter; and the Bishop of Rome, the Successor of Peter; and the supremacy of the Roman Pontiff, the Supremacy of Peter; and communion with Rome, Communion with Peter. "Rome has become the capital of Christendom," says St. Leo the Great, "because it was there that St. Peter established his see." (Serm. in Nativ. Apost.) Since then, pope has succeeded pope, in spite of persecution and death, in spite of the opposition of pagan philosophy and of pagan intrigue, of pagan hate and of pagan enmity. Two hundred and fifty-five popes, till now, have succeeded one another in the See of St. Peter. Of these, seventy-seven are honored by the Church as saints, and twenty-seven have, in imitation of St. Peter, suffered martyrdom for their faith. It was from the center of Rome that the popes governed the Church through the lawful successors of the apostles. Hence the Council of Florence defined that "the Roman Pontiff is the true Vicar of Christ, and the head of the whole Church, and the father and teacher of all Christians: and that to him, in blessed Peter, was delivered, by our Lord Jesus Christ, the full power of feeding, ruling, and governing the whole Church." (Acts of the Seventeenth General Council of Florence, A. D. 1438: L'abbe, vol. xviii, p. 526.) And with the approval of the Second Council of Lyons, the Greeks professed "that the Holy Roman Church enjoys supreme and full primacy and preeminence over the whole Catholic Church, which it truly and humbly acknowledges that it has received, with the plenitude of power from our Lord himself, in the presence of blessed Peter, prince or head of the apostles, whose successor the Roman Pontiff is." (Acts of the Fourteenth General Council—Second of Lyons—A. D. 1274; Labbe, vol. xiv, p. 512.) "If then," says the Vatican Council, "any shall say that the Roman Pontiff has the office merely of inspection or direction, and not full and supreme power of jurisdiction over the Universal Church, not only in things which belong to faith and morals, but also in those which relate to the discipline and government of the Church, spread throughout the world; or assert that he possesses merely the principal part, and not all the fulness, of this supreme power; or that this power which he enjoys is not ordinary and immediate, both over each and all the churches, and over each and all the pastors and the faithful, let him be anathema." (Cap. III.)

14. Who are the lawful successors of the other apostles?

The lawful successors of the other apostles are the bishops of the Roman Catholic Church, who are in communion with the pope.

God the Father sent Christ, his well-beloved Son, to teach his holy will to all mankind. Christ, again, sent his apostles to take his place and continue his work. In like manner, the apostles chose others, ordained them bishops and priests, to continue their work. St. Paul, for instance, ordained Titus, and left him in Crete, to ordain other bishops and priests to succeed him: "I have left thee in Crete," he writes to Titus, "in order that thou shouldst set in order the things that are wanting, and should ordain priests in every city, as I also appointed thee" (Titus i, 5.) Those bishops who were ordained by the apostles, ordained again other bishops and priests, wherever they were needed; and these again, in their turn, ordained others, and so on, in regular succession, down to our own time. Thus, every one of our own bishops and priests is the direct descendant of one or other of the apostles. Therefore, every Catholic bishop can, with truth, say to his flock: "I was consecrated bishop by such a Catholic bishop; he himself was consecrated by such another Catholic bishop, and so on, in a direct line, which reaches to the apostles, themselves. It is thus, through an unbroken line of bishops, that I hold from the apostles their own power to preach to you the word of God, to administer to you the sacraments, and to exercise the spiritual government over your souls. With St. Paul, therefore, I can say to you: 'For Christ we are ambassadors, God, as it were, exhorting by us.'" (2 Corinthians v, 20.)

Indeed, if the Church is the spouse of Christ, the popes, bishops, and priests are her guardians. If the Church is an army ranged in battle, the popes, the bishops, and the priests are her generals. If the Church is a vessel, steering across the storms of persecutions, the popes, bishops, and priests are her pilots. If the Church is the mystic body of Christ, and if the faithful are its members, the popes, the bishops, and priests are the principal members of this body. By their eyes, Jesus Christ watches over his flock; by their feet, he carries to every nation the Gospel of peace; by their hearts, he diffuses everywhere the life of that divine charity without which all is dead. It the Church is the people of acquisition, bought at a great price, the popes, the bishops, and the priests are the leaders, the teachers, the princes, of that chosen generation. If the Church is that sacred edifice, built up by the Divine wisdom itself for the children of God, the popes, the bishops, and the priests are the administrators of this palace; they are the columns of the Church, upon which the whole world rests. God the Father has created the world without the popes, the bishops, and the priests, but it is only through them that he saves it. God the Son redeemed the world without the popes, the bishops, and the priests, but it is only by them that he applies his blood to the souls of men and secures the fruits of his copious Redemption. And you can hardly name a single blessing of the Holy Ghost, without beholding by the side of that blessing the priest as the instrument through which that Divine Spirit communicates his blessing. Yes; if St. Bernard is right in saying that all comes to us through Mary, we are also right in saying that all comes to the people through the popes, the bishops, and the priests,—all happiness, all graces, all heavenly gifts.

§ 3. — GOD THE HOLY GHOST OUR TEACHER

1. Were the apostles to exercise their powers immediately after they had received them?

No; Christ commanded them to wait for the coming of the Holy Ghost. When a king levies soldiers to make war, he must have weapons wherewith to arm them. It would be utterly foolish to send them to fight without arms. It would be simply to sacrifice his men to no purpose, and to invite defeat. Surely God acts with, at least, equal wisdom: "He does not call," says St. Bernardine of Sienna, "without giving, at the same time, to those whom he calls, all that is necessary to accomplish the end for which he calls." (Serm. I, De St. Joseph.) Jesus Christ chose the apostles to continue his work on earth. Their duty was to teach his holy doctrine. To teach it well, it was necessary for them to understand it thoroughly, and to remember it all. But the apostles were at first men without learning, most of them being poor fishermen when called by Christ. They were, naturally enough, full of the prejudices of their nation; their ideas were altogether worldly. Christ had instructed them for three years, in public and in private. Sometimes he spoke to them in parables, at other times he addressed them in plain language. But his parables were to them so many riddles, and his more open instructions they interpreted in a wrong sense. They scarcely knew for what end he had come on earth; they did not as yet understand that the world was to be redeemed by his blood. Even on the day of his ascension, they were figuring to themselves the deliverance of their country from the yoke of the Romans; and their thoughts were of seeing their Master seated, like one of the old Jewish kings, on the temporal throne of King David. Such was their ignorance; such were their ideas. Certainly, as they then were, they were not fit to be sent to preach Christ's doctrine to all nations, or, indeed, any doctrine at all. Moreover, the apostles were to take Christ's place, and continue his work as priests. Christ, as priest, offered his life on the cross for the salvation of mankind; and his desire was that he himself should be offered by the apostles in the sacrifice of the Mass. To be fitted to take the place of Christ as priest, to represent him in his highest character in a worthy manner, it was necessary for the apostles to be like him in all things,—willing, in imitation of their divine Master, to sacrifice, for the sake of his religion, all that was near and dear to them. It was necessary that they should be willing even to lay down their lives for the sake of the faith. In a word, it was necessary for them to be possessed of heroic virtues, for they were to go as lambs among a pack of wolves. If, at the ascension of our Lord, the apostles were not prepared to take Christ's place and continue his work as teachers, they were still less prepared to continue his work as priests. It is true they had been in the school of Jesus Christ for three years; they had witnessed, day by day, his example of charity and meekness, his zeal for the salvation of souls, his spirit of self-sacrifice. Yet, for all that, the apostles had made little progress in virtue. They often yielded to feelings of envy, and to many human weaknesses and imperfections. We find the two sons of Zebedee ambitious; one wishing to sit on the right hand, and the other on the left, of Jesus Christ. On the very eve of Christ's crucifixion there arose among the apostles a dispute for the first place. Finally, the apostles were to be rulers of Christ's kingdom onearth,—the holy Catholic Church.

They were to announce not only to the subjects of the rulers of nations, but also to the rulers themselves, that they were bound to hear the Church like the humblest, and to submit their souls to her guidance, under pain of eternal banishment from the presence of God. Should they dare to command where it was their duty to obey, their mistake would be disastrous to themselves, because "there was no respect of persons with God." (Romans ii, 11.) Such a religion could not be announced without being contradicted, hated, and even most cruelly persecuted, especially by the monarchs of this world, who refuse to recognize anyone superior to themselves. Poor apostles, especially poor St. Peter, the head of the apostles! At the voice of a servant-maid, Peter had denied his divine Master, and taken a solemn oath that he knew him not. And so fearful, so weak, so cowardly were the others that, when their Lord was seized in the garden, they ran away, and left him alone in the hands of his enemies. During his passion, not one of them stood up for his defense; and whilst he was hanging on the cross, St. John alone had the courage to stand at the foot of that cross. They hid themselves, through fear of the Jews; the slightest danger affrighted them; the least obstacle discouraged them. Such were the apostles, even on the day of Christ's ascension into heaven Christ knew them to be uncultivated, and yet he chose them to confound the learning of the wise of this world; he knew them to be ignorant, and yet he selected them to unravel the most ingenious sophistry; he knew them to be weak, and yet he called them to exhaust the cruel ingenuity of all their persecutors. Idols were to crumble before them into dust; men were to be astonished, without knowing why, to find themselves Christians. But God was pleased, says St. Paul, to choose the foolish things of the world, to confound the wise; and the weak things of the world, in Order to confound the strong. (1 Corinthians i, 27). As, at the sound of his voice, the universe came into being out of nothing, so he had only to bless his apostles, and his Church, or kingdom on earth, and a new spiritual world, stood forth, all beautiful, in the midst of nations.

And Christ had repeatedly promised this blessing to the apostles. The Holy Ghost was to bestow it upon them. "The Comforter, the Holy Ghost," he told them, "whom the Father will send in my name, he will teach you all things, and bring all things to your mind, whatsoever I shall have said to you." (John xiv, 26.) For this blessing, Christ commanded the apostles to wait, before leaving Jerusalem to announce the Gospel to all nations. Not long after Christ's ascension, the apostles received this blessing in abundance. According to promise, Christ sent upon them the Holy Ghost, the spirit of life, to animate them; the spirit of grace, to sanctify them; the spirit of wisdom, to enlighten them; the spirit of love, to unite them to himself; the spirit of prudence, to guide them; the spirit of fortitude, to strengthen them; the spirit of piety, to comfort them, and make them fervent; the spirit of peace, to calm their passions; the spirit of purity, to make them pure; the spirit of liberty, to detach them from all earthly things; the spirit of joy, to console them; the spirit of humility, to inspire them with a mean opinion of themselves; the spirit of obedience, to bring them in perfect subjection to the divine will; the spirit of charity, to accompany all their thoughts and actions.

2. When did the Holy Ghost come down upon the apostles?

On the feast of Pentecost, the Holy Ghost came down upon the apostles in the shape of fiery tongues.

After the ascension of our Savior, the apostles assembled together in an upper room in the city of Jerusalem, and remained there for ten days, occupied in prayer, the Blessed Virgin and the holy women being with them. The roofs of the houses in Palestine being flat, the upper room was often the best and largest, as well as the most retired. It was in this upper room that St. Peter proposed the election, by lot, of an apostle to take the place of the apostate Judas. The lot fell upon Matthias, who took at once the place of Judas. The sacred assembly was composed of about one hundred and twenty persons, awaiting the coming of the Holy Spirit. At length, on the tenth day of their retreat, the Jewish feast of Pentecost, while they were all assembled together, "suddenly," about nine o'clock, "there came a sound from heaven, as of a mighty wind coining, and it filled the whole house where they were sitting; and there appeared to them parted tongues, as it were of fire, and it sat upon every one of them. And they were all filled with the Holy Ghost; and they began to speak in divers tongues the wonderful works of God, according as the Holy Ghost gave them to speak." (Acts ii, 2.) No sooner had the Holy Ghost come down upon the apostles, then he at once banished from their minds and hearts error, ignorance, prejudices, worldly motives, earthly desires, and, as Christ had promised, taught them not only some, but all truths. In a moment he changed them completely. A moment before, they were ignorant; but now they are all filled with the most profound knowledge. A moment before, they could not understand the plainest truths; but now they understand the great mysteries of religion. Just a moment before, they were ignorant disciples; but now they are made the teachers of all nations. Such is their eloquence and their power of mind, that they convince the

greatest orators, and confound the most learned philosophers. On the
very day of the descent of the Holy Ghost, St. Peter preached to the
Jews, and converted three thousand persons. Like so many lions, all
the apostles go forth, animated with zeal and charity. No obstacle,
no power, no force, could stop their progress. The sure prospect
of the cruelest death could not prevent them from performing the
duties of their sacred ministry. Their words, animated with the love
of God, penetrated and inflamed the hearts of their hearers, like darts
of fire. The cities of Jerusalem, Antioch, Ephesus, even Rome itself,
the great mistress of the world, listen with rapture and amazement
to the burning words of the fishermen. At the sound of their voices
the temples of the heathen gods fell, as the walls of Jericho fell at the
sound of the trumpet of Josue. Regardless of danger, they preached
Christ crucified, in defiance of all the powers of the world. They
passed from city to city, from province to province, from kingdom
to kingdom, to preach against the most ancient abuses and the most
deeply-rooted vices. The whole world opposed them; but they were
stronger than the world. The cross and gibbet were set up before
them to silence them, but they replied: "We must announce the things
that we have seen and heard; we must obey God more than man."
In a word, they made such rapid progress, they preached with such
wonderful success, that their doctrine reached the extremities of the
world, as then known. It was thus that they established the kingdom
of Christ on earth,—the holy Catholic Church,—not by the force of
arms, not by the severity of cruel laws, not by means of wealth, but
by the strength, light, and courage, planted in their souls by the Holy
Ghost. In defense of Christ's doctrine, they even laid down their lives.
St. Peter was crucified at Rome, with his head down. On the same day
St. Paul, who had been especially appointed Apostle of the Gentiles,
was beheaded in Rome. St. Andrew was crucified in Patras, in Greece.

St. James the Greater was beheaded. St. James the Less was cast down from the battlements of the temple. St. Simon was sawed in two. St. John the Evangelist was cast into a cauldron of boiling oil, and being mercifully preserved, he was banished to the isle of Patmos, where he wrote the Apocalypse. Two years after, he returned to Ephesus, and died at the age of ninety. We learn from tradition that the other apostles also suffered and died for the sake of the Gospel which they preached.

3. How did the apostles prove their divine mission?

By many miracles, which they wrought in the name of Jesus.

If we open the books of the Old Testament, we find, in almost every page, accounts of miracles worked by God in behalf of his people. In every great emergency, and whenever it was expedient to warn, to protect, to teach, or to chastise, we find the hand of God stretched out for the performance of miracles. When our Savior appeared in this world, his birth, his life, his death and resurrection, were a series of miracles. He established his divine mission by the working of miracles. His apostles and disciples did the same, under his eye, and by his positive direction: "Going," said he to them, "preach, saying: The kingdom of heaven is at hand. Heal the sick, raise the dead, cleanse the lepers, cast out devils." (Matthew x, 7, 8.) Christ knew that the heathen nations, blinded as they were with superstition and idolatry, sunk in sensuality, governed by their brutal passions, and having no distinct ideas regarding supernatural things, could not, without any other force or power than the preaching of poor fishermen, be induced to forsake their false gods and worship an invisible God, nor renounce their carnal passions, in the hope of a spiritual reward in another world. Therefore, when he imparted to his apostles the great commission to convert the world to his religion, he granted them, at the same time, the power of miracles; thus, to show that they were really God's ministers, and that he spoke and wrought through them. Hence, we find that the apostles continued to work miracles after the ascension of their Divine Master. The first preaching of the Gospel in Jerusalem, after the day of Pentecost, was accompanied, and rendered effectual, by the miraculous healing of the lame man, at the gate of the temple, by St. Peter and St. John. St. Peter also cured Eneas of the palsy and raised Tabitha to life. His very shadow cured the sick (Acts v, 15): and even the handkerchiefs of St. Paul were the instruments employed by God for signal manifestations of divine power. In a word, the Gospel was introduced and everywhere established by miracles, as St. Mark tells us at the end of his Gospel: "And the apostles, going forth, preached everywhere: the Lord working withal, and confirming their doctrine with miracles that followed."

4. Is, then, the doctrine of the apostles to be received as the doctrine of Christ?

Yes, for Christ said to his apostles: "He that heareth you, heareth me." (Luke x, 16.) "It is not you that speak, but the Holy Ghost" (Mark xiii, 11.)

Allured by no earthly advantage and subdued by no other force than that of the truth preached and confirmed by the miracles of the apostles, the learned and the ignorant, the Jews and the Gentiles, Greeks and barbarians, meekly bent their necks to the yoke of Christ, shook off their ancient prejudices, and professed themselves the followers of a crucified God. To become a Christian, a follower of Christ, in those days, was almost equivalent to certain martyrdom. The most trying of torments were employed against the Christians:

racks and wheels, to stretch and disjoint their limbs; iron teeth, to tear their flesh; fire, gridirons, boiling oil, melted lead, to torture them; wild beasts, to devour them. Some of them were flayed alive or scourged till their bowels burst forth; others were sawed in two; some, again, had their hands and feet cut off, their eyes and teeth plucked out, their nails torn off; some were wrapped in pitch, and used as torches to light up the streets of infidel cities. But their faith was stronger than all torments: it overcame them all, it overcame death itself.

And the faith of the early Christians was so strong, because they beheld in the apostles Jesus Christ himself continuing, in them and through them, the work of redemption for the honor of his heavenly Father and the salvation of mankind. When they heard the apostles preach, they most firmly believed that Jesus Christ preached to them, because he had said to those preachers: "Go and teach all nations; he who heareth you, heareth me." "You despised me not," writes St. Paul to the Galatians, "you did not reject me, but you received me as an angel of God, even as Christ Jesus. I bear you witness that, if it could be done, you would have plucked out your own eyes, and would have given them to me." (Galatians iv, 14, 15.) The same apostle says of the Thessalonians: "We thank God without ceasing: because, when you had received of us the word of the hearing of God, you received it not as the word of men, but, as it is indeed, the word of God, who worketh in you that have believed." (1 Thessalonians ii, 13.) Yes, "I in them" (the apostles and their successors), says Jesus Christ, "and thou, Father, in me. The glory which thou hast given me, I have given them." (John xvii, 22, 23). Indeed, the apostles and their successors are men all divine. The royal prophet says of them: "Ye are gods. "To forgive sins, to cause the Holy Ghost to dwell in the soul, to change bread and wine into the body and blood of Christ, are miracles that can be performed only by God himself. Yet, by the command of God, his priests perform

these miracles every day. They may, therefore, truly be said to be gods;
for, as St. Gregory Nazianzen says, "to have the power of an apostle of
Christ is to be a god on earth, with the commission to make gods of
his fellow-men." Next to God, an apostle, or a successor of an apostle,
ranks highest in power. This truth can be understood only in heaven.
If men upon earth could fully understand this truth, they would die
of love.

What admiration and respect, what love and veneration, would
be elicited for him whom the Lord would, associate with himself
to govern the universe, to rule with him the course of the stars, the
changes of the seasons, and, if you will, to create with him new worlds!
A vocation so marvelous would place this privileged mortal in a rank
apart. But the apostles and all their successors are the objects of a
distinction far more glorious. They are not called, it is true, to direct
the course of the sun, to excite or calm the winds—all that is within
the sphere of nature and time. They are called to a higher office: to
give to heaven the elect; to snatch victims from hell; to sanctify souls;
to concur in the redemption of a world, spiritual and indestructible;
to fill the greatest of kingdoms with inhabitants, all radiant with glory,
divine and everlasting.

Since God, then, has placed the apostles and all their
successors,—the popes, bishops, and priests of the Catholic
Church,—upon the thrones of his own power and sanctity; since he
has given them the titles of "saviors of the world," since he calls them
his "cooperators in the divine work of redemption," what wonder
if he commands all men to hear, to obey, and to honor them, as
they are bound to hear, to obey, and to honor God himself! "He
that heareth you," says he, "heareth me;" "He that toucheth you,
toucheth the apple of mine eye." In the apostles, therefore, and in their
successors, every good Christian sees the ambassadors of the blessed

Trinity: "Go," says Christ to them,— "go and baptize all nations in the name of the Father, and of the Son, and of the Holy Ghost. "In them, therefore, the Christian beholds the representatives of God the Father, to sustain his cause, to make his name respected, to defend his interests, to promote his glory, to vindicate his honor, to adopt for him children, and to prepare them for his service and his kingdom. The good Christian sees, in the apostles and all their successors, the representatives of the Son of God; because, in his name, and by his authority, they preach his Gospel, offer in sacrifice his body and blood, dispense his mysteries and his graces. He sees in them the agents of the Holy Ghost: "It is not you that speak," says Christ, "but the Holy Ghost." (Mark xiii, 11.)

5. Does, then, the Holy Ghost abide with the Church?

Yes, for Christ promised that the Holy Ghost would always abide with the Church.

Our divine Lord made a great promise to all his faithful followers, when he said: If you love me, I will pray to my Father, and he will send you the Holy Spirit, that he may always dwell in you. "If you love me, keep my commandments. And I will ask the Father that he shall give you another Paraclete (Comforter), that he may abide with you forever." (John xiv, 15, 16.) This promise was fulfilled on the tenth day after his ascension into heaven. On that day the apostles did not receive the Holy Ghost for themselves alone; they received him also to communicate him, by themselves and their successors, to all faithful followers of Christ. Indeed, it is not even natural to suppose that the special gifts and powers by which the knowledge of Christ, and faith in him, were to be spread over the world, were to die out with the first few men to whom those gifts and powers were given. St. Luke tells us that, when the apostles heard that Samaria had received the word of God, they sent unto them Peter and John.

These two apostles prayed for them that they might receive the Holy Ghost, who was not as yet come upon Any of them. Then they laid their hands upon them, and they received the Holy Ghost. (Acts viii, 14—17.) Thus did the faithful receive the Holy Ghost by the ministry of the apostles or their successors, both in baptism and confirmation. On this account St. Paul writes: "The charity of God is poured forth in our hearts by the Holy Ghost, who is given to us." (Romans v, 5.) Hence, St. Bonaventure says, that "the just receive, not only the gifts, but also the person, of the Holy Ghost" (1 Sent., d. 14, a. 2, 9, 1), because, when the Holy Ghost infuses his charity and other gifts into a soul, he is so united to his gifts, that he infuses them together with himself. The same is taught by the renowned Master of Sentences (Lib. i, dist. 14 et 15), who quotes St. Augustine and others in support of this doctrine. "Grace," says Suarez, "establishes a most perfect friendship between God and man; and such a friendship requires the presence of the friend, that is, the Holy Ghost, who stays in the soul of his friend, in order to unite himself most intimately with him, and reside in his soul, as in his temple." It is for this reason that St. Paul writes to the Corinthians: "You are the temple of the living God;" as God saith: "I will dwell in them, and walk among them, and I will be their God, and they shall be my people " (Leviticus xxvi, 12); "I will be a father to you, and you shall be my sons and daughters, saith the Lord." (Jeremiah xxxi, 9.) Since that remarkable day on which the Holy Ghost came down upon the apostles, he has never abandoned, and will never abandon, the faithful followers of Christ, the living members of his Church.

6. Why does the Holy Ghost abide with the Church?

To preserve the Church in the purity of doctrine and in the unity of faith.

"Truth," says St. Thomas Aquinas, "is the good— the life of the intellect; whilst falsehood is the evil—the death of the intellect. As long as man remained innocent, it was impossible for man's intellect to believe that to be true which was really false. As, in the body of the first man, there could not be the presence of any evil, so, in like manner, in his soul there could not be the belief in anything false." But, alas, ever since the fall of our first parents, there have been two elements continually combating each other,—truth and falsehood, virtue and vice, true faith and heresy and infidelity. Satan is called in Holy Scripture the father of lies. From the beginning of the world, he tried to turn all religious truths into lies. He practiced this black art in paradise; and having succeeded in making our first parents believe his lying tongue, he has ever since continued to practice it on their descendants, thus to draw them away from God whom he hates, and to spread error and vice among men. But in spite of the efforts made by Satan and his agents,—the enemies of truth,—to destroy and falsify all religious truths, they never succeeded in obscuring it in the Holy Catholic Church. In her, Christ's holy doctrine has always been preserved pure and uncorrupted, because the Holy Ghost, the Spirit of truth, reigns forever in the Church, and abides with her; for which reason, in the Catholic Church, even children have an intuition of truth without fear and confusion, and talk of God and his mysteries as if they had conversed with angels, while they display a clear knowledge of the whole circle of revealed truths, in comparison with which knowledge the wild guesses and perpetual contradictions of the most famous and learned pagans, or unbelieving philosophers or sectaries, are but inarticulate cries.

One day a little Irish girl was weeping to find herself in a Protestant school, to which she had been carried by force, and where it was considered a useful employment of time to blaspheme the Mother of God. "How do you know she is in heaven?" said a grim Protestant spinster to the little girl. The child knew very well that Our Lady is the Queen of heaven, and enthroned by the side of her divine Son, but had never asked herself how she knew it, nor met anyone before who was impudent enough to deny it. She winced for a moment, as if she had received a blow, then flinging back the long hair which fell over her face, this child of a Galway peasant fiercely answered: "How do I know she is in heaven? Why, you Protestants don't believe in purgatory. If she is not in heaven, she must be in hell. It's a pretty son who would send his mother to hell!" Such an answer will surprise no Catholic; it may astonish a Protestant. Other children say like words a hundred times. The gift of faith is a light of the Holy Ghost, which enlightens the minds of the faithful, even of children, to know and to believe that what the Church teaches is a holy and divine doctrine.

7. How does the Holy Ghost preserve the Church in the purity of faith?

By making the head of the Church the infallible teacher in matters of faith and morals.

When our Lord Jesus Christ established his Church, he knew that in all future ages certain men, moved by human weakness or Satanic malice, or by both combined, would arise to corrupt or misinterpret the holy doctrine of his Church; for, men are free agents, and if they will go against God, God, halving given them this most glorious privilege of freedom, does not deprive them of it, even when they use it against himself, though, as he has unmistakably warned them, he will call them to strict account for their use or abuse of man's noblest gift. Now, to remove all doubts about the true meaning of Christ's doctrine, and to preserve it pure and free even from every chance of error, it was necessary that there should be someone privileged by God to state plainly, with divine certainty, that doctrine in all points of faith and morals; in other words, it was necessary that there should be a supreme judge to decide in all disputed points of divine law, from whose sentence there should be no appeal. Without this necessary safeguard, the way was forever open to error, and the work of Christ on earth practically useless.

If every man in the country were to explain the laws of the State as he pleases, there would be nothing but confusion and disorder in society. In like manner, if every man were to interpret the sacred, eternal law of God, the doctrine of Christ, as he pleases, there would be nothing but confusion and disorder in religion. To prevent confusion and disorder in society, human wisdom found it necessary to appoint a supreme judge to decide ultimately in all disputed points of civil law. Now, if even human wisdom sees the necessity of appointing a supreme judge, to decide ultimately in all points of civil law, it is most clear that God, who is infinite wisdom, could and did not fail to appoint a supreme judge to decide ultimately in all points of divine law, in order thus to prevent the possibility of confusion in religion. There never was a time when men were left to themselves to fashion their own religion, to invent their own creed, their own form of worship, and to decide in matters of religion, as they pleased. There always existed on earth a visible teaching authority, to which it was the bounden duty of every man to submit. During the four thousand years that elapsed before the coming of the Redeemer, the doctrines that were to be believed, the feasts that were to be observed, the sacrifices, the ceremonies of worship, everything connected with religion, were regulated by the living, authoritative voice of the patriarchs, the priests, and the prophets. In the Old Law, God appointed a tribunal, presided over by the high priest, to judge in all controversies, both of doctrine and morals. The decision of this tribunal was final, and without appeal. The Jewish historian, Josephus, who was well acquainted with the laws and religion of his own nation, says (lib. 2, contra Appium): "The high priest offers sacrifice to God before the either priests; he guards the laws, judges controversies, punishes the guilty, and whoever disobeys him is punished as one that is impious toward God." But a still greater authority than Josephus, the word of God itself, bears witness to the fact (Deuteronomy xvii, 8—12): "If thou perceive," says Holy Scripture, "that there be among you a hard and doubtful matter in judgment between blood and blood, cause and cause, and thou sees that the words of the judges within the gates do vary, arise and go up to the place which the Lord thy God shall choose. And thou shalt come to the priests and to the judge, that shall be at that time, and thou shalt ask them, and they shall show thee the truth of the judgment. And thou shalt do whatsoever they shall say, and thou shalt follow their sentence. Neither shalt thou decline to the right hand, nor to the left hand. But he that will be proud, and refuse to obey the commandments of the priest who ministered at the time to the Lord thy God, and to the decree of the judge, that man shall die, and thou shalt take away the evil from Israel." Here, then, is clearly a tribunal, appointed by Almighty God himself, to decide in the last resort,—a tribunal from whose sentence there is no appeal. Consider carefully every word of the inspired text. There is no exception, the rule is for all, the terrible sentence is pronounced against every transgressor: whosoever shall refuse to abide by the decision of the high-priest, shall die the death. Witness the punishment of Core, Dathan and Abiron: the earth opened and swallowed them up for refusing to obey. This supreme tribunal remained intact until the coming of the Redeemer.

Our Lord himself assures us of this: "The Scribes and Pharisees have sat on the chair of Moses.

All things, therefore, whatsoever they shall say to you observe and do." (Matthew xxiii, 2.) Again, our Lord assured us that he came not to destroy the law, but to make it perfect. He therefore established, in the New Law, in his Church, that which, in the Old Law, was most necessary for the preservation of faith and morals. He gave to the whole world an infallible judge and teacher in the person of St. Peter, the head of his Church, and in every successor of St. Peter, to decide ultimately in all points of faith and morals. Christ himself assures us that Peter and his successors are the infallible teachers of his religion. He told St. Peter that, by his prayer to his heavenly Father, he had obtained the gift of infallibility for him and all his successors: "I have prayed for thee (Peter), that thy faith fail not; and thou, being once converted, confirm thy brethren." (Luke xxii, 31, 32.) Christ prayed to his heavenly Father that St. Peter and his successors should possess the gift of teaching his religion infallibly, or with divine certainty; because he wished that the never-failing faith of St. Peter and his successors should be forever the foundation-stone of his Church. He assures us of this great truth, when he asked the apostles, "Who do you say that I am?" (Matthew xvi, 15); to which question Peter made answer, saying: "Thou art Christ, the Son of the living God." To this reply of St. Peter, Christ most solemnly answered: "Blessed art thou, Simon Bar-Jona: because flesh and blood hath not revealed it to thee, but my Father who is in heaven. And I say to thee that thou art Peter, and upon this rock I will build my Church." In these words Christ plainly says: As it is my Father who has made known to thee, Peter, that I am his Son, so, also, I make known to the whole world that thou and thy successors shall always know and understand who I am, and what I have taught, because I have entrusted you with my whole flock:

teachers and hearers, priests and people, rulers and subjects: "Feed my lambs, feed my sheep." (John xxi, 16.) Your faith, I most solemnly premise, shall not fail, since no power shall prevail against thee and thy successors, so as to cause you to teach anything else than I myself have taught: "The gates of hell shall not prevail against my Church," built upon your never-failing faith. (Matthew xvi, 18.) Hence it is that within the Church the successor of Peter speaks like his Master, "as one having authority," that he and all the elect of God obey that authority. They know that he who said, "Thou art Cephas (a rock), and upon this rock I will build my Church," lives and reigns in the Holy See. There is his throne on earth. There is the supreme tribunal before which the saints have always pleaded. "To it," as St. Irenaeus wrote, "all the Churches must have recourse;" with it, all the faithful everywhere must always agree." St. Athanasius, driven from his see, appeals to Julius, the Roman Pontiff. St. Dionysius of Alexandria, accused of heresy, implores Pope Stephen to examine and judge his faith. St. Peter of Alexandria has recourse to St. Damasus. St. Cyril of Alexandria flies to St. Celestine. St. Jerome tells the Roman Pontiff, "Who gathers not with thee, scattereth." Tertullian calls him, "the bishop of bishops." St. Ambrose says that where he is "there is the Church." St. Augustine accepts the judgment of St. Innocent as that of heaven. St. Cyprian told Antonianus, "To be united with the See of Rome is to be united to the Catholic Church;" and, when even heretics appealed to the Sovereign Pontiff, pointed out the absurdity of their "going to the Chair of Peter, whence sacerdotal unity takes its rise." The amazing words of our Lord to St. Peter find their sure interpretation in the actual history of the Church, and the loving obedience of the saints. The one is but the fulfilment of the other. Everywhere the Roman Pontiff, —a Victor, a Damasus, a Stephen, an Innocent, or a Gregory,—claims the same supreme authority, and everywhere the saints confess, with acclamation, that he derives it from God. Every part of Christendom bears witness, from the earliest ages, that the Church is built on Peter. At the same moment, as Socrates relates in his history, the Bishops of Constantinople, Gaza, Ancyra, and Adrianople, driven from their sees, commit their cause to Pope Julius. The Council of Antioch adopts the words of Juvenal, Bishop of Jerusalem, that "it is an apostolic tradition that the Church of Antioch should be directed and judged by the Church of Rome." "Peter has spoken by Leo," says the Council of Chalcedon. Churches, the most remote from the center of unity, proclaim the same truth as loudly as those which are contiguous to it. At the Council of Arles, the Bishops of London, York, and Lincoln, confess, in the name of all their colleagues, the rights and prerogatives of the Holy See. When England had finally conquered Wales, and the Bishop of St. Davids was summoned to do homage to the See of Canterbury, he replied that the British bishops had never recognized any superior "except the Holy See." The Church of Scotland gave a similar answer to the Archbishop of York when he claimed jurisdiction over it, and "the answer was approved," as Lingard observes, "by Pope Clement III. "These are only a few examples out of thousands. There is no opposing voice in the whole multitude of the faithful.

It is clear that the infallibility of the pope was implied and assumed by the Fathers of the Church in every word they uttered. Without this conviction, all that the saints said of the Roman Pontiff and his office would have been idle verbiage or criminal exaggeration. Their own fervent confessions prove that the perpetuity of the faith was not a more certain truth to them than the inerrancy of its chief witness. They understood, from the reiterated declarations of our Lord to Peter, unique in the whole history of God's dealings with man, that the Holy See was designed to be the eternal bulwark against heresy, the rock of the Church, the center of unity, and arbiter of the faith. And they said so. They could not affirm this fundamental truth more explicitly than their Lord had done, nor exalt the functions of his Vicar more magnificently than he who gave to him "the keys of the kingdom of heaven." And the councils echoed the same imperishable doctrine. They neither assembled without the pope's permission, nor dared to promulgate their decrees without his sanction.

The pope, by his own motion, often condemned and defined Catholic doctrine, both before and after the first general council; and if the obstinacy of the party condemned by the pope made it advisable to have recourse to general councils, then those councils, after the most mature deliberation, were never found to do anything else than adhere to the sentence already passed by the pope. The Council of Ephesus, in forming its judgment against Nestorius, said that it did so, "following the canons and the epistle of the pope." The same council also ratified, without any further examination, the papal condemnation of Pelagianism.

The Council of Chalcedon, in drawing up its decisions on the point of controversy, did not appeal to the synod which had been held at Constantinople under Flavian; it appealed only to the decree of the pontiff.

In the judgment upon Eutyches, Cecropius, Bishop of Sebaste, declared, in the name of all his brethren, that the Bishop of Rome had sent to them a formulary; that they all followed him, and subscribed his epistle.

The Sixth General Council, in like manner, declared that it adhered to the dogmatic epistle of Pope Agatho, and by it condemned the heresy.

"The Bishop of Rome," say the Greek Synods and doctors of the Church, "has no need of being taught, because he knows, with an unerring knowledge, what is requisite for the unity of the body of the Church." (Alzog's "Univ. Ch. H.," p. 674.)

The decrees of the Fifth General Council, in 381, were not published as binding on conscience before the had been confirmed and declared as sound Catholic doctrine by the pope, for the simple reason that Christ bound himself solemnly only to Peter and his successors, that their faith should not fail; that is, that every one of them would always be so enlightened by the Holy Ghost as to understand the true meaning of his doctrine, and state and teach it plainly with divine certainty.

When the Fathers at Chalcedon said, "Peter hath spoken by Leo," they did not mean, "Peter hath spoken lies by Leo," but that the voice of the pope in every age is the voice of Peter, as his is of the God who said to him, "Feed my sheep." "Peter is not dead," as St. Ambrose said; and when a great saint cried out, long ages ago, to the Roman Pontiff of his day, "Thou judgest all, but art judged by none," he did not propound the senseless doctrine that the Church is subject to a fallible authority, but that the Prince of the Apostles rules her to the end of time, and that therefore the pope was all that St. Bernard and St. Francis of Sales called him in their day—all that the Vatican Council has proclaimed him in ours. It was for all the saints of God an elementary Christian truth that "error can have no access to the Roman Church," as St. Cyprian confessed, because, as St. Ambroise and St. Augustine declared, "the Chair of Peter is the rock which the gates of hell will never overcome." "The faith of the Apostolic See," says Pope Hormisdas, "has always been inviolate;s he has preserved the Christian religion in its integrity and parity; therefore, anathema upon all who depart from this faith." (Alzog's "Univ. Ch. H.," p. 674.)

It has, then, always been the belief of the Catholic Church that the Pope, in his solemn decisions in matters of faith and morals, is infallible; that is, he cannot be deceived nor deceive: in other words, that what the pope teaches when he speaks to all the faithful as chief pastor and teacher of the Church, is infallibly true. This is an article of faith which we must believe as firmly as we believe that there is a God; to say or even to think otherwise is to be an apostate from the faith before God.

"We teach and define," say the Fathers of the Vatican Council, "that it is a dogma (an article of faith) divinely revealed; that the Roman Pontiff, when he speaks ex cathedra,—that is, when, in the discharge of the office of pastor and doctor of all Christians, by virtue of his supreme apostolic authority he defines a doctrine regarding faith or morals to be held by the Universal Church,— by the divine assistance promised to him in blessed Peter, is possessed of that infallibility with which the Divine Redeemer willed that his Church should be endowed for defining doctrine regarding faith or morals; and that, therefore, such definitions of the Roman Pontiff are irreformable of themselves, and not from the consent of the Church. But if anyone—which may God avert!—presume to contradict this our definition, let him be anathema." (Cap. iv.) Now if anyone asks:

8. When does the pope, by the assistance of the Holy Ghost, teach infallibly?

We answer: The pope teaches infallibly when, as teacher of all Christians, he defines a doctrine concerning faith or morals.

We do not claim for the pope infallibility in his opinion, nor in his conversation, nor when writing a book of theology as a private doctor, etc. He is infallible, as the universal father, in all matters of faith and morals; in all facts, natural or supernatural, which affect the faith or moral government of the Church; in all doctrines, logical, scientific, physical, metaphysical, or political, of any kind whatsoever, which imperil the integrity of the faith or the salvation of souls; he is infallible in determining the religious action which the Church has to take in this world, and the means she must use in order to fulfil the duties which God has imposed upon her. Whenever, then, the Holy Father, as Chief Pastor and Teacher of all Christians, proceeds, in briefs, encyclical letters, consistorial allocation, and other apostolic letters, to declare certain truths, or anything that is conducive to the preservation of faith and morals, or to reprobate perverse doctrines, and condemn certain errors, such declarations of truth and condemnation of errors are infallible, or ex-cathedra acts of the pope, and therefore are binding in conscience, and call for our firm interior assent, both of the intellect and the will, even though they do not express an anathema on those who disagree. To refuse such interior assent would be, for a Catholic, a mortal sin, since such a refusal would be a virtual denial of the dogma of infallibility, and we should be heretics were we conscious of such a denial. (St. Alph6nsus Liguori, "Theol. Moral.," lib. i, 104.) It would even be heresy to say that any such definition of truths or condemnations of perverse doctrines are inopportune, as is clear from a brief of Pope Pius IX, dated Nov. 6, 1876, and addressed to a bishop of Germany. The London Tablet, Dec. 16, 1876, writes: "A very important letter from his Holiness, addressed, as it appears from internal evidence, to a bishop in Germany, though the name of that bishop is not forthcoming, has been given to the world by the newspaper entitled La Croix, Though it has been made public not in a very regular manner, yet, as it has been already reproduced by the French Catholic press, we cannot do wrong in noticing it. The Holy Father, after intimating his approval of the bishop's condemnation of some plan, the nature of which is not stated, goes on to deal with the case of certain German priests, who, after having long delayed manifesting their adhesion to the dogmatic definition of the Vatican Council, touching the infallible magisterium of the Roman Pontiff, have at last made their profession to this effect, but declaring, at the same time, either that they had only made up their minds to do so because they saw those German bishops who had defended the opposite opinions in the council accept their definition, or else they admitted, indeed, the dogma defined, but without admitting the opportuneness of the definition? The Holy Father goes on to say that, as the definitions of General Councils are infallible, by reason of the fact that they proceed from the inspiration of the Holy Spirit assisting the Church, they cannot but teach the truth; and that truth does not derive either its force or its character from the assent of men; rather, as it proceeds from God, it requires a full and entire consent, dependent on no condition. Nor could any heresy have ever been proscribed in an efficacious manner, if it had been permissible to the faithful to wait, before submitting to the definition of the truth, for the assent of those who opposed that definition and were condemned by it. 'This doctrine,' adds his Holiness, 'which is the same for the definitions of Ecumenical Councils, and for the definitions of the Supreme Pontiffs, was clearly expressed by the Vatican Council when it taught, at the close of its definitions, that 'the definitions of the Roman Pontiff are irreformable of themselves, and not in virtue of the consent of the Church.' (Sess. iv, c. iv, in fine.) The Supreme Pontiff then passes judgment on the other class of persons just mentioned. 'It is still more absurd,' he says, 'to accept the definition, and persist in saying that it is inopportune. The vicissitudes, indeed, of our times, the errors as numerous as all that have ever existed, the fresh errors which are every day invented for the destruction of the Church, the Vicar of Christ deprived of his liberty, and the bishops of the power, not only of assembling, but even of teaching,—all attest with what opportuneness

Divine Providence permitted that the definition of the pontifical infallibility should be proclaimed at a time when the right rule of belief and conduct was about to be deprived of all other support. But putting all these considerations on one side, if the definitions of Ecumenical Councils are infallible, precisely because they flow from the wisdom and counsel of the Holy Spirit, nothing, surely, can be more absurd than to think that the Holy Spirit teaches, indeed, things which are true, but may still teach them inopportunely? The bishop to whom the letter is addressed is, therefore, instructed to warn any such priests, if there are any in his diocese, that it is not permitted to them so to limit their assent as to make it depend upon an act,—even a praiseworthy act,—of this or that bishop, rather than on the authority of the Church; and that they must adopt the definition 'by a full and entire assent of intelligence and will, unless they would depart from the true faith.'"

In the question of the infallibility and authority of the Apostolic See, there is one thing which we should be careful to bear in mind: Jesus Christ gave to his Church not only gifts and powers, he gave her, also, an infallible knowledge of these gifts and powers. We must believe that she has this knowledge, and knows, with infallible certainty, what she is, and what is in her, and what belongs to her. It is, therefore, not for us to say where the authority of the Church ceases, and where the authority of human experiment begins. The Church alone can judge how far her authority goes. What things come wholly within the domain of science, and what things belong to the region of faith and morals: where the boundary line is to be drawn, and in what attitude we have to place ourselves as to certain subjects,—these things are altogether beyond our power or our right, and are wholly within the judgment of the Apostolic See. It is left to the Church alone to tell us what is and what is not necessary for the salvation of our souls.

If she tells us that certain things are part of the faith which she has to teach, or necessary for this faith, we are bound to believe her. We have no more questions to ask: "No man," say the Fathers of the great Council of Nice, "ever accused the Holy See of a mistake, unless he was himself maintaining an error. The case of St. Cyprian will occur to everyone. The enemies of the Church have never been able to mention a single instance of a pope who departed one hair's-breadth from the true faith of the Church,—a fact which is admitted even by Protestant writers. Even in the midst of the most evil days, the sanctity of the See of Rome was never wholly obscured." (Englehardt, "Ch. Hist.," vol. i, p. 312; Marheineke, "Uni. Ch. Hist.," Erlangen, 1806.) The true explanation of this fact must be sought for in the prayer of Christ, in which a promise is given to Peter and his successors that they shall enjoy immunity from all error in matters of faith (Luke xxii, 32), and to which pointed reference is made by the popes, Leo the Great and Agatho. Pope Leo says, in his Sermon iv, 4: "All are confirmed in Peter, and the assistance of divine grace so regulated, that the grace which is conferred by Christ on Peter passes on through Peter to the other apostles." Let us be humble, and say, with King Oswy: "I say, like you (St. Wilfred), that Peter is the porter of heaven, and that I will not oppose him, but will, on the contrary, obey him in all things, lest, when I come to the doors of the heavenly kingdom, there be none to open them to me, if I am at variance with him who carries the keys. In all my life I will neither do nor approve any thing or any person that may be opposed to him." (Alzog's "Uni. Ch. Hist.," vol. ii, p. 93.)

9. Are, then, the definitions of the Pope new articles of faith?

No; the Holy Father can make no new articles of faith; he merely defines (that is finally determines) what is of faiths according to Holy Scripture and tradition: "The Holy Spirit" say the Fathers of the Vatican Council, "was not promised to the successors of Peter, that by his revelation they might make known new doctrines, but that by his assistance they might inviolably keep, and faithfully expound, the revelation or deposit of faith delivered through the apostles". Hence, when the pope defines any point of doctrine pertaining to Catholic faith, it is as much as to declare that the doctrine in question was revealed to the apostles and has come down to us from the apostles.

"The pope can change nothing that Christ has established, as of faith, or of morals. The pope could not permit Henry VIII to put away his lawful wife and to marry another. The Protestant Episcopal Church had to be invented to perform that task. The pope cannot authorize me to steal what does not belong to me, or to hate my neighbor and wish him evil. The infallibility of the pope is not omnipotence. It does not give him the liberty to do whatever he pleases. On the contrary, the pope is, almost every day, declaring that he cannot do this or the other thing that his persecuting tormentors ask him to do. His infallibility, then, consists in this: that, while the faith that is in him is also in the other bishops and in the faithful, in these it does not so exist that in one or other of them, or even in many of them, it may not fail. But the privilege granted to the successor of St. Peter is that his faith can never fail. His privilege of infallibility is not to change one iota of the faith, but to keep it pure and undefiled. The nonsense about the pope, in virtue, of his infallibility when teaching the Church, coming to meddle in the political party quarrels of countries, where no question of faith or morals is involved, is too drivellingly insensate to be contradicted. The faith and doctrine of the Catholic Church is open and may be read by all men; by Hymen as by the hierarchy, by non-Catholics as by Catholics. This faith and doctrine the Pope of Rome, by the singular gift to Peter by our Lord, is infallible in keeping and declaring." (From the N. Y. Freeman's Journal.)

10. Is man, then, infallible?

No man is infallible of himself; but the pope is infallible, by the assistance of the Holy Ghost, when he teaches anything as Chief Pastor and Doctor of the Church.

The pope, it is true, is man; but, from the beginning of the world, God has spoken through men. He spoke though the patriarchs and the prophets. But the pope is a greater patriarch than Abraham, he is greater than Melchizedek in priesthood, greater than Moses in authority, greater than Samuel in jurisdiction; he is Peter in power, Christ by unction, pastor of pastors, guide of guides; through him the Holy Ghost speaks and teaches the whole flock of Christ. This is the doctrine of the apostles, say the Fathers of the Vatican Council: "And indeed all the venerable Fathers have embraced, and the holy orthodox doctors have venerated and followed, their apostolic doctrine, knowing most fully that this See of holy Peter remains ever free from all blemish of error, according to the divine promise of the Lord our Savior, made to the Prince of his Disciples: 'I have prayed for thee that thy faith fail not, and when thou art converted, confirm thy brethren?

"This gift, then, of truth and never-failing faith was conferred by heaven upon Peter and his successors in this Chair, that they might perform their high office for the salvation of all; that the whole flock of Christ, kept away by them from the poisonous food of error, might be nourished with the pasture of heavenly doctrine; that, the occasion of schism being removed, the whole Church might be kept one, and, resting on its foundation, might stand firm against the gates of hell." (Cap. iv.) It is, then, the Holy Ghost who speaks through the pope; through him he preserves the purity of Christ's doctrine and teaches it free from every blemish of error.

11. How does the Holy Ghost preserve the unity of faith in the Church?

By granting to her members the gift of faith, which enables them to believe all that the Church teaches.

As Christ, by his prayer, obtained the gift of infallibility for Peter and his successors, in like manner he obtained, by his prayer, the gift of faith for the rest of his flock: "Holy Father," he prayed on the eve of his passion, "keep them in thy name whom thou hast given me, that they may be one, as we are also. And not for them only do I pray, but for them also who, through their word, shall believe in me, that they all may be one, as thou, Father, in me, and I in thee; that they may be one in us, that the world may believe that thou hast sent me." (John xvii.) According to the interpreters of holy Scripture, Jesus Christ asks of his heavenly Father that all his followers might participate in the one and in the same Holy Ghost, so that in him, and through him, they might all be united to the other divine persons. Now, all the prayers of Christ were heard by his Father, as he himself tells us, when he prayed to his Father to raise Lazarus from the dead: "Father, I give thanks that thou hast heard me, and I know that thou hears me always." (John xi, 41.) As Peter and his successors then obtained, by Christ's prayer, the gift of teaching infallibly, so, also, the flock of Peter obtained, by Christ's prayer, the gift of believing most firmly all that Peter in person, or through his successors, would teach them. Various, gifts of the same

Holy Spirit are given to different persons, says St. Paul, that each may discharge his own duty: "For in one spirit we were all baptized into one body . . . and in one spirit we all have been made to drink." (1 Corinthians xii, 13.) As the Vicars of Christ are infallible in teaching, so the Church is infallible in believing.

The head of the Catholic Church,—the body of Christ,— being infallible, the whole body shares the inerrancy of the head. Peter and his successors were made infallible in all that relates to faith and morals, not for their own sake simply, but for the sake of their flock, that truth might never be subject to correction, and that all the pastors and the faithful might be eternally secured from error. Adhering to the infallible judgment of Peter, they cannot be deceived. Such is the God-given privilege of the whole Catholic Church. We have a right to be peremptory in condemning every kind of heresy, and we condemn it with an infallible judgment, for we do not speak in our own name, like heretics; no, we speak in the name of him to whom it has been given, as the Vatican Council says, "to be possessed of that infallibility with which the divine Redeemer willed that his Church should be endowed for defining doctrine regarding faith and morals." It is the perpetuity of this undying authority of Peter which distinguishes the Church of Christ from human sects. It alone supplies both the safeguard of Christian truth, and the test of Christian obedience to truth. Without this infallible authority, all is disorder, and the whole plan of redemption a mockery; there is neither Church nor Christianity but only sects and opinions. Outside the Church neither unity nor obedience is possible, because nothing exists which can maintain the one, or enforce the ether. To be separated from the divine authority of the pope, is to be separated from God, and to have no place in the kingdom of Christ: "Where Peter is, there also is the

Church of Christ;" that is, all those who believe and teach as the pope does, form the true Church of Christ.

12. What, then, is the faith of the Roman Catholic?

The faith of the Roman Catholic is a gift of the Holy Ghost, enabling him to believe firmly all that God teaches through his Church.

Our belief in a person's word is firm, in proportion as we think that he is not deceived in his knowledge; that he knows well what he says, because he is wise and prudent; that he will not deceive us, because he loves the truth, and fears God. Thus, in transacting business, we give more credit to a learned or able, than to an ignorant, man; to a learned man who is virtuous, than to one who is not so.

Now, God is the first and essential truth. His knowledge extends to all things and is infinitely perfect; he is essentially true in his words. He knows things only as they are, and can speak them only as he knows them. Therefore, when God speaks, whether it be in his own divine person, or through the apostles and their lawful successors in the Catholic Church, we must listen and obey, simply because it is the voice of God, who can neither deceive nor be deceived. We must have the most respectful, submissive faith in all that he has revealed to us through his Church, and believe her doctrine with the utmost firmness and simplicity, with an unwavering conviction of their reality.

We must believe all the articles of faith more firmly than we believe the proposition that the whole is greater than its part. We should believe them more firmly than what we see with our eyes, hear with our ears, touch with our hands. We should be more certain of these articles of faith than we are of our own existence, which is a reality of which we cannot doubt; yet the things of faith are still more real, having been taught by God, who cannot deceive us. Our knowledge of natural things comes through the senses, which often deceive us. Hence there is nothing true in the universe of which we ought to be so certain as of the mysteries of religion. "Faith," says St. Basil," always powerful and victorious, exercises a greater ascendency over, minds than all the proofs which reason and human science can furnish, because faith obviates all difficulties, not by the light of manifest evidence, but by the weight of the infallible authority of God, which renders them incapable of admitting any doubt." It was thus that Abraham believed when, notwithstanding all the impediments of nature, he felt sure that he should see himself the father of a son, and, through him, of many nations. "He believed in hope against hope," says St. Paul, "that he might be made the father of many nations, according to what was said to him: 'So shall thy seed be? " And he was not weak in faith, for he considered neither his old age, nor that of his wife Sarah. He distrusted not the premise of God, but was strong in faith, giving glory to God, being most fully convinced that whatsoever God has premised he is able to perform.

The faith of Moses was so great, that St. Paul says of him that "he acted with the invisible God as though he were visible."

Similar was the faith of the famous and valiant Count de Montfort, who, being told that our Lord, in the Host, had appeared visibly in the bands of the priest, said to those who urged him to go and see the miracle: "Let those go and see it who doubt it; as for myself, I believe firmly the truth of the mystery of the Eucharist, as our mother, the holy Church, teaches it. Hence, I hope to receive in heaven a crown more brilliant than those of the angels; for they, being face to face with God, have not the power to doubt."

The noble Count St. Eliazer used to say that, with regard to matters of faith, he believed them so firmly that, if all the theologians in the world strove to persuade him to the contrary, their logic would not have the slightest effect on him.

And, in truth, faith ought to take precedence of reason, demonstration, experience, and all other motives of certitude, with the true Christian and new man regenerated in Jesus Christ: "Consider," says St. Augustine, "that you are not called reasonable, but faithful, since, when anyone is baptized, we say, he has become one of the faithful."

We must have this firm faith not only in some but is all the truths which God has made known, although they may be altogether incomprehensible to us. Faith will not allow the rejection of even one; and he who should voluntarily entertain a doubt of one single article, one single point of faith, could not be said to have faith at all. We believe everything that God has revealed, precisely for this reason, that God has said it.

The word of God, who is infallible truth itself, and who cannot deceive nor be deceived, is the why and wherefore of our belief. To say or to think, I believe this article, this truth of faith, but I do not believe that, is as much as to say or to think, I believe that God tells the truth in this point, but he tells it not in that; it is as much as to say, God is capable of telling a lie. This is blasphemy; it is even the denial of God's existence.

And also to say or to think, I cannot believe such an article, or such a mystery of faith, because it is too obscure, too incomprehensible, and contrary to reason, is to exhibit a lamentable lack of reason. To be a man, it is necessary to have reason. Reason is the light of man. But reason tells us that it is necessary to submit to faith, and that there is no sense in him who wishes to subject to his reason the Author of his reason; and that to wish to understand what is above his intelligence, is to be without intelligence.

Reason tells us that our religion would not be divine if it were not above reason. For God would not be God, if he were not incomprehensible; and my soul could not adore him, if my mind could comprehend him. It is one thing to say that such a mystery is contrary to reason, and another to prove it. To prove that a doctrine is contrary to reason, we must have a clear, precise idea of what that doctrine is. We can say, for instance, that it is contrary to reason to assert that a square is a circle, for we have a clear, precise idea of what a square is, and what is a circle. But we cannot say with certainty that a doctrine or a mystery of our holy faith is contrary to reason, for we can never have a full, clear, precise idea of that doctrine or mystery. We cannot have this clear idea, simply because those doctrines are far above reason. We cannot say, for instance, that the doctrine of the Holy Trinity, the doctrine of the three divine persons in one divine substance, is contrary to reason, because we can never have a clear, precise idea either of God's essence, or of the nature of the three divine persons.

And what is true of the Trinity is true also of all the other doctrines and mysteries of our holy faith. They are not against reason, but they are above reason. Reason is above the senses, and faith is above reason.

"Certainly," says St. John Chrysostom, "since the works of God incomparably surpass the capacity of our minds, the thoughts whereby we seek to penetrate the abysses of faith are always accompanied with folly, and resemble labyrinths which it is very easy to enter, but from which it is almost impossible to come forth. These thoughts spring from pride; and as proud minds are ashamed to believe or to admit that which they cannot understand, they entangle themselves in difficulties from which they cannot easily issue. Is it true, then, proud man, that you can understand how the sun and stars were created; how the earth, with all its riches, was called forth from chaos; how the magnet attracts iron; how a single grain of corn sown in the earth produces a thousand other grains? You are not ashamed to own that you cannot answer these things; and when there is question of things of a more sublime nature, of things that are above the comprehension of angels, you will not avow your ignorance—you make bold efforts to understand them. Fool! the shame is not the inability to comprehend them, but the daring to sound them."

Speaking of Rahab, who received the spies, and of whom St. Paul says that her faith saved her from the unhappy fate of her fellow-citizens, St. Chrysostom praises the simplicity of her faith, and adds: "This woman did not examine what the spies said, neither did she reason with herself thus: How can it be possible that the captives and fugitives now wandering in the desert will capture a city so strong and so well provided as ours? Had she argued thus, she had been lost."

Those of the Israelites, on the contrary, who, hearing of the prodigious strength and power of the countries they were to conquer, yielded to diffidence, notwithstanding the divine assurance that they should vanquish their enemies, even without fighting them, were deprived, by their infidelity, of the happiness which God had promised to their faith.

What could be more strange or more opposed to reason than to command a father to sacrifice his only and most innocent son? And yet Abraham put himself in readiness to offer sacrifice without discussing the commandment, or adducing arguments to prove its unreasonableness. He considered only the divinity and wisdom of Him who commanded.

Another person, who wished to show himself more reasonable, refused to strike a prophet, as he had been ordered to do. Such a thing he thought was improper. But his disobedience was soon punished, for a lion rushed upon him and devoured him, not far from the place where the fault had been committed.

Saul having been ordered by God to put the Amalekites to death, with their flocks and herds, found it reasonable to spare the king, and to set aside the best and fattest of the flocks for sacrifice. As a recompense for his fine reasoning on the subject, he was overwhelmed with many evils, and finally lost his kingdom.

The infant at the mother's breast takes what it sees not; sometimes it will even close its eyes when it might see what it takes, as though it confided entirely in its mother, and in the love she bears it; in like manner the soul draws the milk of faith from the bosom of the Church, which she sees not. She reposes on the infinite wisdom and goodness of Jesus Christ, who can teach her nothing but what is true, and give her nothing that is not good. It is on this juice of divine faith that the just man lives, as St. Paul tells us; he avoids not only open heresy, he also diligently shuns, and his heart dissents from, those opinions which approach it more or less closely; and he religiously observes those constitutions and decrees whereby such evil, opinions, either directly or indirectly, have been proscribed and prohibited by the Holy See. For, to be a good Catholic, "it is not sufficient, says the Vatican Council, "to shun heretical pravity, unless those errors also be diligently avoided, which more or less nearly approach it. We, therefore, admonish all men of the further duty of observing those constitutions and decrees by which such erroneous opinions as are not here specifically enumerated, have been proscribed and condemned by this Holy See." (Can. iv.)

The faith of St. Teresa was so firm, that it seemed to her she could convert all heretics from their errors; and so simple, that she said, the less she comprehended a mystery, the more firmly she believed it, and the more devotion it excited in her: she tasted a singular pleasure in not being able to comprehend it. She silenced all objections to a mystery, by saying: "The Son of God, Jesus Christ, has revealed it to us, and we have no more questions to ask."

Indeed, the fact that Jesus Christ has said or done this or that thing, or has taught it to his Church, and commanded her to teach it to all nations, must be for us the weightiest of all reasons to believe it. The famous word of the Pythagoreans, "The master has said it," was with them a foolish idolatry, believing, as they did, that no one could be deceived. Applied, however, to Jesus Christ, it must be a first principle, a sacred axiom, for every Christian. The heavens and the earth shall pass away, but "the truths of the Lord remain forever." (Psalm cxvi, 2.) He has said: "What is great before men is an abomination before God." He has said: "Sooner will a camel pass through the eye of a needle than the rich enter the kingdom of heaven." He has said: "Woe to you who now rejoice, for you shall weep;" "Blessed are those who weep." He has said: "He who renounces not all, and himself also, cannot be my disciple." He has said it. Reason, perhaps, might suggest that these oracles must be explained, softened, modified; that it cannot comprehend how we can find peace in war, glory in contempt, delight in crosses. But the good Christian listens only to his Master: "Christ has said it." He would not have said it, were it not true. The good Christian believes most firmly the doctrine of the Catholic Church, which the apostles have proclaimed, which so many saints and wise men have preached, which the blood of the martyrs has cemented, which miracles have proved, which reason confirms, which the elements and insensible creatures have announced, which the demons themselves are constrained to acknowledge; yes, the good Christian receives the doctrine of the Catholic Church, glorious with so many victories, radiant with so many crowns, laden with the spoils of all its enemies. If, in imitation of the martyrs, the good Christian has not the happiness to die for this doctrine, he endeavors at least to live up to all its precepts.

§ 4. – THE CATHOLIC CHURCH THE GUARDIAN OF DIVINE TRUTH

The Catholic Church is a living society, established by God. It will always remain as God made it. What he constituted the head of the Church, will continue to be the head. What he constituted the teaching authority, will continue to be the teaching authority. What he constituted the subordinate members, or the hearing Church, will always so continue; and the faith which God commissioned his Church to teach to all nations, will always continue the same faith, for the Catholic faith or religion is the word of God, and the word of God is unchangeable. Hence, if anyone asks:

1. Has the word of God been preserved pure and uncorrupted?

We answer: Most assuredly; for it is impossible that the word of God can be corrupted in the infallible Church.

If we consider the ancient Jewish people, it is impossible not to be struck by the wonderful fact of a whole people surpassing all other nations in antiquity, and living throughout in the very midst of universal idolatry and degradation, bearing intact the deposit of the natural, or the primitive religion; that is, of the belief in, and worship of, one only God, spiritual, holy, all-powerful, Father and Judge of all men; such, in fact, as the whole Christian world worships now.

It was not long before all the nations, illumined originally by the light of primitive religion, saw that light expire. They lost themselves in the paths of superstition and idolatry. They wandered farther and farther away from the truth, and nothing could draw them back to the right way. Thus the human mind generally lost sight of the truth which the Jews alone preserved. Is not this a real prodigy in the moral order? How did the Jews alone escape the universal shipwreck of reason? How came it that they alone held fast to the primitive truth, and resisted the tendency of the human mind toward error,—they who were more ancient than all other nations, and consequently might, as they advanced in age, have become corrupted much sooner than the others?

They were naturally not less gross, not less carnal, not less affected by that moral wound which inwardly weakens all mortal men. How are we to explain this grand fact? The preservation of religious truth among this people can be explained only by attributing it to the same means by which truth was first made known to man: the intervention of God.

The same God who incessantly watched over his sacred word before the coming of Christ, has also watched with the same care over the purity of his word after Christ's coming. Hence our Lord says in the Gospel: "It is easier for heaven and earth to pass, than one tittle of the law to fall." (Luke xvi, 17.) The Jewish Church was commanded by God to try, and, after sentence, to stone anyone, whoever he might be, who counselled them to depart from the true

God: so solicitous did God require that Church to be in saving the people from error. Christ requires his Church to be just as solicitous in saving the people from error. Hence she has never failed to cast her stones of condemnation, reprobation, and excommunication, at those who left the truth, taught perverse doctrine, and led their fellow-men into error and perdition. Witness every General Council, witness every Brief, Apostolical Letter, Consistorial Allocution of the pope, condemning and reprobating heresies and errors of the age; witness the condemnation or the prohibition of so many heretical, licentious, and immoral books. In the days of the primitive Church there was, in the marketplace, a great burning of books which had been condemned by the apostles. In the succeeding centuries, the works of heretics were condemned as soon as they appeared. This practice of condemning false and immoral books has been continued to this day. De Lamennais and Gioberti, Rosmini and Ventura,—of whom the two last have been imitators of the humble Fenelon, the two first of the Arrogant Tertullian,— are examples, in our own day, of the ceaseless vigilance of the successors of St. Peter in rebuking and destroying error. The two first resisted the voice of Peter and withered away like a tree blasted by lightning; the two last obeyed his paternal remonstrance, and, by their humility, acquired fresh titles to the love and respect of Christians, to whom they have left so excellent an example. Such is the sleepless fidelity of God's Vicar, and such are the fruits of his divine mission, to preserve the children entrusted to him in the purity and simplicity of our most holy faith. Before his presence error cannot hide her face, and the spirits of darkness, despairing of success, return to the abyss from which they came.

2. How does the Church preserve the word of God?

The Church preserves the word of God, partly in the Holy Scriptures, and partly in tradition.

The Catholic Church possesses a large volume of sacred writings, called the Holy Scriptures, or Holy Writ, or the Bible, or the written word of God. The Church regards the Bible: 1, as an authentic book, because its various parts are written by those authors to whom they are attributed; 2, as a genuine book, because every part of it has come down to us as the author wrote it, without any essential change; 3, as an inspired book, because either God himself revealed the things contained in each part, and which the author could not have known unless by God's revelation; or because God directed the author in the selection of things already known to him, and preserved him from error whilst writing them. Hence, St. Paul recommends this "Scripture inspired by God" to Timothy (2 Timothy iii, 16), and St. Peter calls its writers "holy men of God," who "spoke, inspired by the Holy Ghost." (2 Peter i, 21.) The Fathers of the Church call the Bible a holy and divine book, and frequently tell us that God himself is its author.

The pure preservation of the sacred writings is altogether owing to the parental solicitude of the Catholic Church. The Church existed as a well-organized society, having full divine authority, before there was ever any question of the Scriptures. This is an undeniable fact.

In the ancient law, we see the Jewish Church established and governed; Moses invested with authority; the people going to him to seek the judgment or sentence of God; Aaron clothed with the priesthood; Joshua placed at the head of their armies; the synagogue directed by chiefs,— and as yet the Scriptures had no existence. The first tables of the law, graven by the hand of the Lord, had been broken by Moses; the second were not brought down from Mount Sinai, and given to the people, until some months afterward. It was very much later, according as events succeeded one another, that

Moses wrote the Pentateuch. As for the other books written by the judges, by David, Solomon, and the prophets,—they did not exist till many centuries after the institution and complete development of the ancient Church: and it was only a few years before the coming of our Savior that the list of the canonical books of the first part of the Bible, or the Old Testament, was closed by the Second Book of the Maccabees.

Then our divine Savior comes. He preaches, he commands his disciples to preach throughout the whole world, but he does not write anything, nor does he command anyone else to write. He imparts his own authority to St. Peter and to the other apostles. After his ascension he sends down his Spirit upon them, and from that moment the Catholic Church is established. She assembles in council, to appoint a successor to Judas, or to declare the Jewish ceremonies abolished; she pronounces on the questions concerning the Gentiles; she preaches, she baptizes, she converts the world; she speaks in all things with the voice and authority of God,—and as yet the New Testament is not written. Of all the apostles and disciples there are but seven who have written; and they have written only fragments of history and some letters.

First came St. Matthew, who began to write his Gospel, at the earliest, six years after the ascension of Christ. St. John did not publish his, with his letters and the Apocalypse, till toward the close of the first century; that is, forty years after St. Paul had said to the Romans, "Your faith is spoken of in the whole world." (Romans i, 8.) At the time when St. Luke wrote the Acts of the Apostles, there existed many churches, governed each by its own pastor, as we see in this book of the Acts. The churches of Rome, of Corinth, Colosse, Thessalonica, Galatia, certainly existed before the Epistles to the Romans, Corinthians, Colossians, Thessalonians, and Galatians, were written. The Apocalypse contains exhortations and reproofs addressed to bishops of the churches. At least ten generations of Christians had lived and died before the world knew such a book as the Bible. It was only in the fourth century, when the persecutions were over, that the Church could and did gather together the scattered books which she had carefully preserved. She determined which were canonical (holy and inspired), and which were not. Many books which were considered inspired and supposed to have been written by the apostles or their disciples, were set aside and rejected as spurious, or not inspired. The Catholic Church collected the proper books in one volume; she put this volume into the hands of her children; she told them it was the word of God, and commanded them to believe and receive it as such.

As the art of printing was not invented until more than a thousand years after the authorized collection of the Scriptures, the Church had the Bible copied thousands of times. She translated it into different languages, and continued to watch over its safety, and to guard it with parental care, amidst storms and revolutions, amidst fire and floods, amidst changes and persecutions. She presses it to her bosom as a treasure of priceless value: her children repeatedly shed their blood to preserve it, rather than expose or surrender it to the danger of profanation.

Under the fiery persecutions of Diocletian, hundreds of Christians laid down their lives rather than give up the sacred books; and later on, during the revolution of the middle ages, the first thing always thought of by the monks, who were then the principal transcribers of the Bible, was to transport the sacred volume to the mountains, or to some other place of safety, at the first approach of danger.

As it is the Catholic Church alone that has preserved the sacred Scriptures, so also, the Catholic Church alone can assure us that these writings are inspired by God, have God for their author, are his infallible word. Inspiration is something altogether supernatural, something that cannot be perceived by any of the senses; something which cannot be rendered infallibly certain by feeling or reason, or any merely human testimony, for no man ever saw a prophet or an evangelist converse with God. No sacred writer ever asserted that any of his writings were inspired. No private man, therefore, is able personally to discover, satisfactorily, divine inspiration either in the forty-five books of the Old Testament, or in the twenty-seven of the New. To know what is from God, inspired pr spoken by God, it is necessary to have come from God, and to be guided by God. And the Catholic Church alone is that society which is established and guided by God, to make known to men, with divine, infallible certainty, what is the word of God, and what is not. She has passed her infallible judgment on the holy Bible. The Council of Trent says: "If any one does not receive all these books, with their parts, as sacred and canonical, let him be anathema." After such a solemn declaration of the Church concerning the authenticity and inspiration of the holy books, every Catholic says, with St. Augustine: "For my own part, I should not have believed the Gospel, if I had not been influenced by the authority of the Catholic Church." Luther himself, the apostate monk, could not help making a similar declaration: "We are compelled," he says, "to concede to the Papists that they have the word of God; that, without them, we should have had no knowledge of it at all."(Comment, on St. John, chap, xvi.) Now then, answer to the question of the Catechism:

3. What is Holy Scripture?

Holy Scripture is a collection of books, written under the inspiration of the Holy Ghost, and acknowledged by the Church to be the written word of God, Now,

4. How is the Holy Scripture divided?

Holy Scripture is divided into the books of the Old and of the New Testament, or of the Old and of the New Law.

The Bible is divided into two parts. The first part contains those books which were written before the coming of Christ; and the second part consists of those books which were written after Christ's coming. All the books of the first part, combined, are called the Old Testament, or the Old Law. The word, "testament," means alliance, or covenant. The Old Testament is the alliance, or covenant, which God made with the ancient Jewish people, through his great servant, Moses. It is a contract containing, on the one part, the commands and promises of God; and, on the other, the engagements of the Jewish people to keep God's commands.

The books of the second part of the Bible are called the New Testament. The New Testament is the alliance, or covenant, which God has made with his new people, the Christians, through Jesus Christ, his own beloved Son. This alliance is more perfect than was the ancient one with the Jews.

5. What do the books of the Old and the New Testament contain?

The books of the Old Testament contain the principal truths which God revealed before the coming of Christ; and the books of the New Testament contemn part of the truths which God revealed through Christ and his apostles.

To prevent men from forgetting or altering his law, God commanded Moses to write down all his ordinances. He also afterward inspired the prophets and others to write their prophecies, their instructions, and, in later times, the doctrine and history of the Catholic Church. According to their contents, the books of the Old Testament are divided into three parts:

1. The historical books, twenty-one in number. They are: the five books of Moses: Genesis, Exodus, Leviticus, Numbers, Deuteronomy. These are called the Pentateuch, or the Law. In them are related the creation of the world, the lives of the patriarchs, and the covenant which God made with his people, who were called the Jews, or the Hebrews, or the Israelites. The other historical books contain either the history of the people of God in general, such as: the books of Joshua, that of Judges, the four books of Kings, the two books called Paralipomenon, the books of Esdras, that of Nehemias, and the two books of Maccabees; or they contain the history of certain saints or other illustrious personages, such as: the histories of Job, Ruth, Tobias, Judith and Esther.

2. The moral books, or the books of instruction. These teach men how to lead holy lives; they are: the one hundred and fifty Psalms of David, the Proverbs, Ecclesiastes, the Canticle of Canticles, the book of Wisdom, and Ecclesiasticus.

3. The prophetical books, namely: the books of the four great prophets, Isaias, Jeremias, Ezechiel, and Daniel; to which may be added David, and the twelve minor prophets: Osee, Joel, Amos, Abdias, Jonas, Micheas, Nahum, Habacuc, Sophonias, Aggeus, Zacharias, and Malachias. These are called the minor prophets,

because they wrote less than the first four. The books of the prophets mostly contain prophecies or announcements of future events.

The books of the New Testament are also divided, according to their contents, into three parts:

1.   The historical books (the Gospels written by St. Matthew, St. Mark, St. Luke, and St. John), and the Acts of the Apostles, written by St. Luke.

2.   The books of instruction, which are the fourteen Epistles by St. Paul: one to the Romans, two to the Corinthians, one to the Galatians, one to the Ephesians, one to the Philippians, one to the Colossians, two to the Thessalonians, two to Timothy, one to Titus, one to Philemon, one to the Hebrews; one by St. James; two by St. Peter; three by St. John; and one by St. Jude.

3.   The prophetic book, or the Apocalypse, or Revelation, by St. John. The catalogue of the books of the Old and the New Testament is called the canon of the Scriptures, and hence the sacred writings themselves are called canonical. "These divine writings," says St. Isidore of Pelusium, "which are set before thee in the Church of God, receive as tried gold, they having been tried in the fire by the divine Spirit of the truth. They are steps whereby to ascend to God." (Lib. i, Ep. 369 5 Cyro, 96. Paris, 1638.)

All the sacred truths, however, taught by our divine Savior and his apostles, are not found in the sacred Scriptures. Hence, it is said in the Catechism that the New Testament contains but part of the truths which God revealed by Jesus Christ and his apostles. Several of these truths have been handed down by tradition.

6. What is tradition?

Tradition is that part of Christ's doctrine which is not recorded in the
New Testament

Tradition signifies testimony or truth, handed down by word of mouth from father to son, and generation to generation. By tradition, as here used, is understood the word of God, not written in the sacred books, but preserved in the memory of men in the manner described. In no age did God wish that all he had taught men for their salvation should be fully and clearly recorded in writing. In fact, for two thousand years there was no written word of God. Moses was the first whom God inspired to write down that which he had made known to mankind from the beginning of the world until his time. But God did not inspire Moses to write down a full, clear statement of all religious truth.

Were Noe, or any other of the patriarchs, to come to us with a copy of what Moses wrote about his knowledge of God and the truths revealed by the Lord, he would tell us that he had a wider, clearer, more definite, and more practical knowledge of religious truth, than is conveyed by the words of Moses to the isolated reader. We find, for instance, the distinction made between clean and unclean animals, which distinction evidently had reference to the divine institution of sacrifice, of the origin of which we nowhere read in Scripture. Nor are we told what animals were fit, and what were unfit, for that holy rite. All this Noe would, of course, have known by divine tradition. He was to take by sevens of the clean, and by twos of the unclean.

In the account of the fall of man, there is no express mention made of the evil being who caused the fall, but only of the visible form which he assumed. That it was Satan, all the patriarchs and the Jews knew; but the fact that it was Satan, is mentioned in a part of holy Scripture which was never in the hands of the Jews, viz.: the 12th chapter of the Apocalypse, verse 9. That Henoch prophesied, is nowhere recorded in the Old Testament. Yet the patriarchs, after Henoch, and the Jews knew Henoch's prophecy about our Lord. It has been preserved by tradition, and confirmed by St. Jude the Apostle, 14, 15: "Now of these Henoch also, the seventh from Adam, prophesied, saying: "Behold, the Lord cometh with thousands of his saints, to execute judgment upon all, to reprove all the ungodly for all the works of their ungodliness, whereby they have done ungodly, and of all the hard things which ungodly sinners have spoken against God." Holy Scripture also tells us of Henoch: "Henoch walked with God, and was seen no more, because God took him." (Genesis v, 24.) The expression, "was seen no more," implies his removal from the earth. But we certainly should never have discovered the important fact of his translation in the flesh without other help than those words themselves afford. Throughout the rest of the Old Testament writings there is no clear statement of this fact. We owe our certain knowledge of the real case entirely to the words of St. Paul, who gives an explanation of it in his Epistle to the Hebrews: "By faith Henoch was translated, that he should not see death, and he was not found, because God had translated him: for before his translation he had testimony that he pleased God." (Hebrews xi, 5.) The knowledge of the fact, however, was preserved traditionally among God's people, and the truth of the tradition is confirmed by an inspired writer. Henoch is still living and in the flesh.

In the whole period before the Deluge, we have but one recorded revelation respecting man's spiritual interests, and that is the statement made to the serpent: "And the Lord God said to the serpent: Because thou hast done this thing, thou art cursed among all cattle and beasts of the earth: upon thy breast shalt thou go, and earth shalt thou eat all the days of thy life. I will put enmities between thee and the woman, and thy seed and her seed; she shall crush thy head, and thou shalt lie in wait for her heel." (Genesis iii, 14, 15.)

Now that statement, by itself, is evidently quite inadequate as a foundation for such a living, practical system of religion as existed at that time. It requires the existence of a divinely appointed teaching Church, with its groundwork of traditional knowledge, to give a value to that statement. The patriarchs before the Flood could not possibly have obtained from that brief statement all the knowledge of the truth which they undoubtedly had. They knew the extent and value of that statement by the teaching of the divine system in which they lived, and which they humbly followed.

Even when we come to Abraham, who seems to have lived in the very light of God's countenance, we find that the revelation made to him is brief and indistinct. Surely, in the words, "in thy seed," there is not enough whereon to build the whole religion of Abraham.

The main feature, however, of the patriarchal Church, was sacrifice, which requires more particular notice. We do not read anywhere of the institution of the rite of sacrifice, nor of the meaning of the rite, nor is there any command mentioned for offering sacrifice till we come to the Mosaic time; but allusions in the book of Genesis show that sacrifices were continually going on, and in some cases, as for instance, Gen. xv., they were sacrifices of a very peculiar nature, and of a highly ceremonial character. We find Abraham, by God's command, offering not merely a lamb or a bullock, but "a cow of three years old, and a she-goat of three years, and a ram of three years; a turtle also, and a pigeon." (Genesis xv, 9.) The offeror of such sacrifices learned a great deal by his habit of sacrificing. He was schooled by it into a due acknowledgment of God as his Creator, taught humility, and a dependence upon something with which God had provided him to become acceptable in his presence. The tendency of every sacrifice manifestly was to impress upon man, practically, a sense of his own unworthiness to appear before God without some atonement; to teach him that without some death or suffering, undergone on his account, he could not worship God properly; to make him, so far as he could then be made, a Christian. A sense, then, of sinfulness, and of the necessity of atonement, was the practical habit formed by sacrifices; and so mankind were trained in a state of preparation for the Gospel and its benefits.

What, then, is the light in which we are to regard these brief revelations of holy Scripture? We are to look upon them as solemn declarations, full of deep meaning and import, presupposing a divine teaching system, but clothed and wrapped up, as it were; not speaking clearly, if at all, to persons who knew nothing else than those words, yet giving sufficient knowledge to those living under a divinely appointed teacher of traditional knowledge. There was a patriarchal body, a patriarchal church, in which there was a system of religious education, clear and distinct, so far as it went; a ceremonial and certain sacraments, by which men were drawn toward God, and taught the knowledge of the truth. That patriarchal church, or body, simply because it was God's ordinance, was a guide sure and infallible, to the extent of the revelation then made known. It had all the essentials of a teacher from God. Its knowledge, though partial, was clear, and its utterance distinct and infallible.

This is a most important thing to bear in mind, because infidelity, rationalism, and heresy, in every form, are always taking advantage of the brevity of holy Scripture, its want of explicitness, to the disparagement of its teaching, and of religion in general. For instance, th efact that the doctrines of the immortality of the soul, and the resurrection of the body, are not explicitly stated in the books of Moses, has given occasion for asserting that those truths were not known at that time; and that all that holy men of old were looking to, all that, in fact, the Church of Israel desired and hoped for, lay on this side the grave; and that life and immortality were in no sense brought to light before the coming of the Gospel. Such a distinction between former dispensation and the Christian is used as an argument against the Christian revelation.

We ought, then, to remember that the patriarchs, and the patriarchal body generally, had a clear, definite, practical knowledge of religious truth,—a wider knowledge than the mere words of holy Scripture, had they possessed them, could have conveyed to isolated minds. They infallibly preserved, by divine tradition, the religious truths and the promises of God.

From the beginning of the world to the time of Moses, the faithful followers of God believed in an unwritten divine revelation or in tradition. From the time of Closes, almost to the time of the coming of the Redeemer, those, also, who were saved outside the Jewish people, had faith in tradition. It was also by tradition alone that the Jews knew several religious truths: such as the Trinity, original sin, the spirituality and immortality of the soul, the future incarnation. It was a tradition among the Jews that, besides the written revelation, Moses also received, on Mount Sinai, an oral and traditional revelation, which he transmitted to the priests. To this tradition our Savior appealed. (Matthew xxiii, 2.) Moses, the judges, King David, and others of the inspired writers, repeatedly referred the Jews to it. The traditions of the Pharisees and of the heathens only are condemned.

There has ever been a Church of God, a society possessing and preserving a full and clear traditional knowledge of divine truth, independent of all writing, or collection of writings. Of course, this is so under the Gospel dispensation. Our blessed Lord founded his Church, committed to her the deposit of truth, commissioned her to teach that truth to all nations, and promised to be with her so teaching till he should come again; and to that teaching he enjoined obedience under the severest menace:

"He that believeth not shall be condemned." (Mark xvi, 15.) Those doctrines which our Lord and Savior Jesus Christ taught his apostles by word of mouth, but which they have not committed to writing, together with those which the Holy Ghost dictated to them, and which they were to transmit to the Universal Church, are called the Christian traditions, or the word of God, not written in the New Testament. Holy Scripture itself and the early Fathers of the Church tell us that the whole doctrine of Christ and his apostles was not written down: "There are also," says St. John, at the end of his Gospel, "many other things which Jesus did, which, if they were written every one, the world itself, I think, would not be able to contain the books that should be written." (Chap, xxi, 25.) "All things," writes St. Epiphanius, "are not found in the holy Scripture, for the apostles have taught us some by tradition, some by writing." Whence, for instance, do we know that the Old and the New Testament are inspired writings; that the Sunday is to be kept holy, instead of Saturday; that the baptism conferred upon infants by heretics is valid; that baptism is necessary for children; that the receiving of holy communion is not necessary for the salvation of infants? These and other doctrinal or moral truths we know only by tradition.

7. How has the unwritten word of God come down to us?

The unwritten word of God has come down to us by the constant and invariable teaching of the Church.

The apostles taught the truths which they had learned from Christ. They took great care to instruct their disciples thoroughly and make them capable of so instructing Others. Thus, their pure and holy doctrine was delivered to the first bishops and priests of the Roman Catholic Church. By them it was, in like manner, handed down to their successors, and so on, unimpaired, to those who, at the present time, teach in the Catholic Church. This we know from what St. Paul writes to the Bishop Timothy, and from the early Fathers of the Church: "And the things which thou hast heard of me before many witnesses," writes St. Paul, "the same commend (entrust) to faithful men, who shall be fit to teach others." (2 Timothy ii, 2.) St. Polycarp, Bishop of Smyrna, who was acquainted with many of Christ's disciples, and especially with St. John, writes: "I have always taught what I have received from the apostles."

"We received the Gospels from the apostles," says St. Clement; "they were sent by Jesus Christ; Jesus Christ was sent by God. Receiving command, and by the resurrection of our Lord fully secured, and strengthened by the Holy Spirit, the apostles went out, announcing the coming of the kingdom of God. They preached through the country and towns, and appointed bishops and deacons, their first fruits, and whom they had proved by the spirit. These our apostles knew, through Jesus Christ, that disputes concerning episcopacy would arise; wherefore they appointed those of whom I have spoken, and thus established the series of future succession, that, when they should die, other approved men might enter on their ministry." (Ep. i, ad Cor., Tuter P. P. Apost., t. i, p. 171: Amstel. 1724.) The pastors of the Church, then, taught what they received. Christ left his revelation living in the divine authority of the pastors of his Church; by these it is left also living in the unanimous consent of the Fathers and Doctors of the Church; in the decrees and decisions of General Councils and of the Sovereign Pontiffs; in the liturgies or other forms of prayer; in the acts of the martyrs; in the public and solemn administration of the sacraments; in the catechisms and books of instruction of Christian writers; in the faith, the prayers, the religious practices of the Christian family, and the Christian monuments of the Church. The Catholic Church is the living Gospel. Those who have seen the grand cathedrals in Europe tell us that there they found expressed, in the most striking forms of the Romanesque and Gothic styles, the precept of prayer, the faith in the Real Presence, and in the holy sacrifice of the Mass, the distinction between clergy and people, and the preeminence of bishops over simple priests; that there they read the principal truths of the Gospel in the pictures and emblems on the window-glass. And those who have visited the catacombs of Rome tell us that there they saw altars for the celebration of the Mass; the bones of martyrs under the stone upon which Jesus Christ was offered; tribunals of penance, where the Christians, during the first three centuries, confessed their sins, before receiving holy communion; that there they found sculptures representing Christ crucified, his ever blessed Virgin Mother Mary, his holy apostles, the primacy of St. Peter, the belief in purgatory, the invocation of saints, and the practice of baptizing infants.

Now, this is the Gospel written in the blood of martyrs on the tombs and vaults of these catacombs, engraved in the very bowels of Rome, inlaid in stone and in marble, as precisely and clearly as in our catechisms. Again, were we to examine the documents of old libraries, the books of the Greek and Latin Fathers, of the writers of controversy of every country and of every century, we should find the Gospel spoken and proclaimed in all languages, as on the day of Pentecost. Finally, if we recall to our mind the universal religious practices: the frequent use of the sign of the cross, the practice of fasting in Lent, prayer for the dead, repeating the Apostles' Creed,—are they not the living Gospel? Indeed, the Catholic Church and the Gospel are one. Where else could we find the "Thou art Peter,"—that is, the Church founded upon Peter? Where else should we find the "I am with you all days,"—that is, an episcopate uninterrupted from the days of Jesus Christ to our own time? Where else should we find the "Whosesoever sins you shall forgive, they are forgiven them,"— that is, the ministry of the forgiveness of sins? Where else, indeed, should we find the sacrifice of which the apostle speaks—the realization of the words of St. Paul, "We have an altar,"—that is, the universal and perpetual sacrifice announced by the prophets, the sacrifice according to the rite of the high-priest of Salem, the sacrifice under the appearance of bread and wine, the "priest forever, according to the order of Melchizedek"?

All these are facts which most eloquently bear witness to the Gospel truths of the Catholic Church; they are witnesses which no heresy can silence; they are barriers in defense of her Scriptural and traditional truths, which no subtlety can undermine, no boldness surmount.

8. Must we believe the unwritten word of God just as firmly as the written?

Yes, because the one is the word of God just as well as the other.

The doctrines taught by Jesus Christ and his apostles, which have not been written in the New Testament, are no less true than those which are there written. The apostles taught the true doctrine of Christ not less by their preaching than by their writings; and the Holy Ghost expressed his will as well by their tongues as by their pens. "Therefore, brethren," writes St. Paul, "stand fast, and hold the traditions which you have learned, whether by word or by our epistle." (2 Thessalonians ii, 14.) "It is, then, evident," writes St. John

Chrysostom, "that the apostles taught many things without writing, which we must believe as firmly as those which are written." (Hom. iv, on 2d Epist. to the Thessal.)

Hence, "if you are a Christian," says Tertullian, "believe what has been handed down." (De Prescript, xix.) To refuse to believe in the unwritten word of God is as much as to say to the Lord: "I will believe in thy word—in all that thou tell, on condition, that thou take the trouble to give it to me in writing." What folly, what impiety is this! Such impiety is abhorred and condemned by the Catholic Church. "There are," says the Council of Trent, "truths and rules of conduct contained in unwritten teaching, which, being received by the apostles from the lips of Christ himself, or delivered by the apostles themselves, under the dictation of the Holy Ghost, have come down as from hand to hand, even to us. These traditions the Council receives and venerates with the like piety and reverence as it does the holy Scriptures; and if any one knowingly and deliberately holds the aforesaid traditions in contempt, let him be anathema." (Sess. iv.) "Let us, therefore," says St. John Chrysostom, "account the tradition of the Church worthy of faith. It is tradition—ask no more." (Hom. iv, in Epist. ii, Thess., n. 2.) "It never was," says St. Vincent of Lerins, "it nowhere is, it never will be, allowable for Catholic Christians to teach any other doctrine than that which they have received; and it always has been, everywhere is, and will be, their duty to anathematize those who do otherwise." (Commonit. adv. Haereses.) The infallible rule of faith which Christ left for all men is to believe all that his Church teaches. Wherefore, "that only is of divine faith which God has revealed, and which the Church proposes to our belief." Not to believe what the Church teaches is "to be a heathen and a publican," a great sinner before God. Certain it is, that whatever truth the Catholic Church proposes to our belief, it is contained either in holy

Scripture or in tradition. But the authoritative reason for believing it, is the divine, infallible teaching authority of the Church. We need her unerring voice, especially in the interpretation of holy Scripture. Hence it is asked in the Catechism:

9. Is it easy for everyone to understand the Holy Scripture?

And the answer is: No; for, what St, Peter says of the Epistles of St. Paul may be applied to many other passages of holy Scripture, namely, "There are certain things in his (St. Paul's Epistles which are hard to be understood, which the unlearned and unstable wrest, as they also do the other Scriptures, to their own destruction." (2 Peter iii, 16.)

Evidence of this simple truth is seen every day. Protestant sects, such as the Mormons, build systems of the grossest immorality on perverted texts of Scripture. Only recently, members of an English sect called the Peculiar People were brought up for trial in the civil courts, for having caused the death of a child. They refused to call in the services of a doctor when the child was sick, justifying their conduct by such Scriptural texts as: "The Lord shall heal the sick man," "Not a bone of him ye shall break," etc.

Luther declared on his deathbed: "We are mere schoolboys, incapable of thoroughly understanding one single verse of Scripture; and it is with difficulty we succeed in learning the A, B, C of it. Five years' hard labor will be required to understand Virgil's Georgies; twenty years' experience to be master of Cicero's Epistles; and a hundred years' intercourse with the prophets Elias, Eliseus, John the Baptist, Christ, and the apostles, to know the Scriptures! Alas, poor human nature!" (Florimond Remond, b. iii, c. ii, fol. 287; Laign, Vita Lutheri, fol. 4.) The Scriptures greatly differ from all human writings.

These can be understood at once, provided the mind is applied to them, and be sufficiently disciplined to follow the author's train of thought. There is no such thing as meaning hidden behind meaning in human writings. Once we have mastered them, we know the whole of their contents. Not so with holy Scripture. After we have critically studied the language of the Scripture; after we have accumulated all external information bearing on its matter; after we have availed ourselves of all the aid which the Church provides for her children, even then we have not exhausted its meaning.

The sense of holy Scripture cannot, as it were, be mapped, or its contents catalogued; but after all our diligence, to the end of our lives, and to the end of the Church, it must be an unexplored and unsubdued land, with heights and valleys, forests and streams, on the right and left of our path, and close about us, full of concealed wonders and choice treasures. Of no doctrine whatever, which does not actually contradict what has been delivered, can it be peremptorily asserted that it is not in Scripture; of no reader, whatever be his study of it, can it be said that he has mastered every doctrine which it contains.

This peculiarity of the holy Scripture, namely, that a great deal more meaning is implied in the word of God than is expressed, constitutes the great difficulty in the way of discovering its sense. The word of God is, indeed, a word holy and adorable; but a word that remains silent under every interpretation. When difficulties and doubts arise, then I must have some external guide or interpreter that shall solve those difficulties, and satisfy my doubts, and that guide or interpreter must be unerring.

10. Who is the infallible interpreter of Holy Scripture?

The Catholic Church alone is the infallible interpreter of holy Scripture.

We learn the sense of Scripture in the same way as we learn the rest of Christian Doctrine, that is, by consulting and listening reverently to our divine teacher, the Catholic Church; for the sense of Scripture was divinely impressed upon the mind of the Church by her divine Founder, from the beginning of her existence; that sense being, in matter of fact, nothing more nor less than the deposit of faith, which it was the Church's duty and office to guard, interpret, and develop, according as occasion should serve. "The apostles," says St. Irenaeus, "carefully entrusted the Scriptures to their successors; and to whom the Scriptures were entrusted, to them also was committed the interpretation of Scripture." Accordingly, the Church has decreed, in the Council of Trent, that no one should presume to interpret the Scriptures in a sense contrary to that which she has held and holds, or contrary to the unanimous consent of the Fathers: "No prophecy of Scripture," says St. Peter, "is made by private interpretation." (2 Peter i, 20.)

The Church may make known the sense of any passage of Scripture in two ways: directly or indirectly. She makes it known directly, either by a solemn definition, or by the universal consent of the Church, from the earliest times. She makes it known indirectly, when she tells us that we are to interpret Scripture according to the analogy of faith; that is, in such a way that our interpretation shall be in harmony with her teaching upon all other points of Christian Doctrine.

As to the unanimous assent of the Church, we may learn this from the writings of the Fathers, who themselves were but exponents of the mind of the one living, divine Teacher. But in order to be bound by the interpretation of the Fathers, the Council of Trent tells us that that interpretation must be morally unanimous, and, moreover, on some point in connection with faith or morals. But,

11. Does not the Church forbid the reading of the Bible?

No; not the reading, but the private interpretation, of the Bible is forbidden.

The Scriptures contain, indeed, the revealed mysteries of divine faith. They are, undoubtedly, the most excellent of all writings. They are written by men inspired by God, and are not the words of men, but the infallible word of God, which can save our souls. (1 Thessalonians ii, 13; James i, 21.) But then they ought to be read, even by the learned, with the spirit of humility, and with a fear of mistaking their true sense, as many have in all ages. Monseigneur de Cheverus, in his sermons, often dwelt on the necessity of some teaching authority to render unwavering the faith of the learned as well as of the ignorant. To convince Protestants of this necessity, he often repeated, in his discourses to them, these simple words: "Every day, my brethren, I read the holy Scripture like yourselves; I read it with reflection and prayer, having previously invoked the Holy Ghost, and yet, at almost every page, I find many things that I cannot understand, and I find the great necessity of some speaking authority, which may point out to me the meaning of the text, and render my faith firm." And his hearers immediately made the application to themselves. "If Monseigneur de Cheverus," said they, "who is more learned than we, cannot comprehend the sacred Scripture, how is it that our ministers tell us that the Bible is to each of us a full and clear rule of faith, easily understood of itself, and requiring no aid in understanding its meaning?" Taking occasion from the admission that even the most learned cannot agree as to matters of faith, the zealous bishop pointed out how wisely God came to aid human weakness in the discovery of truth, by appointing a living, speaking authority, which, drawing its origin from Christ or his apostles, has descended down to us by an uninterrupted succession of pastors, professing, at all times and in all places, and without the least variation, the same holy doctrine as was taught and professed by the apostles.

The Bible is, indeed, the book of books, or the best book. Hence the Church encourages the faithful to read the holy Scriptures; for, says Pope Pius VI, "they are the most abundant sources, which ought to be left open to everyone, to draw from them purity of morals and of doctrine, to uproot the errors which are so widely spread in these corrupt times." To guard, however, the faithful against corrupted Bibles, and against erroneous interpretations, the chief pastors of the Church have decreed that, with regard to reading the Bible in the vernacular, we should have the learning and piety requisite for it, and that the translation should be approved by the Holy See or accompanied with explanations by a bishop. The reading of the Bible will always be attended with great spiritual advantage, if it is read with becoming reverence, humility, and pious dispositions. It is, then, false, utterly false, to say that the Catholic Church forbids us to read the Bible. We are not forbidden to read the Bible, but we are forbidden to interpret it according to our own whim, giving the word of God any meaning which we choose to give it. And,

12. Why does the Church forbid the private interpretation, of the Bible?

Because numberless heresies have risen from the private interpretation of the Bible.

From the time of the apostles to the present day, there have risen unlearned men, as well as men accomplished in every kind of learning, who undertook to interpret the Bible according to their own private opinions. The consequence was, that the ignorant were led into errors, for want of knowledge, and the learned, through pride and self-sufficiency. Instead of interpreting Scripture according to the teaching of the Church, and learning from her what they should believe, they have tried to teach the Church false and perverse doctrines of their own. They avail themselves of the Scriptures to prove their errors. They say that they have the Scriptures on their side, which are the fountain of truth. But these deluded men do not consider that the truth is found, not by reading, but by understanding, the holy Scriptures. This arrogance in interpreting the Bible according to their fancy proceeds from pride. But God resists the proud and withholds from them the light of faith. In punishment for their pride and want of submission to the teaching of his Church, he permits such men to fall into all kinds of errors, absurdities, and vices; he permits the holy Scriptures, which are a great fountain of truth, to become to them a great fountain of errors. So that to them may be applied the words of our divine Savior: "You err, not knowing the Scriptures" (Matthew xxii, 29); and of St. Peter: "They wrest the Scriptures to their own destruction." (2 Peter iii, 16.)

The Adamites pretended to find in the book of Genesis that they were as pure as our first parents and need not be ashamed of being naked any more than Adam and Eve before the fall. Arius pretended to find, in forty-two passages of the Bible, that the Son of God was not equal to the Father. Macedonius maintained that from holy Scripture he could prove that the Holy Ghost was not God; and Pelagius asserted, on the authority of holy Scripture, that man could work out his salvation without the grace of God. Luther asserted that he found in Isaias that man was not free; and Calvin tried to prove from Scripture that it is impossible for man to keep the commandments.

There is no error so monstrous, no crime so heinous, no practice so detestable, which perverse men have not endeavored to justify by some passage of Scripture. St. Augustine asks, "Whence have risen heresies and those pernicious errors that lead men to everlasting perdition?" and he answers: "They have risen from this: that men understand the Scriptures wrongly, and then maintain presumptuously and boldly what they thus understand wrongly." (In Joan. tr. xviii.) Thus, "the Gospel," as St. Jerome observes, "is, for them, not the Gospel of Christ any longer, but the gospel of man, or of the devil: for the Gospel consists, not in the words, but in the sense, of Scripture, wherefore, by false interpretation, the Gospel of Christ becomes the gospel of man, or of the devil." "My thoughts, saith the Lord, are not as your thoughts, neither are your ways my ways; for, as the heavens are exalted above the earth, even so are my ways exalted above your ways, and my thoughts above your thoughts?' (Isaiah 1, 8, 9.) Who, then, shall, by his private reason, pretend to know, to judge, to demonstrate, to interpret, the unsearchable ways of God, and the incomprehensible, divine mysteries hidden in the holy Scripture? "How can I understand it, if no one explains it to me?" (Acts viii.)

To sum up what has been said: In the order of time, the Catholic Church precedes the Scripture. There was no time when a visible and speaking divine authority did not exist, to which submission was not due. Before the coming of Jesus Christ, that authority among the Jews was in the synagogue. When the synagogue was on the point of failing, Jesus Christ himself appeared; when this divine personage withdrew, he left his authority to his Church, and with her his Holy Spirit. All the truths which we believe to be divine, and which are the objects of our faith, were taught by the Church, and believed by millions of Christians, long before they were committed to writing, and formed what is called the New Testament. And those truths would have remained to the end of the world, pure and unaltered, had that primitive state continued; that is, had it never seemed good to any of the apostolic men, as it did to St. Luke, to commit to writing what they had learned from Christ. He did it, he says, that Theophilus, to whom he writes, might "know the verity of these words in which he had been instructed."

A Catholic, therefore, never forms his faith by reading the Scriptures, his faith is already formed before he begins to read; his reading serves only to confirm what he always believed: that is, it confirms the doctrine which the Church had already taught him. Consequently, if these books had not existed, the belief in the facts and truths of Christianity would have been the same; and it would not be weakened if those books were no longer to exist.

As the Catholic Church made known to the Christians those facts and truths long before they were recorded in writing, she alone could afterward rightly decide, and infallibly state, what books did, and what did not, contain the pure doctrine of Christ and his apostles; she alone could and did know what books were, and what were not, divinely inspired; she alone could and did make that inspiration an object of faith; she alone can, with infallible authority, give the true meaning, and determine the legitimate use, of the holy Scriptures.

Although the Scripture, the true word of God, is not to us a rule of faith, taken independently of the teaching authority of the pastors of the Church, the successors of the apostles, yet it is not inferior to the Church in excellence and dignity. It is inspired, holy, and divine. Hence, it is the custom of the Church to erect a throne in the middle of councils, on which she places the sacred books as presiding over the assembly, occupying, as it were, the first place, and deciding with supreme authority. When celebrating Mass, she wishes that the faithful, during the reading of the Gospel, should all rise, and remain standing, to show their reverence for the sacred truths. We venerate the Scriptures as a sacred deposit bequeathed to us by the kindest of parents, containing truths of the highest moment, practical lessons of saving morality, and facts of history relating to the life of our divine Savior, and the conduct of his disciples, eminently interesting and instructive. For all this we are very grateful.

Besides, the Scriptures come forward with a powerful aid, to support, by the evidence of their contents, both the divine authority of the Church, and the divine truths of the faith which we have received from her, applying that aid to each article, and giving a luster to the whole. So Theophilus, when he read that admirable narration which St. Luke compiled for him, was more and more confirmed in the verity of things in which he had been instructed. (St. Luke i, 1-4.)

For those, however, who reject the divine authority of the Church, the holy Scriptures can no longer be authentic and inspired writings—they are for them no longer the word of God; for they have no one who can tell them, with divine certainty, what books are, and what are not, divinely inspired; they have no one who, in the name of God, can command them to believe in the divine inspiration of the writers of those books. Explaining them as they do, according to their fancy, and translating them in a way favorable to their errors, they have, in the Scriptures, not the Gospel of Christ, but that of man or the devil, calculated only to confirm the ignorant in their errors, and the learned in their pride and self-sufficiency. We read, in the Gospel of St. Matthew and of St. Luke, that Satan hid himself under the shade of the Scripture when he tempted our divine Savior. He quoted passages from holy Scripture, to tempt him to ambition and presumption. But he is answered: "Begone, Satan: it is written, Thou shalt not tempt the Lord thy God." Satan, being overcome, left for a time. But not long after, under the mask of Arius, Nestorius, Pelagius, Luther, Calvin,

John Knox, Henry VIII, and a host of other heresiarchs, he renewed his attacks on Jesus Christ, in the person of the Catholic Church. This demon is heresy, which hides itself under the shade of Scripture. Were Satan to utter blasphemies, he would be known at once, and men would flee from him in horror. So he deceives them under the appearance of good; he repeats passages from holy Scripture, and men naturally listen to him, and are apt to believe and follow him. But the good Catholic answers him: "Begone, Satan! It is written, He that will not hear the Church, let him be to thee as the heathen and the publican." (Matthew xviii, 16.) This is the great, the infallible, and the only rule of faith, that leads to him who gave it,—Jesus Christ.

The heretics and Catholics to whom St. Dominic preached the Gospel, put together in writing the strongest arguments in defense of their respective doctrines. The Catholic arguments were the work of St. Dominic, who confirmed the Catholic doctrine, by many passages of holy Scripture. The heretics, too, quoted holy Scripture in confirmation of their doctrine. It was proposed that both writings should be committed to the flames, in order that God might declare, by his own interposition, which cause he favored. Accordingly, a great fire was made, and the two writings were cast into it: that of the heretics was immediately consumed to ashes, whilst that of the Catholics remained unhurt, after it had been cast into the fire three times and taken out again.

This public miracle happened at Fanjaux; the fruit of it was the conversion of a great number of heretics of both sexes. The same kind of miracle happened at Montreal. St. Dominic drew up in writing a short exposition of the Catholic faith, with proof of each article from the New Testament. This writing he gave to the heretics to examine. Their ministers and chiefs, after much altercation about it, agreed to throw it into the fire, saying that, if it burned, they would regard the doctrine which it contained as false. Being cast thrice into the flames, it was not damaged.

Let us unceasingly thank Almighty God for the grace of being children of the Catholic Church. St. Francis de Sales exclaims: "O dear Lord! many and great are the blessings thou hast heaped on me, and I thank thee for them. But how shall I be ever able to thank thee for enlightening me with th yholy faith? O God! the beauty of thy holy faith appears to me so enchanting, that I am dying with love of it; and I imagine I ought to enshrine this precious gift in a heart all perfumed with devotion." St. Teresa never ceased to thank God for having made her a daughter of the holy Catholic Church. Her consolation at the hour of death was to cry out: "I die a child of the holy Church, I die a child of the holy Church."

THE NINTH
ARTICLE OF THE
APOSTLES' CREED

THE HOLY CATHOLIC CHURCH

FOR love of man, God created the boundless universe, with its stars and countless worlds, and he made the universe, the temple of his endless love. The stars of heaven, as they sweep along in silent harmony, are ever singing a wondrous song, and the sweet burden of their song is, "God is love and truth."

This world is the temple of God's love and truth. The green earth, with its flowers, is the carpeted floor. The clear sky above is the vaulted dome: its pillars are the mountains, white with eternal snow. The mists and vapor that are ever ascending, like the smoke of sacrifice, remind us of the thoughts of love and gratitude that should ever go up to heaven from our hearts. The whispering of the winds, the rush of the storm, the murmuring of the brook, and the roar of the cataract, are the music that raises our hearts to God. And when God had finished that wondrous temple of his love, "He saw that it was good." (Genesis i, 25 .)

For love of man, God has raised a still more wondrous temple.—the temple of his holy Church. Millions and millions of chosen souls have aided in building this wondrous temple. Its foundation was laid at the gates of paradise. The patriarchs and prophets have labored at it, through the long ages of hope and expectation. It was completed, in the fulness of time, by the Only Begotten of the Father, our Lord Jesus Christ. This temple of love was consecrated by the Holy Ghost on that wonderful day of love, the Feast of Pentecost. The summit of this glorious temple of love now rises to the highest heavens, and to the throne of the living God himself. In its depth, it reaches to that region of suffering where those are detained who are to be cleansed from all stain, before entering into the joys of heaven. In its width, it extends over all the earth, and shuts out no one who is willing to enter its portals. In this new creation, far more than in the old, God looks on those things that he made, and sees that they are "very good." What God does, is done well— is a perfect work. The establishment of the Catholic Church is the grand work of his power; it is the greatest fact in history,—a fact so great, that there would be no history without it; a fact permanent, entering into the concerns of all nations on the face of the earth, appearing again and again on the records of time, and benefiting, perceived or unperceived, directly or indirectly, socially, morally, and supernaturally, every member of the human family.

From the beginning of the world God always had but one Church to teach his religion to men, and lead them to heaven; Satan, too, from the beginning, has tried to have a church and a worship of his own. He found followers among the angels to refuse submission to God's holy will. Need we wonder at seeing him find followers among men? As the faithful servants of God are known and distinguished by their ready obedience to the divine authority of the Catholic Church, so those who are deceived by Satan are known by their want of submission to the divine authority of the Church. They form churches of their own, in opposition to the true Church of God. In the ninth century, the Greeks separated from the Roman Catholic Church, and formed a church of their own, called the Greek Church. In the beginning of the sixteenth century, Martin Luther, an apostate friar, preached a doctrine of his own; he gained many followers in Germany, who left the Catholic Church, and formed what is called and known as the Lutheran, or Protestant, Church. In 1531, Henry VIII, King of England, fell away from the Catholic Church, and made himself the supreme head of the English, or Anglican Church. These, and other churches, are the work of man. No doubt, everyone who is acquainted with the life of our Lord and is asked:

1. How many churches did Christ establish?

Will answer: Christ established but one church.

Indeed, as there is but one Christ, so there is, and can be, but one Church of Christ. The Church is called the body of Christ. Now, as Christ has but one body, so he can have but one Church. Christ himself tells us plainly that he established but one Church. He did not say to St. Peter, Upon thee I will build my churches: he said, "Upon thee I will build my Church." He never said, The gates of hell shall not prevail against my churches; he said, "The gates of hell shall not prevail against my Church." In fact, that our Lord established but one Church, is self-evident; it needs no proof. We are as certain of it as we are that there is but one God. St. Paul asserts this in the clearest terms: "One Lord, one faith, one baptism;" that is, as there is, and can be, but one Lord, so there is, and can be, but one faith, one religion, one Church. And as our Lord established but one Church, it follows, necessarily, that all other churches are not the work of Jesus Christ. They are the work of man; the Church of Christ, the Catholic Church, alone is the work of God.

All the works of God have something divine and supernatural about them,—something that at once proclaims their divine origin; something that distinguishes them, in an unmistakable manner, from the works of man. As the Catholic Church is the work of God, she has something about her to show that she is from God; she has marks graven on her which make it impossible for one to be mistaken about her being the true Church of Christ; she has the most incontestable proofs of her divine mission and authority, to convince all who wish to be convinced.

2. By what marks is the Church of Christ easily known?

By these four: The Church of Christ is: 1, one; 2, she is holy; 3, she is Catholic; and, 4, she is apostolic.

Above all, perfect unity must be found in the Church of Christ; for Christ calls his Church a "building," a "kingdom," a "city," a "flock," a "house," a "body." To establish, insure, and preserve unity, he made St. Peter the foundation of the building, the chief ruler of the kingdom, the key-holder of the city and house, the principal shepherd of the flock, the head of the body. And on the eve of his passion, Christ asked for a unity in his Church, like that which unites the three divine persons in one and the same nature: "Father," he prayed, "keep them whom thou hast given me, that they maybe one, even as we are one." (John xvii, 11.) Moreover, he prayed that this union might last forever, and that it should be the distinctive mark of his Church: "I pray, also," he says, "for all those who, through their word, shall believe in me, that they may all be one, as thou, Father, in me, and I in thee, that the world may believe that thou hast sent me." (John xx, 21.) The apostles express very clearly the necessity of unity and show that it is a distinctive mark of the true Church: "Be careful," says St. Paul, "to keep the unity of the spirit in the bond of peace. One body and one spirit, one Lord, one faith, one baptism."

Unity, then, is a distinctive mark, and an essential condition of the Church of Christ. That Church which has no unity, cannot be the true Church; and that Church which has unity, must certainly be divine.

In the Church of Christ holiness also must be found, no less than unity. Christ shed his blood for no other purpose than to form for himself, says St. Paul, a pure Church, "without spot or wrinkle, or any such thing; that it should be holy and without blemish." (Ephesians v, 25.) Moreover, as the Church of Christ teaches the true faith, holiness must be the result of this faith, since Christ says: "A good tree cannot bring forth evil fruit." (Matthew vii, 18.) According to Christ's promise, miracles will be performed by the true believers of his Church, and bear "witness to her holiness." (Mark xvi, 17.)

The Church, however, is not composed of the elect alone, for Christ compares her to a net which draws out of the sea "good and bad fish" (Matthew xiii, 47); to a field where the cockle grows together with the wheat, until the day of the harvest. (Matthew xiii, 30.)

Again, during his public life, Christ declared repeatedly that his unalterable purpose was to unite, in one religious society, all mankind, of every age and clime, and afford his followers the means to free themselves from sin and become reconciled to God; to grow in purity and holiness of life, and thus enter into life everlasting. He spoke always and everywhere, in language most clear and explicit, of this note of universality, as one peculiar to his kingdom. (John x, 16; Matthew xxviii, 19.) All the prophecies relative to the Messiah spoke of the whole human race as the flock of Christ, whose kingdom was to extend its bounds "till it embraced all pagan nations." (Matthew xv, 24; Psalm cix, 2.) Christ's Church, therefore, must be Catholic, or universal.

Finally, Christ has most solemnly promised to be with his apostles to the end of the world, and he has made St. Peter the first Bishop of Rome, the foundation of the Church, and her supreme head. Christ's Church, therefore, must be apostolic. Holy Scripture itself gives us this full information about the marks of the true Church of Christ. And if it is asked:

3. Which Church is one, holy, Catholic and apostolic?

The answer is: The Roman Catholic Church alone is one, holy, Catholic, and apostolic.

It is easy to

4. Show how the Catholic Church is one.

The Catholic Church is one, because all her members are united: 1, in one faith; 2, in one worship; 3, under one infallible head.

1. The Catholic Church is one, because all her members are united in one faith.

Unity is especially divine. It exists in its perfection only in the adorable Trinity. Wherever we find unity in created things, we may be sure that it is an image and reflection of God. Now, in this world, there is one society, and only one, in which unity has always existed, and has never been broken. This society is the Catholic Church. This society is the most numerous, the first, and the most ancient of all the communities that call themselves Christian. The Catholic Church is found in all kingdoms and states; it reaches from pole to pole, from east to west; embraces all ranks and classes of men. The members of the Catholic Church differ from one another in their character, in their education, in their modes of thought; they differ in their language, in their habits of life, in their sympathies and prejudices; in a word, they differ from one another in everything that distinguishes man from man. But in one thing they are all united: in religion. In religion, alone, they are all of one mind and one heart. In this wonderful society you will find the passionate Italian, with his glowing imagination; you will find, also, the stolid and tenacious Englishman; the lively and brilliant Frenchman; and the quiet, thoughtful German. You will find there the stately Spaniard; the witty, impulsive Irishman, and the acute and practical American. All these, and so many other races, though they contrast violently with one another in every natural gift and habit; though they retain all their distinctive peculiarities as men and citizens, yet in religion they are all one—absolutely one. Throughout the wholeCatholic world, the myriads of every nation, climate, and language, nobles and peasants, monarchs and slaves, philosophers and little children, there exists a unity of faith and doctrine, so divine and absolute, so spontaneous and yet so perfect, so unshackled and yet so complete, that a cardinal in Rome or a neophyte in China, a mathematician in Holland or a wood-cutter in Syria, or a little child anywhere, would give, in substance, the same answer to any question u pon any doctrine of the Church.

2. When their children are born, all bring them to be regenerated in the same waters of baptism. When they become unfaithful to their baptismal vows, and sin against God's commandments, they all have recourse to the same tribunal of penance. They all seek strength at the same eucharistic table, and, animated by the same faith, they receive truly the body and blood of Jesus Christ. In sickness, when they are about to appear before their God, they all send for the priest of the Church, and receive the sacrament of Extreme Unction. They all are one, not only in faith, but also in worship.

And what is more natural than this oneness in worship? Christ, who taught us our religion, has also taught us how to worship his heavenly Father in a manner worthy of his divine majesty. He instituted the holy sacrifice of the Mass, in which he is at once the High-Priest and the Victim. Through the hands of his priests, he offers himself for us to his heavenly Father as a sacrifice of adoration, of thanksgiving, of atonement, and of impetration. Since the institution of the Mass, paradise blooms again, the heavens are purple, the angels shine in white, and men are exhilarated. This sublime and profound mystery, which scandalizes obstinate unbelievers, and arouses the pride of Protestants, is, nevertheless, that which renews the face of the earth, satisfies the justice of God. redeems man unto salvation, opens heaven, sanctifies the world, and disarms hell. It is this mastery which has engendered a more holy religion, a more spiritual worship, and a purer virtue among men, because it is more interior; from it sprin g the most efficacious sacrament, more abundant graces, more sublime ceremonies, more perfect laws; it is that tender adoption of men, as children of God, substituted for the more ancient alliance between God and man, which was founded upon fear. This mystery is the striking manifestation of all truths, and the censure of all errors; all vices find their condemnation therein, all virtues their principle, all merits their recompense; it is, in short, the foundation of faith, the support of hope, and the most powerful motive for the love of God.

The holy Mass is the sun of Christianity, and the summary of all that is grand, and magnificent, and most prodigious, both in the triumphant and in the militant Church of God. The angels almost envy us this divine sacrifice. Protestants and infidels may say, with a sneer, that it is the pomp and glitter of our ceremonies and altars that draw the faithful to the church. Not so. The fickle nature of man cannot be charmed long by such transitory things.

Our altars, indeed, we adorn, we decorate our churches, we embellish the priestly vestments, we display the gorgeous ceremonies of the Church, but not to attract the people; we do all this simply because our Lord Jesus Christ is present there, our Savior and our God, surrounded by countless myriads of angels. This is the grand source of the magnificence of our architecture, the gorgeousness of our vestments, the diversity of our ornaments, the sound of our organs, the religious harmony of our voices, and the grandeur and order of all our ceremonies, both in the consecration and dedication of our churches, and the solemn celebration of the Mass.

This is the reason why we adorn ourselves with our gayest attire, why we rifle the gardens of their sweetest and choicest flowers to decorate our altars and scatter them in lavish profusion before the feet of our sacramental King. This is the reason why our sacred altars glitter and sparkle with cheerful lights, while clouds of sweet-smelling incense float up and around the sacred Victim.

It is related of Frederick II, King of Prussia, that, after having assisted at a solemn high Mass, celebrated in the church of Breslau by Cardinal Tringendorf, he remarked: "The Calvinists treat God as an inferior, the Lutherans treat him as an equal, but the Catholics treat him as God." Yes, indeed; it is only the Catholic Church that is the home for our dear Savior. His presence fills her halls to overflowing with joy and gladness. Her propitiatory altars are the anchors of hope for the sinner, her sanctuaries, the antechambers of heaven. Take away the blessed sacrament, and you take away her Savior. Give her the blessed sacrament, and you give her a glory, an honor, a triumph, the greatest possible this side of paradise. Her altars are the altars of joy, because they are the altars of the Saving Victim for the sins of the world; for which reason the robed priest begins the tremendous sacrifice with the antiphon: "I will go unto the altar of God, to God who rejoices my youth."

This sacrifice of adoration, of thanksgiving, of atonement, and of impetration, is offered up daily, nay, hourly, all over the world. To it come the simple peasant from his woods, the shepherd from the mountains, the man of business, the solemn religious, the devout student, the holy recluse, the laboring youth, the innocent child, with its baptismal robe unsullied, the penitent sinner who has atoned, or who is atoning, for having stained the purity of his soul: all, all draw grace and strength, and consolation and virtue, from this ever-flowing fountain of spiritual riches, in proportion to the measure of their faith, confidence, fervor, and devotion. To this fountain of healing water, the poor walk free and favored, as in presence of nature; they can approach it as nearly as kings and can enjoy equally the splendor and loveliness of the altar of God. Here ends the land of malediction. Here God is before all, and all are before God; his children, his creatures— nothing more, nothing less—all alike in this. No one marshals you, no one heeds you; here you may kneel and weep in secret, or lie prostrate before the Good Shepherd and the Lamb of God, in the blessed sacrament; here each sun that rises will find you more consoled, with healthier looks, less pale; here the workings of an uneasy conscience are soothed and made straight; or rather, here it is that you find time and opportunity for reconciliation with God.

Here the poor sinner is assisted to enter upon the way of salvation; here he is supplied with that living water, of which those who drink shall never more feel thirst; here we find the female sex, gifted with great faith and ardent devotion, turning their hearts to the Catholic altar, whether in joy or sorrow, in sickness or in health, like the innocent child, who always runs thither for help where he trusts most; here the poor pilgrim, wearied with fatigue, kneels down on the altar-steps, to thank Him who has watched over him during a long and perilous journey; here a districted mother comes into the temple to pray for the recovery of her son, whom the physicians have given over; here God is our Father, the angels and saints our friends.

O how glorious, how sublime, is the worship of the Catholic Church, as she celebrates daily, hourly, the triumphal march of the Prince of Peace around the world which he has redeemed! Hour after hour, in all parts of the world, the solemn anthems of Catholic worship roll heavenward, like "the noise of many waters." Minute after minute, hour after hour, day after day, month after month, year after year, and century after century, the glorious anthems of the Catholic Church have rolled on unbroken through the long lapse of eighteen hundred changeful, fleeting years. The unnumbered voices of every age, and sex, and rank, which have sounded from that hour when the angelic harmonies charmed the midnight air of Bethlehem, even to this very moment,—all seem borne to our ears in one overpowering flood of sweetest, heavenliest harmony.

3. The Catholic Church is one, because all her members are united under one infallible head.

Yes; more than two hundred millions of Christians venerate and obey the Holy Father, Pope Pius IX, as the successor of St. Peter, the supreme, earthly chief of the immortal Church of Jesus Christ; the father of souls; the guide of consciences; the sovereign judge of the religious interests of humanity; the head of Catholic Christendom; the mouth of Christ's Church, ever living and open to teach the universe; the center of Christian faith and unity; the light of truth, kindled to illuminate the world; the adamantine base of a divine edifice, which the powers of darkness can never shake; the cornerstone upon which the city of God here below reposes; the prince of priests, the father of fathers, the heir of apostles; a greater patriarch than

Abraham, greater than Melchizedek in priesthood, than Moses in
authority, than Samuel in jurisdiction: in a word, Peter in power,
Christ by unction, pastor of pastors, guide of guides, the cardinal joint
of all the churches, the keystone of the Catholic arch, the impregnable
citadel of the communion of the children of God. Were the holy
Pontiff, Pius IX, permitted to go abroad amid his children, every knee
would bend before him, in token of cheerful obedience; every voice
would salute him, in proof of the deepest veneration, and every tongue
would bless him with untold affection; head and body, ruler and
subjects, the shepherd and the flock, the Sovereign Pontiff and the
people, would be seen to be one heart and one soul. All Catholics live
in the heart of the Father of the Faithful; and he lives in the hearts
of all Catholics, the Holy Ghost, the Spirit of truth, abiding with
them, and uniting them all in one faith, in one worship, and under one
head: "Therefore," says St. Jerome, "was one of the twelve set over all
the others as the recognized head, in order that all occasion of schism
might be removed." (Opp. T. ii, p. 279.)

This miracle of unity of human minds and hearts in all things has
been perpetuated, from age to age, in a world where everything else
is changing, and is perpetuated silently and peacefully, without effort
and without constraint. So irresistible is the mysterious power that
thus joins together so many human hearts, that even the convert of
yesterday, whether he lives in the very center of European civilization,
or amid the savage tribes of Africa, feels already the sweet spell upon
him, and finds his heart beating in unison with the great heart of the
Church, as if he had been suckled at her breast, and had lain in her
bosom from infancy.

In the whole history of the human race there is no record of any
such miracle as this. Even were all the dead to rise from their graves,
and to crowd our streets and thoroughfares, it would not be a greater

miracle. Like the Jews of old, the men of the present generation "desire a sign," in order that they may believe; and now here is a sign, a standing miracle, more luminous, more dazzling, than the noonday sun. "Truly the finger of God is here."

One day a certain Protestant of Pennsylvania came to Archbishop Kenrick, of Baltimore, to tell him that he wished to become a Catholic. "What induced you," asked the archbishop, "to take this step?" "The bugs, the bugs!" he replied. "What do you mean by that?" "I have often noticed," said he, "how in nature animals follow their leader, and are kept united together by him. The same must be true in religion: only that one can be of divine origin which has a leader whom all are bound to follow. As I find this only in the Catholic Church, I feel convinced that she is the true Church, in which alone I can be saved." If St. Paul could say to the heathens, "You might have found out the true God by his works, if you had cared to do so," surely God may say, in the great day, to the children out of the Catholic Church: "You might have known the true Church by her unity, if you had not closed your eyes."

The next mark by which Christ wished his Church to be distinguished is that of holiness. But, in speaking of the holiness of the Catholic Church, we do not mean to say that every member of the Church is holy. The field of the Church is wide and has weeds as well as wheat. In the very company chosen by our Lord Jesus Christ himself, there was a Peter who denied him, and a Judas who betrayed him. So it is at the present day. So it will be to the end of time. Should, then, anyone ask:

5. Show how the Catholic Church is holy?

We answer: The Catholic Church is holy: 1, in Jesus Christ, her Founder; 2, in her doctrine, which is Christ's doctrine; 3, in her means of grace,

the proper use of which makes us holy; 4, in many of her members, whose
holiness has been confirmed by miracles and extraordinary gifts.

1. The Catholic Church is holy in her Founder, who is our Lord Jesus Christ, the Son of God. But what mind of man or angel can conceive the greatness of the holiness of Jesus Christ, which is, indeed, infinite? To say that his holiness is greater than that of all the saints and angels united, is to fall infinitely below it. Jesus Christ, as God, is infinite holiness itself, and the sum of ou rconception of holiness is but the smallest atom of the holiness of God. David, contemplating the divine holiness, and seeing that he could not, and never would, be able to comprehend it, could only exclaim: "O Lord! who is like unto thee?" (Psalm xxxiv, 10.) O Lord! what holiness shall ever be found like to thine? It is an utter impossibility for any human or angelic understanding to conceive an adequate idea of the holiness of Christ. All we can say is, that his holiness is infinite. The Catholic Church, then, is holy in her divine Founder.

2. The Catholic Church is also holy in her doctrine, which is the doctrine of Christ and his holy apostles, and his doctrine is the expression of the will of his heavenly Father:

"My doctrine is not mine, but of him that sent me." (John vii, 16.) As the will of God is most holy, so also the doctrine expressing the holy will of God must be most holy. Hence, the book containing the word of God is called the holy Bible, or holy Scripture. Every action and every word of our Savior breathes holiness, inspires holiness, and leads to holiness. Therefore, he calls those blessed who learn his doctrine: "Blessed are your ears, because they hear. For, amen I say to you, many prophets and just men have desired to hear the things that you hear, and have not heard them." (Matthew xiii, 16.) Hence, all those who live up to this doctrine are called saints: "You are a chosen generation—a holy nation," says St. Peter of the Christians. (1 Peter i i, 9.)

The very enemies of the Catholic Church bear witness to the holiness of her doctrine. Why have so many fallen away from her faith? It is because they had not courage enough to live up to her holy precepts. Why is it that so many do not embrace the Catholic faith who know that the Catholic Church is the only true Church of Christ? It is because they are afraid of her holy morals. Even the most wicked feel naturally convinced that the Catholic religion is holy: a fault in a Catholic is considered,—and considered rightly,—more grave than in one who is not a Catholic.

3. The Church is holy in her means of grace. It is her office to make men holy. She holds out to her children not only the holy example and doctrine of her divine Founder as the pathway to holiness, she also offers to them the means of grace, which enable them to live up to her holy doctrine. By his divine example and holy doctrine Christ showed us the narrow road that leads to heaven. But what would it avail us to know the road to heaven, if we had no strength to walk on that strait, and, to fallen humanity, hard road? This strength we have not of ourselves. God is the greatest supernatural good. We can, then, acquire this good only by supernatural strength, that is, by the help of Almighty God. By his sufferings and death, Christ obtained for us all the graces necessary to live up to his holy doctrine, to overcome all the evil inclinations of fallen nature, all the temptations, all the trials and struggles of life. These graces he wished to be applied to our souls by means of the sacraments and prayer, and he appointed his Church to sanctify her children by these means of grace.

The child is born in sin; the Church cleanses it in baptism and makes it a child of God. The child is weak; the Church strengthens it in confirmation, makes it a brave soldier, to battle with the world, the flesh, and the devil. The child is wounded, falls into sin; the Church, like the good physician, probes the wounds, and pours into the bleeding heart the oil and wine of hope and consolation, in the sacrament of penance. The child is hungry and weary; the Church feeds it with heavenly food, nourishes and refreshes it with the precious body and blood of our Lord Jesus Christ. The heart of the young man feels the fire of that love which first came from God, and which has become unholy only by abuse; and the Church, like a fond mother, sanctifies and preserves this natural love of the bridegroom and the bride. In the holy sacrament of marriage, she blesses this love before the altar of God, and declares its bonds perpetual. And should the heart of the young man aspire to a higher and holier destiny; should he desire, in his inmost soul, to soar high above the weakening tenderness of mere human love; should he desire to become the savior of his fellow-men, the cooperator with God himself in the great work of redemption, the holy Church leads him by the hand, she "blesses, sanctifies, and consecrates" him before the altar of God; she makes him a priest forever, a priest of the Most High God.

At last, when her child is dying, the holy Catholic Church comes to his bedside with sanctifying oil and the prayer of faith; she administers to him the sacrament of Extreme Unction, to strengthen and console him in his fearful death-struggle. But her love does not end at the bed of death. She opens wide the doors of her temple; she offers an asylum even to the dead body of her child. She blesses that body which was once the temple of the living God, and she even consecrates the very ground in which that body is laid to rest.

The love of the Church for her children does not pause even at the grave. Day after day she offers up her prayers; day after day she offers up the holy sacrifice of the altar for the souls of her children departed. The husband may forget the wife of his bosom, the mother may forget the child of her heart, but the holy Church does not forget her children, not even in death: her love is divine, it is eternal. And in this love the Church is impartial: she is just to all. As the holy spouse of Christ, she loves justice and hates iniquity. She has spurned the anointed king from the temple of God, until he repented of his crime; and on the head, of the lowly monk, who spent his days in labor and prayer, she has placed the triple crown.

At one moment she bathes with baptismal dew the peasant's child; and at another, she boldly confronts the imperial might that dares assail her holy altar. Now the Church is accused of despotism, because she upholds the rights of lawful authority; and again, she is accused of Arrogance, because she dares to protect the poor, the downtrodden, and the friendless.

She blesses all things that are good in this world; she protects and encourages the fine arts. Truth is the essence of order, the essence of beauty. Religious truth is heavenly order, is supernatural beauty. The Church is the living spouse of heavenly truth; she must, therefore, be the friend, the protector, of all beauty and order, and so she has proved to be for over eighteen hundred years.

In the Church, all that is good and beautiful in art or nature has been purified as in a heavenly crucible and consecrated to the service of religion. The poet seeks to please the imaginations of men, and the Church unfolds before him the annals of Christianity. She tells him of the august sacrifice of infinite love, which is her soul and life, and she tells him of her heroic sufferings, of her martyr faith; and the poet draws holy inspiration from these touching records, and incites men to a higher, to a holier life.

The painter and the sculptor seek to place before our eyes the happiest, the most sublime of conceptions; and the Church bids them look into her treasure-house, where they find the most perfect models of every virtue, — models of pure, of noble, of heroic self-sacrifice.

The architect seeks to build up a monument of strength, and intellect, and beauty; and the Church unlocks for him the sublime, mysterious meanings of her ceremonies and symbols. Guided by her inspiration, he teaches the lifeless stone, he teaches the spreading arch, the pointed spire, to speak to men of faith, of hope, of love; he teaches them to speak of prayer, of sacrifice, of heaven.

The orator strives to nerve men for the solemn duties, the grand conflicts of life; the Church of Christ, touches his lips with living fire from the altar, and his eloquence flows on in an impetuous stream of "thoughts that breathe, and words that burn."

The musician seeks to weave his entrancing spells around ear, and heart, and soul; and the Church breathes into his soul the glorious, wondrous melodies which she has borrowed from the angels of heaven, and her music seems like beatific worship, and the worship on earth like beatific music.

4. The Church is holy in many of her members. What is more natural than this? A mother that teaches her children so holy a doctrine, sets before them constantly the example of her divine Founder, that they may live and die as he did. A mother that has such powerful means to sanctify her children, cannot but be holy in the fruits of sanctity, in the saints, and in the sacred institutions which she has produced.

To be convinced of the personal sanctity of millions of her children, we have but to open the annals of Church history. There we read of thousands of men and women who fulfilled the saying of Christ: "Whosoever shall lose his life for my sake and the Gospel, shall save it." (Mark viii, 35.) Such was the havoc made during the early persecutions of the Church, that her martyrs alone amount to thirty thousand for every day in the year.

How many thousands of the children of the Church followed that spying of the Lord: "If thou wilt be perfect, go, sell what thou hast, and give to the poor, and come, follow me!" (Matthew xix, 21.) And, "Every one that hath left house, or brethren, or sisters, or father, or mother, or wife, or children, or lands, for my name's sake, shall receive a hundred-fold, and shall possess life everlasting." (Matthew xix, 29.) Astonishing, indeed, is the number of those who have followed this saying of our Lord, by embracing the religious life.

St. Athanasius writes that in his time there were monasteries like tabernacles, full of heavenly choirs of people, who spent their time in singing psalms, in reading and praying; that they occupied a large extent of land, and made, as it were, a town among themselves. Suc himmense numbers resorted to the religious life in Palestine, that Isidore was the superior of one thousand monks, and his successor, Apollonius, of five thousand in the same monastery. In the cloistered community of Oryrynchus there were ten thousand monks. Upon a hill in Nitria, about twenty miles from Alexandria, there were five hundred monasteries under one superior. Palladius relates that he saw a city in which there were more monasteries than houses of seculars, "so that, every street and corner ringing with the divine praises, the whole city seemed a church." He also testifies to having seen multitudes of monks in Memphis and Babylon, and that not far from Thebes he met with a Father of three thousand monks. St. Pachomius, who lived about three hundred years after Christ, had seven thousand disciples, besides one thousand in his own house: and Serapion had ten thousand monks under his jurisdiction.

Theodoret records that there were also multitudes of religious women throughout the East, in Palestine, Egypt, Asia, Pontus, Cilicia,

Syria, and also in Europe: "Since our Savior," he says, "was born of a Virgin Mother, the fields of holy virgins are everywhere multiplied."

Nor was the great increase of religious houses confined to the early ages of the Church, for Trithemius, who died about the year 1516, says that, in his time, the province of Ments alone contained one hundred and twenty-four abbeys; and that there was a time when they had fifteen thousand abbeys, besides priories and other small monasteries, belonging to his order.

St. Bernard, in his Life of St. Malachy, records that, in Ireland, there was a monastery out of which many thousands of monks had come forth: "A holy place indeed," he says, "and fruitful in saints, bringing forth abundant fruit to God, insomuch that one man alone of that holy congregation, whose name was Luanus, is reported to have been the founder of one hundred monasteries. And these swarms of saints have not only spread themselves in Ireland and Scotland, but have also gone into foreign parts; for St. Columba, coming from thence into France, built the monastery of Luxovium, and raised there a great people, their number being so great that the divine praises were sung by them day and night without intermission. St. Columba founded one hundred monasteries, of which thirty-seven were in Ireland, a country which was, for centuries, known all over Europe as the Island of Saints and of Doctors." According to Archdall, there were in Ireland seven hundred and forty-two religious houses.

St. Bernard, in the space of thirty years that be was abbot, founded one hundred and sixty monasteries. So rapid was the progress of his order that, in the space of fifty years from its establishment, it had acquired five hundred abbeys; and at one time no fewer than eight hundred were dependent on Clairvaux.

The Franciscans seem to have been particularly blessed in the speedy and extensive propagation of their order, for, about the year

1600, one branch of this order, called the Observantines, is said to have numbered one hundred thousand members. This order reckons at present two hundred thousand men and three hundred thousand sisters, including the tertiaries. It possesses two hundred and fifty-two provinces and twenty-six thousand convents, of which five are in Palestine, and over thirty in Turkey. More than eighty-nine emperors, kings and queens have been admitted into the order, which has, moreover, the glory of having furnished three thousand saints, or beatified persons, of whom seventeen hundred are martyrs.

Nor is the Church less holy in many of her members, in our day. Who really takes Christian care of the poor, the sick, and the friendless, but the Catholic Church? She has founded such orders as the Sisters of Charity, the Sisters of Mercy, the Sisters of St. Joseph, and so many others, in order to administer to their wants.

Where can you find, outside of the Catholic Church, that young and beautiful virgin, who lays at the foot of the cross her youth, her wealth, and her beauty; who sacrifices all earthly hope and love, to spend her days in a loathsome hospital, and to watch, during the long, dull night, by the bedside of the sick and dying? The charitable, heroic deeds of these holy virgins have already brought conviction to the minds and hearts of many non-Catholics.

St. John the Evangelist tells us that our Savior cured one day a young man who had been born blind. The Pharisees heard of this, and were filled with rage and envy. They took the young man aside and said to him: "Give glory to God; that man that cured you is a sinner." "Well," said the young man, "whether he be a sinner or not, I cannot say. But one thing I do know, and tha tis, that he has cured me. God does not hear sinners. If this man were not from God, he could not do such things." (John ix.) This was the argument of the young man in the Gospel; this, too, is the simple argument of every honest non-Catholic.

The bigots and Protestant preachers say to the returned soldier, to the young man who has just come forth from the hospital where he suffered during a long and painful illness: "The Catholic Church is sinful and corrupt." "Well," the young man answers, "whether she is corrupt or not, I do not know; but one thing I do know, and that is, that I was at the point of death, and now I am well: and I owe it, after God, to the good Sisters of the Catholic Church. They waited on me in the hospital, in the battlefield; they nursed me as tenderly as a mother or a sister could have done and they did it without pay, without any human motive or reward. Now, a bad tree cannot bring forth such good fruit. If the Catholic Church were as sinful and corrupt as you say, God would not give her children such heroic devotedness."

Behold, again, the holy charity of the Catholic Church toward the very outcasts of society, —those poor, fallen creatures, that have become the dishonor of their sex! See how closely she imitates her divine spouse, our Lord Jesus Christ! Jesus is present at a great feast. A poor, sinful woman, notorious on account of her wicked life, falls prostrate at his feet. She washes his feet with her tears and wipes them with her hair. The Pharisees are shocked and scandalized. They say in their hearts:

"This man is no prophet; if he were a prophet, he would know what kind of a woman that is who kneels at his feet; he would spurn her from him." But Jesus knows well the sinful life of Magdalen, and yet he does not reject her. On the contrary, he defends her before them all, and says to her: "My child, go in peace, thy sins are forgiven thee!"

Ah, how full of mercy and compassion is the heart of Jesus Christ! Now look upon his spouse, the holy Catholic Church, and see if she is not worthy of her heavenly Bridegroom! The unfortunate woman whom many have helped to drag into destruction, has not now a hand stretched out to save her. The world that allured and ruined her despises her and laughs her to scorn. The proud, self-righteous Pharisee turns away from her in horror and disgust. The grace of God at last touches her heart. She sees herself abandoned by all; she turns her despairing eyes to God. Friendless, homeless, and alone, she wanders through the dark by-ways of this valley of tears till at last she stands at the ever-open portals of the holy Catholic Church. She enters, she falls at the feet of the priest of Jesus Christ. She weeps, she repents, she is forgiven.

See those pure virgin nuns, who are justly called the Daughters of the Good Shepherd! They have sworn, before the altar of God, to devote their whole life to the reformation of these poor outcasts of society,—these unhappy victims of a heartless world. See how gently they receive the fallen one, how kindly they treat her! See how she enters the convent chapel, and at the very feet of Jesus, in the blessed sacrament, she pours out her prayers, and sighs, and tears! She experiences at last that there is rest for the weary, that there is hope for the sinner; that there is, indeed, a heaven on earth, in the holy Catholic C hurch.

In every age, and in every country through which the Catholic religion has spread, there have been many Catholics who showed, in their daily conduct, that they complied with the words of St. Paul: "This is the will of God, your sanctification." (1 Thessalonians iv, 3.) They were scrupulous keepers of the commandments of God, fulfilling the whole law and the prophets. How could it be otherwise? Jesus Christ, in the blessed sacrament,—this divine food, the source of all sanctity,—never ceases to bring forth holy bishops, like St. Charles Borromeo, St. Francis de Sales, St. Alphonsus Liguori; holy priests, like St. Vincent de Paul, St. Francis Xavier, St. Peter Claver: holy virgins, like St. Teresa, St. Catharine of Sienna, St. Zitta, St. Rose of

Lima; holy widows, like St. Frances de Chantal; holy martyrs, like
Borie, Gagelin, and so many others.

That God confirmed the holiness of his servants by many miracles
and extraordinary gifts, may be read in the Lives of the Saints, or in
any Church history. "Amen, amen, I say to you," said Christ, "he that
believes in me, the works that I do he also shall do, and greater than
these shall he do" (John xiv, 12); and, "These signs shall follow them
that believe: In my name they shall cast out devils, they shall speak
with new tongues, they shall take up serpents, they shall lay their hands
upon the sick, and they shall recover." (Mark xvi, 17, 18.) Accordingly,
we read that Saints Paphnutius, Remigius, Otto, Robert, Dominic,
and many others, cast out the devil from possessed persons. When St.
Bernardine of Sienna, St. Anthony of Padua, St Francis Xavier, and
others, preached to an audience composed of people from different
countries, everyone believed he heard his own tongue spoken. St.
Hilary, St. Magnus, St. Patrick, and others, banished snakes and other
reptiles. St. Gregory Thaumaturgus moved a mountain, to obtain a
site for a Church. St. Patrick, St. Martin, St. Benedict, St. Dominic, St.
Anthony, St. Francis of Paula, and many others, raised dead persons
to life. St. Francis Xavier raised twenty-five, and St. John Capistran,
thirty dead persons to life. St. Stanislas the Martyr restored a man to
life who had died three years before and presented him before the court
to testify that he had bought from him a certain piece of ground for
his church, and that he had paid him in full.

The Catholic Church, then, is holy in her doctrine and means of
grace; she is holy in all those of her members who live up to her holy
doctrine. She is holy in the strenuous efforts which she has always
made to put down errors, correct abuses, destroy sin, and cure all
kinds of evils. Anyone who reads, for instance, the acts of the Council
of Trent cannot fail to notice that one-half of its chapters treat of

the great work of reformation. In this council the Church proscribes duels, reduces liturgies to unity, banishes profane airs and secular music from her temples, institutes seminaries for the education of the clergy, establishes, at cathedrals, free-schools and lectures on holy Scripture, for the instruction of the people; she reminds her pastors that they are bound to continence, to residence, to frequent and diligent preaching; she interdicts all appearance of simony and venality in the distribution of ecclesiastical offices, in preaching indulgences, and in administering the sacraments.

(NB - In uprooting evils, in putting down errors, and heresies, and the like, the Church never used violent means, such as confiscation of goods, banishment, exile, bloodshed and death. The Church has always taught her children to suffer persecution for the sake of Christ, but never to commence it and carry it on. Her spirit is to love her enemies, to pray for their conversion, and to return good for evil. Hence she has, at all times, invariably condemned such actions of Catholic monarch's as were opposed to this spirit of meekness and charity. King Ferdinand established what is called "The Spanish Inquisition." He had good reason to believe that the Moors and the Jews were enemies to his government. In those days outspoken heresy was looked upon as an offence against religion as well as against the State. Accordingly, he erected a civil tribunal for the trial of those of his subjects who were suspected of heresy and disloyalty. By this civil tribunal the Moors and Jews were oppressed,

not so much on account of their heresy, but rather on account of their rebellious spirit, arising from heresy. The object, therefore, of the Spanish Inquisition was to preserve the integrity of the kingdom, rather than that of the Catholic religion. From the beginning of the action of this political institution, Pope Sixtus IV was exceedingly displeased with it. He urged his objections so strongly, that the ambassadors of both courts were ordered to leave their respective stations, and Ferdinand commanded all his subjects to leave Rome. The pope also commanded that the Inquisition should not be established in any other province. The Holy Father did all in his power to stop the prosecutions, and to soften the punishments in other cases. He also insisted that the civil rights and the property of every condemned person should be restored to him, or, if he was dead, to his children. Pope Leo X excommunicated the Inquisitors of Toledo. Pope Paul III lamented bitterly the condition of the Spanish Inquisition, and assisted those who were opposing its introduction into Naples. Pope Pius IV aided St. Charles Borromeo in keeping it out of Milan. The statement of these facts is verified by Llorente's work, or by Professor Hefele's (of Tubingen) Epitome of Llorente, in his "Ximenes." The excesses of the Spanish Inquisition would not have taken place had the court of Spain been obedient to the briefs and commands of the popes. Whenever temporal princes persist in meddling with matters which do not pertain to

their province, they will always pass the limits of justice. It would be great folly for anyone to blame the Church for those excesses of her members which she disowns, abhors, and condemns. No Protestant or infidel could even produce a brief of a pope or an act of a council sanctioning religious persecution. The Catholic Church is indeed opposed to heresy; but the only weapons she uses to extirpate it are, to explain her doctrine to all non-Catholics, and to be charitable and meek toward them.)

Thus the tree is pruned, but not uprooted; the pastors, those heavenly physicians, cure their patients, but do not kill them; the clergy and the religious orders are reformed, but the priesthood and the religious state are not abolished; incontinence is suppressed, though universal marriage is not preached; the weeds in the field of the Lord are plucked up, but the good seed is preserved. This is a reformation, not of the Church, but by the Church, —a reformation to bring about which, she was established by Christ; a reformation which she accomplishes by her general councils, by her zealous bishops and holy priests, by her fervent religious orders and congregations of both sexes, and by so many pious confraternities. But the Church herself, her doctrine, her means of grace, her order of government, are all divine and holy, and therefore can never be reformed: it would be a monstrous impiety to say that she could be reformed.

What a glorious Church is ours! What power but that of God could make her so divinely one in her faith, in her morality, in her worship, in her government? What holiness but that of the Lord could make her so holy in her Founder, in her doctrine, in her sacraments, in her members? What more natural than that the Lord of all power and of all holiness should make this Church Catholic, as to time, place, and doctrine? But,

6. What does the word Catholic mean?

The word Catholic means Universal,

Now it is easy to—

7. Show how the Roman Church is Catholic, or Universal.

The Roman Church is Catholic: 1, because she has existed in all ages; 2, because she teaches all nations; and, 3, because she maintains all truths.

1. The Roman Church is Catholic, because she has existed in all ages. This Church is Catholic, or universal, in her duration. She goes back, without a break, through the apostles to Jesus Christ, through Jesus Christ to the origin of the chosen people, and through Abraham and the patriarchs even to our first parents in paradise. The enemies of God hate his holy Church; they hate the pope, they hate the bishops and the priests; they grind their teeth, they foam at the mouth, they tremble with rage, and seem as if they would tear into pieces all the popes, bishops and priests that have ever lived, from Peter to the present day. Why? Because Jesus Christ continues to live in Peter, and in his successors; he speaks to the world and teaches it, through them, like one having authority. It is for this very reason that the Church will remain forever; for, truth and justice being in the end always victorious, the Church will not cease to bless and to triumph. All the works of the earth have perished, time has obliterated them. The

Catholic Church remains; she will endure until she passes from her earthly exile to her country in heaven.

Human theories and systems have flitted across her path, like birds of night, but have vanished; numberless sects have, like so many waves, dashed themselves to froth against this rock, or, recoiling, have been lost in the vast ocean of forgetfulness. Kingdoms and empires that once existed in inimitable worldly grandeur, are no more; dynasties have died out, and have been replaced by others.

Theories and scepters and crowns have withstood the Church; but, immutable, like God, who laid her foundation, she is the firm, unshaken center, round which the weal and woe of nations move: weal to them if they adhere to her, woe to them if they separate from her. If the world takes from the Catholic Church the cross of gold, she will bless the world with one of wood. If necessary, her pastors and all her children can suffer and die for the faith, but the Catholic Church remains: she is immortal.

We cannot but smile when we hear men talk of the downfall of the Catholic Church. What could hell and its agents do more than they have already done for her destruction? They have employed tortures for the body, but they could not reach the spirit; they have tried heresy, or the denial of revealed truth, to such an extent that we can see no room for any new heresy; they have, by the hand of schism, torn whole countries from the unity of the Church; but what she lost on one side of the globe, she gained ten fold on theother. All these assaults have ignominiously failed to verify the prophecies of hell, that "the Catholic Church shall fall."

Look, for instance, at the tremendous effort of the so-called Reformation, together with its twin sister, the unbelief of the nineteenth century! Whole legions of Church reformers, together with armies of philosophers, armed with negation, and a thousand-and-one systems of paganism, furiously attacked the Chair of Peter, and swore that the Papacy should fall, and, with it, the whole Church. Three hundred years are over, and the Catholic Church is still alive, and more vigorous than ever. She is the glorious Church of all ages. And as Christ made her Catholic, or universal, as to time, so also he made her Catholic as to place.

2. She teaches all nations: "Going therefore," said our Lord to his apostles, "teach ye all nations;" and, "You shall be witnesses unto me in Jerusalem, and in all Judea, and Samaria, and even to the uttermost part of the earth." More than fifteen hundred years ago there hung in the catacombs of Rome a lamp shaped in the form of a ship, at whose helm sat St. Peter, steering with one hand, and with the other giving his blessing. On one side of this miniature ship were engraved the words, "Peter dies not;" and on the other, the words of our Savior, "I have prayed for thee." (Luke xxii, 32.)

There could not be a more beautiful symbol of the Catholic Church. She is the lamp which has dispelled the darkness of heathenism, and has furnished the nations with the brilliant light of truth; the Church is a ship, which has carried this light safely, through the storms of ages, to the ends of the earth, bringing with it blessings to the nations, and gathering into its apostolic net, as it sailed along, the perishing children of men. And at the helm sits the poor fisherman of Galilee, St. Peter, in the person of the pope, together with his assistants, the Catholic bishops and priests, directing the course of the vessel, now to this, now to that distressed country, now to this, now to that sorrowing people, to carry to them, not gold, not silver, but what is infinitely more precious,— faith; and with faith, true civilization, based upon the unchangeable principles of supernatural morality, true prosperity, true happiness, and peace on earth and for eternity.

It was not by the circulation of the Bible, by Bible societies or by money, but by the living voice of the Roman Church, —it was through the popes, the Catholic bishops and priests, that Christianity, at the end of the third century, covered the whole then known world. The Capitoline temple, and with it the many shrines of idolatry, the golden house of Nero, and with it Roman excess and Roman cruelty, the throne of the Caesars, and with it Roman oppression and Roman injustice, had all passed away, and there stood the Rome of the Fathers of the Church,—the Rome which has yet to do such wonders in the w orld.

"And the light shone into the darkness." Pope after pope, the principal bearers of the light of the true faith, sent forth to the nations bishops and missionaries, full of the spirit of self-sacrifice, solely devoted to their great task; and by the inflamed zeal, the fervent piety, the earnest prayers and penances, the astounding miracles, the bright examples and spotless lives of these apostolic men, new tribes and new nations were gained for Christ, year after year. Thus, St. Austin carried the light of faith to England, St. Patrick to Ireland, St. Boniface to Germany. The Frieslanders, the Moravians, the Prussians, the Swedes, the Picts, the Scots, the Franks, and hundreds of others, were brought to the bosom of the Church through the preaching and labors of the bishops and priests of the Roman Catholic Church. Driven from one country, their influence was made to act on another. When Solisman, the Sultan, threatened to wipe out Christianity from Europe, Roman Catholic bishops and priests went to the East Indies, to China, and Japan. When Europe failed in its fidelity, and listened to the siren voice of heresy, Catholic bishops and priests were sent to the newly-discovered continent of America, and to the West Indies.

Gregory XVI devised plans for missions to the interior of Africa,—missions which are yet working winders. This great work of enlightening the world with the true light of the Catholic religion, the Church accomplished, more particularly by those astonishing organizations called religions orders.

Besides carrying the light of faith to all nations, those religious orders did another thing: they civilized the countries to which they had been sent.

In the pagan world, education was an edifice built up on the principles of slavery. The motto was: "Odi profanum vulgus et arceo"—I hate and shun the common people. Education was the privilege of the aristocracy. The great mass of people was studiously kept in ignorance of the treasures of the mind. This state of things was done away with by the Roman Catholic Church, when she established the monastic institutions of the West. The whole of Europe was soon covered with schools, not only for the wealthy, but even for the poorest of the poor. Education was systematized, and an emulation was created for learning, such as the world had never seen before. Italy, Germany, France, England, and Spain had their universities; but, side by side with these, their colleges, gymnasiums, parish and village schools, as numerous as the churches and monasteries which the efforts of the Holy See had scattered, with lavish hand, over the length and breadth of the land.

And where was the source of all this light? At Rome, For, when the barbarian hordes poured down upon Europe from the Caspian Mountains, it was the popes who saved civilization. They collected, in the Vatican, the manuscripts of the ancient authors, gathered from all parts of the earth at enormous expense. The barbarians, who destroyed everything by fire and sword, had already advanced as far as Rome. Attila, who called himself "the Scourge of God," stood before its walls; there were no emperor, no pretorian guard, no legions present, to save the ancient capital of the world. But there was a pope: Leo I. And

Leo went forth, and by entreaties, and threats of God's displeasure, induced the dreaded king of the Huns to retire. Scarcely had Attila retired before Genseric, King of the Vandals, made his appearance, invited by Eudoxia, the empress, to the plunder of Rome. Leo met him and obtained from him the lives and the honor of the Romans, and the sparing of the public monuments which adorned the city in such numbers. Thus, Leo the Great saved Europe from barbarism. To the name of Leo might be added those of Gregory I, Sylvester II, Gregory XIII, Benedict XIV, Julius III, Paul III, Leo X, Clement VIII, John XX, and a host of others, who must be looked upon as the preservers of science and the arts, even amid the very fearful torrent of barbarism that was spreading itself, like an inundation, over the whole of Europe. The principle of the Catholic Church has ever been this: "By the knowledge of divine things, and the guidance of an infallible teacher, the human mind must gain certainty in regard to the sublimest problems, the great questions of life; by them the origin, the end, the aim and limit of man's activity, must be made known, for then only can he venture fearlessly upon the sphere of human efforts, and human developments, and human science." And, truly, never has science gained the ascendency outside of the Church that it has always held in the Church. And what is true of science is true, also, of the arts. It is true of architecture, of sculpture, and of painting. We need only point to the Basilica of Peter, to the museums and libraries of Rome. It is to Rome the youthful artist always turns his steps, in order to drink in, at the monuments of art and of science, the genius and inspiration he seeks for in vain in his own country. He feels, only too keenly, that railroads and telegraphs, steamships and power-looms, banking-houses and stock-companies, though good and useful institutions, are not the mothers of genius, nor the schools of inspiration; and therefore he leaves his country, and goes to Rome, and there feasts on the fruits gathered by the hands of St. Peter's successors, and returns home with a name which will live for ages in the memory of those who have learned to appreciate the true and the beautiful.

The depravity of man shows itself in the constant endeavor to shake off the restraint placed by law and duty upon his will: and to this we must ascribe the licentiousness which has at all times afflicted society. Passion acknowledges no law, and spares neither rights nor conventions; where it has the power, it exercises it to the advantage of self, and to the detriment of social order. The Church is, by its very constitution, Catholic, and hence looks upon all men as brothers of the same family. She acknowledges not the natural right of one man over another; and hence her Catholicity lays a heavy restraint upon all the efforts of self-love, and curbs, with a mighty hand, the temerity of those who would destroy the harmony of life, implied in the idea of Catholicity.

One of the first principles of all social happiness is, that before the law of nature, and before the face of God, all men are equal. This principle is based on the unity of the human race, the origin of all men from one common father. If we study the history of paganism, we find that all heathen nations overturned this great principle, since we find among all heathen nations the evil of slavery. Prior to the coming of Christ, the great majority of men were looked upon as a higher development of the animal, as animated instruments, which might be bought and sold, given away and pawned; which might be tormented, maltreated, or murdered; as beings, in a word, for whom the idea of right, duty, pity, mercy, and law, had no existence. Who can read, without a feeling of intense horror, the accounts left us of the treatment of their slaves by the Romans? There was no law that could restrain in the least the wantonness, the cruelty, the licentious excess of the master, who, as master, possessed the absolute right to do with his slaves whatsoever he pleased. To remove this stain of slavery has ever been the aim of the Catholic Church. "Since the Savior and Creator of the world," says Pope Gregory I, in his celebrated decree, "wished to become man, in order, by grace and liberty, to break the chains of our slavery, it is right and good to bestow again upon man, whom nature has permitted to be born free, but whom the law of nations has brought under the yoke of slavery, the blessing of his original liberty." Through all the middle ages,— called by Protestants the dark ages of the worlds—the echo of these words of Gregory I is heard; and, in the thirteenth century, Pope Pius II could say: "Thanks be to God and the Apostolic See, the yoke of slavery does no longer disgrace any European nation." Since then, slavery was again introduced into Africa and the newly-discovered regions of America, and again the popes raised their voices in the interest of liberty. Pius VII, even at the time when Napoleon had robbed him of his liberty, and held him captive in a foreign land, became the defender of the negro. Gregory XVI, on the 3rd of November 1839, insisted, in a special Bull, on the abolition of the slave trade, and spoke in a strain as if he had lived and sat side by side with Gregory I, thirteen hundred years before. But here let us observe, that not only the vindication of liberty for all, not only the abolition of slavery, but the very mode of action followed in this matter by the popes, has gained for the Church immortal honor, and the esteem of all good men. When the Church abolished slavery in any country where it existed, the popes did not compel masters, by harshness or threats, to manumit their slaves; they did not bring into action the base intrigues, the low chicanery, the canting hypocrisy, of modern statesmen; they did not raise armies, and send them into the lands of their masters to burn and to pillage, to lay waste and to destroy; they did not slaughter, by their schemes, over a million of free men, and another million of slaves; they did not make widows' and orphans without number; they did not impoverish the land, and lay upon their subjects burdens which would crush them into very dust. Nothing of all this. That is not the way in which the Church abolished slavery. The popes sent bishops and priests into those countries where slavery existed, to enlighten the minds of the masters, and convince them that slaves were men, and consequently had immortal souls like other people.The pastors of the Church infused into the hearts of masters a deep love for Jesus Christ, and consequently a deep love for souls. They taught masters to look upon slaves as created by the same God, redeemed by the same Jesus Christ, destined for the same glory. The consequence was, that the relations of slave and master became the relations of brother to brother; the master began to love his slave, and to ameliorate his condition, till at last, forced by his own acknowledged principles, he granted to him his liberty. Thus, it was that slavery was abolished by the preaching of the popes, bishops and priests. The great barrier to all the healthy, permanent, and free development of nations was thus broken down; the blessings, the privileges of society, were made equally attainable by the masses, and ceased to be the special monopoly of a few, who, for the most part, had nothing to recommend them except their wealth.

It is thus that the Catholic Church has accomplished the great work of enlightening society. She has shed the light of faith over the East and the West, over the North and the South, and with the faith she has established the principles of true science on their natural bases. She has imparted education to the masses, wherever she was left free to adopt her own, and untrammeled by civil interference. She has fostered and protected the arts and the sciences; and today, if all the libraries, and all the museums, and all the galleries of art in the world were destroyed, Rome alone would possess quite enough to supply the want, as it did in former ages, when others supplied themselves by plundering Rome. She has abolished slavery, and established human freedom. She truly is what she is called: Catholic for all ages, Catholic fo rall nations, and—

3. She is Catholic, because she maintains all truths.

The Roman Church is universal, or catholic, as to doctrine. Her doctrine is the same everywhere. What she teaches in one country, she also teaches in another. Her doctrine in one place is her doctrine in another. There can be in the Roman Church no new doctrine, no local belief, no creed in which the whole Church has not been united—the Church uniting to condemn all variations from this belief. New discipline, new practices, new orders, new methods, may be adopted by the Church, according to the requirements of her work; but there can be no doctrine which has not existed from the beginning, as it was received from Christ and the apostles. A doctrine, to be truly Catholic, must have been believed in all places, at all times, and by all the faithful. By this test of catholicity, or universality, antiquity and consent, all questions of faith are tried and decided. Doctrines and articles of faith may be newly defined, as, for instance, that of the Immaculate Conception or of the Infallibility of the Pope, but there can be no new doctrine. Novelty is a quality of heresy; for, though some errors may be very old, yet they are new as compared with the truth. In every case, the truth must first appear before its corresponding error. The denial of any truth supposes its previous assertion. Like the divine Founder of the Roman Catholic Church, her doctrine is the same yesterday, today, and forever.

"Some years ago," writes Mr. Marshal, a distinguished English convert, "I was present, officially, at the examination of an English primary school, in which the children displayed such unusual accuracy and intelligence, as long as the questions turned only upon secular subjects, that I was anxious to ascertain whether they could reason as well about the truths of the Catechism as they could about those of grammar and arithmetic. I communicated my desire to their clergyman, who kindly permitted me to have recourse to a test which I had employed on other occasions. I requested him to interrogate them on the Notes of the Church, and when they had explained in the usual manner the meaning of the word Catholic, I took up the examination, with the consent of the priest, and addressed the following question to the class: 'You say the Church is Catholic because she is everywhere. Now, I have visited many countries, in all parts of the world, and I never came to one in which I did not find heresy. If, then, the Church is Catholic because she is everywhere, why is not heresy Catholic, since heresy is everywhere, also?' 'If you please, sir,' answered a little girl, about twelve years of age, 'the Church is everywhere, and everywhere the same; heresy may be everywhere too, but it is everywhere diffe rent.'"

The Church is unceasingly assailed by new errors, yet she always and everywhere is consistent with herself; she explains and develops her earlier definitions, without even the shadow of change appearing; she has declared, hundreds of times, that she can introduce no innovations, that she has no power to originate anything in matters of faith and morals, but that it is her right and office to maintain the divine doctrine as contained in Scripture and tradition. She has convoked nineteen General Council, and in each pronounced a solemn anathema on all who in the least deviated from the faith. In all ages she has undergone the cruelest persecutions, because she maintains all truths, and for this very reason she will be persecuted to the end of the world. But rather than yield one iota of her doctrine, she is willing to make every sacrifice: she permits whole countries to leave her, her pastors to be murdered, her children to be imprisoned and exiled, rather than permit one tittle of the law to be abolished. See, for instance, what she has done and suffered in upholding the dignity of the sacrament of marriage, — the corner-stone of society!

See the workings of Catholic and Protestant doctrines of marriage in society! Take the common instance of a man in whose heart there is a fearful struggle between conscience on the one hand, and blind, brutish passion on the other! His wife, —that wife whom he once loved so dearly,—has become hateful to him. Perhaps she has lost the charm of beauty which once fascinated his heart. Another stands before him—she is young, she is beautiful. Protestantism, like the tempter of hell, whispers in his ear: "Sue for a divorce. The marriage bond can be broken. Youth and beauty may yet be yours?' And the voice of conscience, the voice of God, is stifled. Brutish passion conquers. Divorce is sought and obtained, and the poor wife is cast away, and left heart-broken and companionless. And the children of such a marriage, —who shall care for them? Who shall teach them the virtues of obedience and charity? How can they respect a divorced mother, an adulterous father? No, these children become naturally the curse of society. They fill our prisons, our hospitals, the brothels.

On the contrary, if that man is a Catholic, the holy Church speaks to him in solemn warning: "See!" she says, "you took that wife in the day of her early joy and beauty. She gave you her young heart before the altar. You swore before God and his angels to be faithful to her until death. I declare to you, then, that, at the peril of your immortal soul, you must keep that union perpetual.

That union shall end only when you have stood by her death-bed, when you have knelt at her grave."

The Catholic Church has always regarded Christian marriage as the corner-stone of society; and at that cornerstone have the pastors of the Church stood guard for eighteen centuries, insisting that Christian marriage is one, holy and indissoluble. Woman, weak and unprotected, has always found at Rome that guarantee which was refused her by him who had sworn at the altar of God to love her and to cherish her till death. Whilst in the nations which Protestantism tore from the bosom of the Church, the sacred laws of matrimony are trampled in the dust; whilst the statistics of these nations hold up to the world the sad spectacle of divorces almost as numerous as marriages, of separations of husband from wife, and wife from husband, for the most trivial causes, thus granting to lust the widest margin of license, and legalizing concubinage and adultery; whilst the nineteenth century records in its annals the existence of a community of licentious polygamists within the borders of one of the most civilized countries of the earth, we have yet to see the decree emanating from Rome that would permit even a beggar to repudiate his lawful wife, in order to give his affections to an adulteress.

The female portion of our race would always have sunk back into a new slavery, had not the popes entered the breach for the protection of the unity, the sanctity, the indissolubility of matrimony. In the midst of the barbarous ages, during which the conqueror and warrior swayed the scepter of empire, and kings and petty tyrants acknowledge no other right but that of force, it was the popes that opposed their authority, like a wall of brass, to the sensuality and the passions of the mighty ones of the earth and stood forth as the protectors of innocence and outraged virtue, as the champions of the rights of women, against the wanton excesses of tyrannical husbands, by enforcing, in their full severity, the laws of Christian marriage. If Christian Europe is not covered with harems; if polygamy has never gained a foothold in Europe; if, with the indissolubility and sanctity of matrimony, the palladium of European civilization has been saved from destruction, it is all owing to the pastors of the Church. "If the popes," says the Protestant Von Muller,—"if the popes could hold up no other merit than that which they gained by protecting monogamy against the brutal lusts of those in power, notwithstanding bribes, threats, and persecutions, that fact alone would render them immortal f or all future ages."

And how had they to battle till they had gained this merit? What sufferings had they to endure, what trials to undergo? When King Lothair, in the ninth century, repudiated his lawful wife, in order to live with a concubine, Pope Nicholas I at once took upon himself the defense of the rights and of the honor of the unhappy wife. All the arts of an intriguing policy were plied, but Nicholas remained unshaken; threats were used, but Nicholas remained firm. At last, the king's brother, Louis II, appears with an army before the walls of Rome, to compel the pope to yield. It is useless— Nicholas swerves not from the line of duty. Rome is besieged; the priests and people are maltreated and plundered; sanctuaries are desecrated; the cross is torn down and trampled underfoot, and, in the midst of these scenes of blood and sacrilege, Nicholas flies to the Church of St. Peter. There he is besieged by the army of the emperor for two days and two nights; left without food or drink, he is willing to die of starvation on the tomb of St. Peter, rather than yield to a brutal tyrant, and sacrifice the sanctity of Christian marriage, the law of life of Christian society. And the perseverance of Nicholas I was crowned with victory. He had to contend against a licentious king, who was tired of restraint; against an emperor, who, with an army at his heels, came to enforce his brother's unjust demands; against two councils of venal bishops: the one at Metz, the other at Aix-la-Chapelle, who had sanctioned the scandals of the adulterous monarch. Yet, with all this opposition, and the suffering it cost him, the pope succeeded in procuring the acknowledgment of the rights of an injured woman. And during succeeding ages we find Gregory V carrying on a similar combat against King Robert, and Urban II against King Philip of France. In the thirteenth century, Philip Augustus, mightier than his predecessors, set to work all the levers of power, to move the pope to divorce him from his wife, Ingelburgis. Hear the noble answer of the great Innocent III:— "Since, by the grace of God, we have the firm and unshaken will never to separate ourselves from justice and truth, neither moved by petitions, nor bribed by presents, neither induced by love, nor intimidated by hate, we will continue to go on in the royal path, turning neither to the rightnor to the left; and we judge without any respect to persons, since God himself does not respect persons."

After the death of his first wife, Isabella, Philip Augustus wished to gain the favor of Denmark by marrying Ingelbifrgis. The union had hardly been solemnized, when he wished to be divorced from her. A council of venal bishops assembled at Compiegne and annulled his lawful marriage. The queen, poor woman, was summoned before her judges, and the sentence was read and translated to her. She could not speak the language of France, so her only cry was, "Rome!" And Rome heard her cry of distress and came to her rescue. Innocent III needed the alliance of France in the troubles in which he was engaged with Germany; Innocent III needed the assistance of France for the Crusade; yet Innocent III sent Peter of Capua as legate to France. A council is convoked by the legate of the Pope: Philip refuses to appear, in spite of the summons, and his whole kingdom is placed under interdict. Philip's rage knows no bounds; bishops are banished, his lawful wife is imprisoned, and the king vents his rage on the clergy of France. The barons, at last, appeal to the sword. The king complains to the pope of the harshness of the legate; and when Innocent only confirms the sentence of the legate, the king exclaims, "Happy Saladin! he had no pope!" Yet the king was forced to obey. When he asked the barons assembled in council, "What must I do?" their answer was, "Obey the pope; put away Agnes, and restore Ingelburgis." And, thanks to the severity of Innocent III, Philip repudiated the concubine, and restored Ingelburgis to her rights, as wife and queen.

Hear what the Protestant Hurter says in his Life of Innocent: "If Christianity has not been thrown aside, as a worthless creed, into some isolated corner of the world; if it has not, like the sects of India, been reduced to a mere theory; if its European vitality has outlived the voluptuous effeminacy of the East, it is due to the watchful severity of the Roman Pontiffs—to their increasing care to maintain the principles of authority in the Church."

As often as we look toward England, we are reminded of the words of Innocent III to Philip Augustus. We see Clement using them as his principles in his conduct toward the royal brute, Henry VIII. Catharine of Aragon, the lawful wife of Henry, had been repudiated by her disgraceful husband, and it was again to Rome she appealed for protection. Clement remonstrated with Henry. The monarch calls the pope hard names. Clement repeats, "Thou shalt not commit adultery!" Henry threatens to tear England from the Church-—he does it; still Clement insists, "Thou shalt not commit adultery!" The blood of Fisher and Moore is shed at Tyburn; still the pope repeats, "Thou shalt not commit adultery!" The firmness of the pope cost England's loss to the Church. It cost the pope bitter tears, and he prayed to heaven not to visit on the people of England the crimes of the despot; he prayed for the conversion of the nation; but to sacrifice the sanctity, the indissolubility of matrimony,—that he could never do; to abandon helpless woman to the brutality of men who were tired of the restraints of morality,—no, that the pope could never permit. If the court, if the palace, if the domestic hearth, refused a shelter, Rome was always open, a refuge to injured and down-trodden innocence.

"One must obey God more than man." This has ever been the language of the Church, whenever there was question of defending the laws of God against the powers of the earth; and in thus defending the laws of God, she has always shown herself Catholic, Oh, how sad would be the state of society were the popes, the bishops, and priests to be banished from the earth! The bonds that unite the husband and wife, the child and the parent, the friend and the friend, would be broken. Peace and justice would flee from the earth. Robbery, murder, hatred, lust, and all the other crimes condemned by the Gospel, would prevail. Faith would no longer elevate the souls of men to heaven. Hope, the sweet consoler of the afflicted, of the widow and the orphan, would flee away, and in her stead would reign black despair, terror, and suicide. Where would we find the sweet virtue of charity, if the popes, the bishops, and priests were to disappear forever? Where would we find that charity which consoles the poor and forsaken, which lovingly dries the tears of the widow and the orphan, — that charity which soothes the sick man in his sufferings, and binds up the wounds of the bleeding defender of his country? Where would we find that charity which casts a spark of divine fire into the hearts of so many religious, bidding them abandon home, friends, and everything that is near and dear to them in this world, to go among strangers, among savage tribes, and gain there, in return for their heroism, nothing but outrage, suffering, and death? Where, I ask, would we find this charity, if the popes, the bishops, and priests were to disappear forever?

Let a parish be for many years without a priest, and the people thereof will become the blind victims of error, of superstition, and of all kinds of vices. Show me an age, a country, a nation, without priests, and I will show you an age, a country, a nation, without morals, without virtue. Yes, if "religion and science, liberty and justice, principle and right," are no tempty sounds—if they have a meaning, they owe their energetic existence in the world to the "salt of the earth,"—to the popes, bishops, and priests of the Catholic Church.

Finally, the Church, one, holy and Catholic, is also apostolic. Now, should some one ask :

8. Show how the Catholic Church is apostolic.

We answer: The Catholic Church is apostolic, because her chief pastor, the pope, is the lawful successor of St. Peter, and the bishops are the lawful successors of the other apostles, from whom they have their doctrine, their orders, and their mission, through an unbroken succession of bishops.

The Catholic Church can show precisely how she obtained possession of the divine authority of the apostles. The Roman Pontiff, Pius IX, can name the two hundred and fifty-three popes who, without a break, handed down the authority of St. Peter, the head of the apostles, even to himself. He can tell the day and hour of his election and consecration, which are consigned to imperishable monuments.

Every bishop of the Catholic Church can also show the authentic titles which prove the transmission of the apostolic authority from the pontiff, who founded his Church, down to himself, the validity of his ordination, and the legitimate character of his mission. Every priest receives his authority from his bishop. Thus, there is not a break in those glorious lines of bishops, which each episcopal see, and above all sees, that of Peter, can show alike to friend and foe. Here nothing is arbitrary, nothing uncertain. The apostolic ministry is perpetuated, under the presidency of the head of the apostles, with the perpetual presence and assistance of Him who promised to be with his own, even to the end of the world. Thus the authority of the minister of our altars does not depend on the power of any temporal monarch, nor on the people; it depends solely on the head and chief pastor in the apostolical hierarchy. What noble independence this! It is the security of the faithful, and constitutes both the greatness of the Church, and the dignity of her pastors.

In the beginning of the thirteenth century the pope sent ambassadors to the famous Tartar monarch, Jengis Khan. The Tartars asked the ambassadors, "Who is the pope? Is he not an old man at least five hundred years of age?" They might have said twelve hundred, and they would have been right; for, as Pius IX has said so truly, "Simon may die, but Peter lives forever:" and Peter will live until time shall have ended its course. Pius IX is to us Peter; for each pontiff, as he comes, reigns upon Peter's throne, speaks with his voice, binds and looses with his hands, opens and closes the kingdom with the keys which Peter once took from the pierced hands of his divine Master: and he will hold those keys of life and death till the number of the elect is filled, and the last of the redeemed enters his Father's house.

The Church taught and governed in our days by the pope and bishops, differs not in its essential character from the Church taught and governed by Peter and the apostles. Let us see how Peter exercises the authority conferred on him, and, through him, upon all his successors, by Jesus Christ. After the resurrection of our Savior, who appeared to Peter first of all the apostles, he is the first to proclaim that resurrection to all the people, and he confirms the truth of his testimony by a miracle. (Acts ii, 14 and, iii, 15.) After the ascension of our Lord, Peter assembled the apostles and some disciples in the upper-chamber, and addressed them thus, "The Scripture must needs be fulfilled," which foretells the defection of Judas, and his place being taken by another. We, therefore, must choose one from among us, who has been a witness to the miracles and resurrection of the Son of God, to take his place. (Acts i, 16.) Is the Gospel to be preached

to the Gentiles? It is Peter to whom the solution of the difficulty
is revealed; it is he who decides, "all holding their peace, and giving
glory to God." (Acts iii, 18.) Peter first received the Gentiles into the
Church (Acts x), after having been the first to introduce the Jews into
her sacred fold. At a later period, the question of circumcision and the
ceremonies of the law came up. Peter at once rose up and explained the
common faith. All listened in silence. A decree was made in which the
faith on this point was determined forever. Peter visited the Christians
of Joppe, Lydda, Galilee, Pontus, Galatia, Cappadocia, Asia, Bithynia,
etc. (Acts ix.) Everywhere he founded new congregations of Christian
s and visited them all in his office of Supreme Pastor. From Jerusalem
he went to Antioch, from Antioch to Borne, where he combated
the heresy of Simon the Magician, and finally sealed his glorious
apostleship by dying a martyr's death.

As the lawful successor of the Prince of the Apostles, the pope
decides, without appeal, matters of faith and morals, convokes general
councils, presides over and confirms them, founds churches, visits
them in person, or by his delegates, appoints bishops, confirms
them in the faith, and acts in all as the Supreme Head and Pastor
of the Catholic Church. Peter took possession, for himself and
his successors, of all the prerogatives and duties of the Sovereign Pon
tificate.

Now let us see how the apostles exercise the authority conferred
on them by Christ. From the Acts of the Apostles we learn that they
teach and preach the Gospel, they baptize and impose hands,—that
is, give confirmation,— they found churches, and give them pastors;
they choose one to succeed Judas; in the Council of Jerusalem,
they regulate whatever concerns faith and discipline, saying, "It has
seemed good to the Holy Ghost and to us" (Acts xv, 82); they resolv
e difficulties, and repress scandals that arise, and, if necessary, they

excommunicate him who deserves to be cut off from the communion of the faithful, till he truly repents; they command the Christians to avoid teachers who were not sent by Christ (Titus iii, 10), and to receive their oral traditions as well as their written instructions (2 Thessalonians ii, 14); they clearly teach that the Church is founded upon the apostolic ministry (Ephesians ii, 20); that Christ appointed apostles, pastors, doctors, in a word, a teaching and governing body, to accomplish the work of sanctifying the elect, that "we be not carried about with every wind of doctrine" (Ephesians iv, 12-14); they also teach that the Holy Ghost has appointed bishops to rule the Church of God (Acts xx, 28); that the reading of holy Scripture "is profitable," to those especially who "teach and reprove others, " yet that they contain difficult passages, "which the unlearned wrest" from their true meaning "to their own destruction." (2 Peter iii, 16.) What is all this but precisely what the bishops of the Catholic Church practice today? They teach, decide on points of faith and morals, give confirmation, ordain priests; they govern, punish, excommunicate, grant indulgences, recommend the faithful not to become familiar with heretics; they assemble in council, to regulate in matters concerning faith, morals, and discipline; and all this they do in the name of the Holy Ghost, who has promised them his assistance. They teach that the unwritten word of God is to be received with the same faith as the written; and each bishop says, with the great apostle, that he is "appointed by the Holy Spirit" to govern his Church. Thus, we see that the Church of Jesus Christ, as described by St. Luke, St. Paul, St. James, and the others, is precisely the same as the Church which is called one, holy, Catholic and Apostolic, Now,

9. Why is the Catholic Church called Roman?

The Catholic Church is called Roman: 1, because the visible head of the Church is Bishop of Rome; 2, because St. Peter and his successors fixed their see in Rome; 3, because all the Catholic Churches in the world profess their union with the Roman Church.

The Catholic Church is called Roman, because at Rome the pope, as visible head of the Church, has fixed his see. St. Peter was the first pope and first bishop of Rome. After having preached in Jerusalem and presided for seven years over the Church of Antioch, he left St. Ignatius in his place at Antioch, and went to Rome, where he fixed his see. He was, however, often absent to perform his apostolical duties in other countries. He came to Rome in A. D. 40. Having remained there for some considerable time, he went back to the East, but returned to Rome not long after. In 49, on account of some tumult raised by the Jews against the Christians, St. Peter and St. Paul were banished from Rome by Claudius, but they were soon allowed to return. St. Peter returned again to the East, and in 51 was present at the General Council held at Jerusalem by the apostles, where, in a discourse, he showed that the Gentile converts were not bound by the Jewish ceremonies. St. Peter went back to Rome afew years previous to his martyrdom, in the reign of the Emperor Nero. But before his final return thither, he preached the Gospel over all Italy? and likewise in other provinces of the West. When again in Rome, he and St. Paul, by their prayer, put an end to the magical delusions of Simon Magus. Enraged at this, the tyrant Nero put both apostles into the Mamertine prison. After an imprisonment of eight months, St. Peter was scourged, and then crucified with his head downward. He chose this manner of crucifixion, because he believed himself unworthy to suffer and die in the same way as his divine Master. According to Eusebius and Others, he held possession of the See of Rome for about twenty-five years, assisted by St. Paul, who shared with him the honor of having founded Christian Rome.

St. Peter, then, the Prince of the Apostles, who first occupied the Apostolic See, transmitted, by the command of God, to the pontiffs, who even to the end of time should occupy his see, his primacy in the apostolate and in the pastoral charge, together with all the authority which he had received from God our Savior. Hence the Greeks, in 1274, subscribed this profession of faith, which was presented to them by Gregory X: "The holy Roman Church possesses a supreme and complete primacy and authority over the whole Catholic Church; she acknowledges truly and humbly that she received it, together with plenary authority, from the Savior himself, in the person of Peter, the Prince or Head of the Apostles, of whom the Roman Pontiff is the successor; and as she is bound more than the other churches to defend the truth of religion, so, if any questions arise concerning the faith, they ought to be determined by her judgment. Whoever considers himself wronged in any matter which pertains to the Church, can appeal to her tribunal; and in all the causes which relate to ecclesiastical jurisdiction, recourse may be had to her judgment. All churches are subject to her, and the prelates who govern them owe respect and obedience to her. The plenitude of power belongs to her in such a manner that the other churches are admitted by her to a share in her solicitude. Several of these, especially the patriarchal churches, have been honored with various privileges by the Roman Church, without prejudice to her prerogatives, which she must preserve whether in General Councils or in certain other cases." (Labbe, t. xi, p. 965.)

In the fourteenth century, it is true, several popes resided at Avignon, in France, yet they did not cease, on that account, to be the Bishops of Rome and the heirs of St. Peter. Rome is, indeed, the capital of Christendom, and is justly called the Eternal City, for it has always

been the center of Catholic unity, and the see of the successors of St. P
eter.

From St. Peter's time every succeeding head of the Church was
Bishop of Rome, and, seated in the Chair of Peter, governed the
Church as her Sovereign Pontiff, as the visible representative of
ecclesiastical unity, as the supreme teacher and guardian of the faith, as
the supreme legislator and interpreter of the canons, as the legitimate
superior of all bishops, as the final judge of councils, enjoying the
primacy both of honor and jurisdiction; so that the pagan historian,
Ammianus Marcellinus, styled Pope Liberius "the overseer of the
Christian religion;" and the Fathers, the Councils, the Doctors of the
Church, ecclesiastical writers, and the saints of all ages, have called
the Bishop of Rome pope, that is, father, because lie is the common
spiritual father of all Christians. They have called him also the Most
Holy Father, the Universal Bishop of the Church, the Vicar of Christ,
the Pastor of pastors, theJudge of judges. They have given him the title
of Sovereign Pontiff, because he is superior to all either pontiffs or
bishops, not only as to honor, but also as to jurisdiction, and because
he exercises supreme authority in the Universal Church. On account
of this primacy or supremacy which the head of the Church has
received immediately from God, in the person of Peter, the Council
of Trent defines that the faithful, of whatever dignity, —be they
kings or emperors, bishops, primates, or patriarchs,—owe him a real
and true obedience. The same council declares that it pertains to him
to provide the churches with pastors to determine the impediments
which make marriage null and to dispense with them, to convoke
a General Council, to confirm its decrees, to resolve the doubts
raised by them, to create cardinals, to appoint bishops, to watch over
the reform of studies, to correct abuses, to decide the most grave
causes in which bishops are concerned; he can reserve to himself the

absolving from certain grave crimes, absolve those who have possessed themselves of ecclesiastical property: without his judgment nothing of importance can be established in the Church.

Here it may be asked:

10. Did this power of the pope also include the power to depose temporal rulers?

The London Tablet, Dec. 5, 1874, answers this question as follows: "We firmly believe that the deposing power actually exerted by more than one Roman Pontiff, and owing its efficacy to the spontaneous assent of the Christian conscience, is manifestly included among the gifts of Peter. We believe it, among other reasons, because no power can be wanting to his supreme jurisdiction, of which the safety of the Christian commonwealth, committed to his oversight, may at any time require the exercise. He is God's vicegerent. The Church, which is God's kingdom on earth, was built by her divine Founder "upon this rock." The Almighty Architect might have chosen another foundation, but he chose this, and the gates of hell have not been able to subvert it. It is true that St. Peter never used the deposing power, but that was because Christendom had not yet begun to exist; it is equally true that neither Pius IX nor any of his successors are ever likely to use it, but that is because Christendom has ceased to exist. There is a great host of Christians—more than ever there were—but there is no longer any Christendom. There is not in the whole world so much as a solitary state, unless it be one of the South American republics, which even professes to shape its policy by the law of God, much less by the counsels of his Vicar. They did so for many ages, to their own advantage, but they have ceased to do it. Only the Moslem now affects to do everything 'in the name of Allah.' Governments are no

longer Christian. Their very composition proves it. Even in the cabinet
of one who is called, as if in derision, 'His Apostolic Majesty,' there
are two Jews. Everyone knows how the rest are formed; they might
all write over their council doors, if they were candid enough, 'No
truth here.' For them, as Gibbon would say, all religions are 'equally
true and equally false.' Some princes encourage their own children
to change their religion, in order to make a good marriage. Others,
while professing to honor Peter, sit down to table with miscreants
whom he has excommunicated. Christendom no longer exists. If it
did, certain crowned malefactors, who make a treaty with Atheists
and Freemasons, and persecute bishops, would probably find that, as
St. Ambrose says, 'Peter is not dead.' But if Christendom should ever
be restored, which does not seem likely, we profess our unhesitating
conviction that the deposing power of God's Vicar would revive with it

.

"When states were wholly Catholic, as they were for a good many
centuries, when all men believed, with the saints and martyrs, that it
was to the pope that the Almighty said, 'Whatsoever thou shalt bind
on earth, shall be bound in heaven;' when the supreme authority of
the Holy See was at once the bulwark of thrones, and part of the
public law of Europe; when Caesar said to bishops, presided over by
the papal legates, as Constantine, the master of the world, said to the
Fathers at Nice, 'Nos a vobis rede judicamur,'—nobody disputed that,
as members of the Christian commonwealth, kings and princes were
subject, by the law of God, to the authority of the Roman Pontiff. It wa
s his office to restrain, by all the means which the decree of God and
the faith of Christians gave him, any abuse of their power by which
either the interests of religion or the just rights of Christian people
were prejudiced. He was at once the guardian of the faith, and the
Only invincible enemy of tyrants. The most eminent non-Catholic

writers have confessed that Christianity was preserved from what
Guizot calls 'the tyranny of brute force,' mainly by that vigilant and
fearless intervention of the Holy See, for which, as some of them
sorrowfully admit, no substitute can now be found. But it is evident
that the extreme penalty of deposition, the application of which is
now transferred from the pope to the mob, could only be enforced
in a state of society which has long since passed away, and is never like
ly to return.

"The only remonstrants against the spiritual authority, even when
its judgments were most formidable, were worthless princes, who
wished to filch the revenues of episcopal sees, and a few depraved
prelates, who wished to curry favor with such princes. The Church
lived in those days, as Emerson observes with true American candor,
'by the love of the people.' They knew who was their friend. His
judgments had no terror for them. The modern jealousy of the Holy
See, which has only transferred all spiritual authority, as Professor
Merivale remarks, 'from the Church to the State,' has been as fatal to
liberty as to religion. The state most violently opposed to the Holy
See at this day is Prussia, and the only representatives of liberty in
Prussia are the Catholic bishops and clergy. Even German Protestants
witness against the ruthless enslavement of mind and conscience in a
country in which only two institutions now remain: the barrack and
the goal. What Neander would have said of the present tyranny in
Prussia, we may judge from his own words: 'Beautiful,' he exclaims,
'and worthy the frankness becoming a bishop, is the language of
St. Hilary of Poitiers to Constantius.' And what did the saint say
to Caesar, who ruled after the fashion of Bismarck and his master?
'Tyrannus non jam humanorum, sed divinorum es. Antichristum
praevenis et arcanorum mysteria ejus operaris.' It was a strong thing
to say to Caesar sitting in his purple robe. If St. Hilary lived in our

day, he would soon be in a Prussian prison, with the learned Neander, if he ventured to applaud him, in the next cell. It was the popes, says Hurter, who saved Christianity 'from the tyranny of the temporal power, and from becoming a mere State function, like religion among the Pagans.' It was well for Hurter that his lot was not cast in the age of Bismarck. Even Leibnitz would have been deemed a mortal enemy by the Prussian Constantius. It was the inventor of the integral calculus who actually proposed, though a Protestant, 'to establish in Rome a tribunal to decide controversies between sovereigns, and to make the pope its president, as he really did, in former ages, figure as judge between Christian princes. But ecclesiastics should, at the same time, resume their ancient authority, and an interdict or an excommunication should make kings and kingdoms tremble, as in the days of Nicholas I or Gregory VII.' Leibnitz would evidently be out of place in contemporary Prussian society. They have no room there for such as he was, except in their prisons: and those cheerful abodes will soon be too full to hold any more.

"If popes no longer depose bad princes 'by the authority of Peter? there are others who depose good ones without any authority at all. To depose them more effectually, they have taken to cutting off their heads. Cromwell and his fellows did it in England; Mirabeau and his friends in France. These energetic anti-popes did not object at all to deposition, provided it was inflicted by themselves. They object to it still less now: it has become a habit. Englishmen deposed James II, after murdering his father, and put a Dutchman in his place.

In other lands they are always deposing somebody. The earth is strewn with deposed sovereigns. Sometimes they depose one another, to steal what does not belong to them. One of them has deposed the pope himself, at least for a time, and all the rest clap their hands. They do not see that by this last felony they have undermined every throne in Europe. Perhaps in a few years there will not be a king left to be deposed. Since the secular was substituted everywhere for the spiritual authority, kings have fared badly. The popes only rebuked them when they did evil: the mob is less discriminating. And the difference between the deposing power of the popes and that of the mob is this, that the first used it, like fathers, for the benefit of religion and society; the second, like wild beasts, for the destruction of both."

There is, therefore, among all true Catholics, but one unanimous voice as to the supreme authority of the head of the Roman Church, viz.: that Jesus, the Son of God and of man, gave to Peter and his successors that fulness of jurisdiction and power which will keep the Church in safety till he comes back in the day of judgment; and to deny that supreme authority is to be at sea, drifting about with the currents of opinion, and tossed on the troubled waves of Protestantism, Calvinism, Quakerism, Mormonism, Spiritualism, and all the other isms and sophisms.

Now, in order that the great power and authority bestowed upon St. Peter should be often present to our minds, that apostle is represented with keys in his hand. He holds two: one a symbol of his jurisdiction, and the other of his orders. One key is turned toward heaven, to show that St. Peter had the power of opening or closing it; the other is directed toward the earth, to show that he had full authority over the faithful, and the power of imposing laws upon t hem.

The pope, however, is not only the head of the Church, he is also a temporal prince. In the establishment of his Church, our divine Savior did not consult the civil authorities; neither Herod nor Pilate was asked for approval. If those rulers had not lived at all, they could not have been more completely ignored, so far as establishing the Church, preaching and teaching the doctrine of Christ, and performing all th

e offices of the Christian ministry, go. Caesar and his officers had
no voice in this. They had authority in the kingdoms of the world,
but none whatever in the kingdom of God. It was established, and
to be spread and to last forever, whether they willed it or not. The
apostles, especially the head of the apostles, and their successors, are
to exercise their power in perfect freedom. They are freely to teach
what is true, freely to condemn what is false; freely to denounce the
crimes of men and of governments; freely to constitute the hierarchy
in various countries; freely to let persons have recourse to them in
their doubts, and freely to reply to them; freely to condemn those who
refuse obedience to the Church; freely to separate from the Church
those who have separated themselves from her, by persisting in error
or in disobedience; freely to define religious and moral truths, that is,
give laws binding on minds in believing, and on consciences in acting.
The ruler of nations and the lord of many legions, though he had not
been consulted at all in the establishment of the Church, was bound
to hear her voice, like the humblest peasant, and submit his soul to
her guidance, under pain of eternal banishment from the presence of
God. He might pretend to command when it was his duty to obey,
but the mistake was sure to be disastrous to himself, as indeed the final r
esult proved.

When the divine Master had finished his work, and his Vicar
reigned in his place, the independence of the spiritual power, in its
own province, was, if possible, still more evident. We know what the
attitude of the apostles toward the State was. In questions of the soul,
they set it at naught. They taught loyalty to Caesar in all that religion
does not condemn, as their successors do at this day, so that among
Christians was found a host of martyrs, but not a single conspirator
or assassin; but when Caesar required disloyalty to God, the apostles
and the Christians bade him defiance. They knew the penalty and

accepted it. It was perfectly understood that Caesar, like other beasts of prey, had claws and teeth, and could use them. He did use them with considerable effect. He had soldiers, lictors, prisons, axes, and scaffolds. But such engines, destructive as they were, could only hurt the flesh; and the apostles and Christians were told not to "fear them that kill the body, and are not able to kill the soul." They were warned that they would be "brought before governors," but that they were not even to take thought what they should say. The divine Master would teach them what to say.

The conditions of the combat between Christ and Caesar, between the spiritual and the secular power, will never cease. In order that the head of his Church might enjoy perfect freedom in the exercise of his power, under God's providence the pope became a temporal prince. He obtained his temporal power before Constantine abandoned Rome, and it was confirmed and completed by Charlemagne, more than a thousand years ago. God inspired Christian princes to attach a principality to the Holy See, called the Patrimony of St. Peter,—the States of the Church: "It has been the will of God," says Pius IX, "that the princes of the earth, even those who are not in communion with the Church of Rome, should defend and maintain the temporal sovereignty of the Holy See, which has been, by a disposition of divine Providence, enjoyed for many centuries by the Roman Pontiffs. The possession of that temporal dominion enables the reigning pope to exercise his supreme apostolical authority in the government of the Universal Church with that liberty which is necessary to fulfil the duties of his apostolical office and procure the salvation of the flock of Christ." (Allocution, May 10th, 1850.)

The pope, then, possesses his territory under a title higher and older than any government in the world. Napoleon I sought to destroy this temporal power of the pope, but was forced at last to admit the necessity of papal independence: "The pope," he said, "is not at Paris; it is well: we reverence his authority precisely because he "is not at Vienna nor at Madrid. At Vienna and at Madrid they feel the same with regard to Paris. It is, therefore, better that he should be neither with us nor with any of our rivals, but in Rome, his ancient seat, holding an equal balance between all sovereigns. This is the work of the centuries, and they have done well. The temporal power is the wisest and best institution that could be imagined in the government o f souls."

The temporal dominion of the pope being a moral necessity for the well-being of the Church, the Holy Father and the bishops have pronounced anathema against all those who impugn it. History, indeed, sometimes shows us the Supreme Pontiff under another aspect. There were times when his triple crown crumbled, when his scepter shrunk to a hollow reed, when his throne became a shadow, and his home a dungeon. But God permitted this only to show us how inestimable is human virtue, when compared with human grandeur. Human grandeur may perish, but virtue is immortal. God permitted it, to prove to the scoffing infidel world that the simplicity of the patriarchs, the piety of the saints, the patience of the martyrs, have not as yet vanished from the earth. God permitted it, in fine, to show the rabid enemies of our holy faith that, though our common father were in chains, though his motives were calumniated, and though his kingly power were destroyed, yet the Church, the holy Catholic Church of Jesus Christ, is still able to guide and to support her children, and to confound, if she cannot reclaim, her enemies.

The pontiff is firm, immovable as a rock. No threats can awe, no promise can tempt, no sufferings can appall him. With exile, the dungeon, and death before his eyes, he dashes away the proffered cup, in which the pearl of his liberty is to be dissolved: "Non possumus" is his bold and noble language. "We can die, but we cannot give up the rights of the Church." The Catholic world cannot, and will not, submit and agree to the sacrilegious occupation of the Papal States by any government. The voices of more than two hundred millions of Catholics will ring from every land under the sun, demanding perfect liberty of action for their common spiritual father, and the undisturbed possession of the Patrimony of St. Peter. The spirit of opposition to the temporal power of the pope is but the spirit of modern Paganism, which aims at the destruction of civil government, the rights of justice, the law of God and of man. All justice-loving men admit this. The opposers of the temporal power start from the pagan principle of separation of the temporal from the spiritual; they are either bigots, or infidels, or vain and frothy theorizers, or corrupt politicians of the Masonic sect, or restless demagogues; and if they be Christians, their faith sits as lightly on their conscience as a feather on the back of a whirlwind: they are all pervaded by the pestilential spirit of modern Paganism. When a government becomes indifferent in religious matters, wishes to assume supreme control over the asylums of suffering humanity, secularizes churches and schools, caring only for the mere literary or arithmetical education of its subjects; when it makes laws infringing on the rights of conscience or property; when it interferes with the sacraments and the rites of the Church, then it is pagan in spirit. It endeavors to prevent men from attaining the end of creation; it ceases to be a free government, or to fulfil the end for which all governments were instituted. Every temporal ruler who denies the pope's rights to his temporal power, will soon find his own abolished.

As the Papacy is of divine right, so also is the Episcopacy of divine right. Christ willed that there should be bishops to assist the pope in the government of the Church. For this reason, St. Paul says, "The

Holy Ghost hath placed you bishops to rule the Church of God." The word "bishop" means overseer, inspector, or superintendent.

The choice of a bishop has to be made, or at least to be confirmed, by the pope; from him each bishop holds his jurisdiction over the territory assigned to him by the pope. Episcopal jurisdiction has been instituted by Christ in such a manner that each bishop should receive his jurisdiction from the pope, who makes the bishops sharers in the power of the keys which Christ gave to Peter alone, and, in his person, to his successors: "The Lord," says Tertullian, " has given the keys to St. Peter, and, through him to the Church." St. Gregory of Nyssa says the same, in other words: "Through Peter, Christ has given the keys of the kingdom of heaven to the bishops." As Peter and his successors alone have received the keys of the kingdom of God, they alone can communicate the use of them to the rest of the pastors. From Peter and his successors, the bishops hold the jurisdiction which they exercise in their dioceses; it is by him that they hold, in their dioceses, the place of Christ, as priests, as pontiffs, as doctors, as legislators, as judges, as heads and pastors of the faithful under their jurisdiction, and are, as St. Paul says, ambassadors for Jesus Christ, God's coadjutors, who exhort the faithful by their mouth; for all this is what constitutes jurisdiction. This doctrine has been solemnly declared by Pius IX, in his Encyclical Letter of Nov. 9th, 1846, addressed to the archbishops and bishops of the Catholic Church: "Come with an open heart," he says, "and with full confidence, to the See of the blessed Peter, Prince of the Apostles, the center of Catholic unity, and the summit of the episcopacy, whence the episcopacy itself derives its origin and its auth ority".

[NB: When the pope is elected according to established regulations, and if he consents to his election, he becomes at once invested with authority over the Universal Church, though he be neither a bishop nor a priest,nor deacon, nor subdeacon, but a mere cleric. He is capable of performing every act belonging to papal jurisdiction; he can, for instance, grant indulgences, pass censures, grant dispensations, appoint canons, institute bishops, create cardinals. But the peculiar power of the priesthood and the episcopacy, such as forgiving sins, administering the sacraments of confirmation and of holy orders, he cannot exercise until he has first been consecrated. From what has been said, it follows that the Papacy, the Sovereign Pontificate, is a dignity, not of orders, but of jurisdiction. If the pope be a bishop at the time of his election, he receives no other consecration. Being clothed with the episcopal character, he is on an equality with the other bishops; but as pope, and vested with the dignity and authority of head of the Church, he is superior to all the past ors of the Church.

If, at the time of his election, the pope is not in holy orders, he can receive them all on the same day. The privilege of consecrating a pope who is no bishop at the time of his election, belongs to the Bishop of Ostia.

When the pope is elected he changes his name, because he is the successor of St. Peter, whose name was changed by Jesus Christ.

The pope can be taken from any rank of the ecclesiastical hierarchy. In the early ages of the Church, subdeacons were but seldom raised to the dignity of the Papacy ; but deacons were often elected. Priests were seldom chosen to fill that high office, and the appointment of bishops to it was of very rare occurrence. The first pope raised from the episcopal office to the papal throne was Formosa, Bishop of Oporto, who was elected in 891. The discipline of the Church, in this respect, has undergone a great change; for, from about the end of the thirteenth century, it was the ordinary practice to select the pope from among the bishops, and from 1592 to 1775 we find but three popes elected who were no bishops at the time of their election. In our times, Clement XIV, Pius V, and Gregory XVI, were the only persons who were simple priests at the time of their elevation to the Papacy. The pope is elected by the cardinals. For many centuries the pope was elected by the Roman clergy, and the faithful took a very active part in the election; but, for many years past, the election has been confined to the cardinals, who are the princes and senators of the Church, and are vested with a dignity inferior only to that of the pope.

The learned are divided in their opinions in reference to the origin of cardinals, and the derivation of the name cardinal, Some think that cardinal comes from the word cardo, cardinalis, a hinge on which a gate or a door turns; because the cardinals are the hinges or pivots on which the government of the Church rolls. According to Baronius, Bellarmine, and other liturgical writers, the officiating priests of the parishes and churches of Rome were the first cardinals; and they were so called because, when they accompanied the pope to the altar, they stood ad cornua, that is, at the corners or angles of it. Besides the churches served by priests, there were a great many hospitals, the administration of which was entrusted to deacons. These deacons also attended the pope whenever he officiated, and, with the priests of the parishes, stood at the corners of the altar; hence, the distinction between the cardinal priests and the cardinal deacons. The titular bishops of the sees in the vicinity of Rome, called suburbicarian bishops, attended the pope on all solemn ceremonies, and took up their positions, like the priests and deacons of whom we have just spoken, at the corners of the altar, and hence the origin of cardinal archbishops. The latter, in virtue of their episcopal consecration, have always taken precedence over the cardinal priests and cardinal deacons.

The dignity of cardinal, in the sense in which that word is now understood, is the highest in the Church, next to that of the pope. The cardinals are the princes and senators of the Church, the councilors of the pope, his coadjutors and vicars in the functions of the Sovereign Pontificate.They form the consistory, or the council of the pope, who selects them from all nations, to aid him in the government of the Ch urch.

By a Bull of Sixtus V, published in 1586, the number of cardinals was fixed at seventy. They are divided into three orders, namely: six cardinal bishops, fifty cardinal priests, and fourteen cardinal deacons.

The six cardinals of the first order are the Bishops of Ostia, Porto, Palestrina, Albano, Sabine, and Frescati, suffragans of the Patriarchate of the West. The cardinal priests are nearly all bishops, but, as they have only the title of priests, they belong to the second order. The cardinal deacons are so called, because their title is only that of deacon.

In the council held at Lyons, in 1248, Pope Innocent IV presented to the cardinals the red hat, as a sign of their being obliged, if necessary, to shed their blood for the cause of God and of his Church. In 1464, Paul III presented them with the red cassock and cap. In 1630, the title of Eminence was given to them exclusively, by an order of Urban VIII. But the choicest and most glorious of their privileges is that of electing the pope. The cardinals cannot, whilst the Holy See is vacant, exercise papal jurisdiction, nor have they the power of making laws, unless the interests of religion may urgently require it. (Collegium Cardinalium sede papali vacante nullam habet potestatem condendi leges.— Reiffenstuel.) The body of cardinals is called the College of Cardinals, or Sacred College. The assembly of cardinals, when they meet for the purpose of electing a pope, takes the name of Conclave. The word conclave is also applied to the place in which they meet for the purpose of the election, which is now the Quirinal Palace, where as many rooms have been prepared as there are cardinals, and where they remain shut up till the election has taken place. They meet once a day in the chapel of the palace, where a scrutiny is made of their votes, which are written and placed in an urn. This is repeated every day till two-thirds, at least, of the votes are in favor of one candidate for the Pontifical Chair, who is then considered duly elected.

The pope may resign his power and authority. In the history of the Church we find more than one instance of a pope laying down his dignity and power, after having exercised them for some time. St. Celestine V, who, from a devout hermit, was raised to the Chair of Peter, abdicated his functions after a reign of scarcely four months and was succeeded by Cardinal Cajetan, under the name of Boniface VIII. Alarmed at the responsibility of the office and finding the performance of his usual exercises of prayer and meditation impracticable, he determined to go back to his former solitude, and in a Consistory held at Naples, he abdicated the Pontifical Chair, assumed his former name of Peter, put on again his old religious habit, and entreated those around to select an efficient successor. In the annals of the Church we find the names of others who willingly laid aside the power and authority conferred on them as Vicars of Christ.

Everything connected with the dying moments of the pope is invested with that solemnity and gravity suited to the high and holy office which, during life, he had fulfilled. His domestic prelates and the chief dignitaries of his household are summoned around his bed. He then makes a profession of his faith, grants particular favors to all about him, requests their prayers, and receives from the hands of the Sacristan Prelate the holy Viaticum, and from the Cardinal Penitentiary a plenary indulgence. If his state will allow of it, he summons before him the College of Cardinals, in the presence of whom he renews his profession of faith. He recommends to them the Church of God, and engages them to select, as his successor, the person whom they believe most worthy to feed the sheep and the lambs. The domestic prelates remain at his bedside when he is in the agony of death, and the Sacristan Priest recites the recommendation of the departing soul, and a part of the passion. Scarcely has the pope breathed his last, when the Cardinal Camerlingo, preceded by the master of the ceremonies, repairs to the palace, and takes up his position at the foot of the bed, on which the deceased pope lies, his face covered with a white veil. The cardinal kneels down, and offers up a short prayer. He then stands up, and the attendants uncover the face of the pope. The Camerlingo approaches the body, strikes three times the head of the deceased with a small silver hammer, and calls out his name three times. He then turns toward the assistants, and says, "The pope is indeed dead." (Power's Catechism.)]

Episcopal consecration, however, is not necessary for the exercise of episcopal jurisdiction; all that is necessary is, that the election of a bishop should be confirmed by the pope. This confirmation of the pope gives to the bishop-elect canonical institution and confers on him jurisdiction over all the faithful of the territory which has been assigned to him. This jurisdiction, received from the pope, may also be taken away by the pope. Bishops, however, cannot be deprived of the power which is essentially connected with orders and the episcopal character, because that power is received immediately from God. Should, therefore, a bishop become a heretic, he still retains his episcopal character, in virtue of which he validly, though unlawfully, confers confirmation, holy orders, and offers the holy sacrifice of the Mass.

All bishops are on an equality as to their episcopal character, but the jurisdiction of some,—of patriarchs, metropolitans, and archbishops,—is more extended than that of others. This privilege of greater power is conferred by the pope alone, as he may think fit to grant to this or that bishop a greater or less share of the supreme authority which he holds over all the churches.

In the early ages of the Church, the title patriarch (sovereign father, chief father) was given to the titular bishops of the sees of the most important cities, such as Alexandria, Constantinople, Jerusalem, and Antioch. The Patriarch of Rome has always been considered the universal patriarch. The bishops presiding over the capital cities of the empire were called metropolitans, but, in later times, archbishops, that is, chief bishops. The patriarchal churches were established by the Holy See, wherein the power rests of extending or limiting the jurisdiction of any bishop; for, "everything," says St. Leo, "which Christ has given to the other bishops, has been given through St. P eter."

Besides the pope and the bishops, there are other legitimate pastors, called parish priests, who are subject to their respective bishops; for, as the bishop possesses the plenitude of the priesthood, he enjoys by divine righty that is, by Christ's institution, a superiority not only of precedence and of honor, but even of authority, over all his priests, who, without his good-will and pleasure, can do nothing in regard to ecclesiastical matters. He is the pastor of his whole diocese. He can, therefore, give to this or that priest jurisdiction more or less extended.

For good reasons he can also restrict the jurisdiction which he had given, and even withdraw it altogether.

In the early ages of Christianity, there was but one Church in each city or town, in which the faithful assembled under the presidency of the bishop. But when, in the course of time, the number of Christians had considerably increased, and bishops were unable to attend to the spiritual wants of their flock, dioceses were divided into parishes; that is, a union of many families, who assemble in a particular church, called parochial church, to assist at the holy sacrifice of the Mass, and the other duties of religion. Each parochial church is attended by a priest called the parish priest, whose duty it is to instruct the people in the way of salvation, and administer to them the sacraments of baptism, holy eucharist, penance, matrimony, and extreme unction. From a custom long established, the parish priest can dispense his parishioners in matters of fasting and abstinence, and in the observation of Sundays and holy days. Parish priests are often assisted in their labor by other priests, called vicars or coadjutors. Every parish, then, has three immediate pastors: the pope, the bishop, and the parish priest.

All the particular churches in the world profess their union with the Church pf Rome. She is the mistress of all others: "To be united with the See of Rome," says St. Cyprian, "is to be united with the Catholic Church, for the Church of Rome is the principal Church; the Bishop of Rome, the chief bishop; the episcopal throne of this Church is the throne of Peter, the source and center of ecclesiastical unity; and therefore all bishops of the world must, either directly or indirectly, be in communication with Rome, in order that, by thus communicating with her, the union of all may be preserved." And St. Irenaeus, who lived in the first century, declares that, instead of scrutinizing the doctrine delivered by Christ and his apostles, and searching tradition, it is enough to inquire what is the teaching of the Church of Rome: "For it is necessary," says he, "that the whole Church,—that is, the faithful of the whole world,—should be in communion with this Church, on account of its more powerful authority; in which communion the faithful of the whole world have preserved the tradition that was delivered by the apostles. When, therefore, you know the faith of this Church, you have also learned the faith of the others." (Contr. Haeret. iii, 3, n. 2.) "Whoever," says St.

Jerome, "is not in communion with the Church of Rome, is outside the Church." (Adv. Jovian., lib. i, n. 26.)

The One, Holy, Catholic, Apostolic and Roman Church, then, unites all the distinguishing marks of her divine institution and mission. Nowhere do these distinctive marks of the Church of Christ appear with more luster than in those holy assemblies, called General Councils. The Church's unity appears most strikingly in the union of all the members to the same supreme head who convoked the council, presides over it, confirms and executes its decrees. The sanctity of the Church is clearly seen in her condemnation of errors, and extirpation of abuses. The catholicity of the Church is seen in the convocation of the pastors of the whole Christian world; and the apostolicity of the Church is manifest in the assembly of all the bishops, the successors of the apostles, who are convoked, heard, and called to judge in matters of faith and morals, to regulate discipline, to acknowledge the authority of tradition, to confirm the doctrine of the apostles, and, after their return to their respective dioceses, to communicate to their diocesans "what hath seemed good to the Holy Ghost and to them;" at which the hearts of all the faithful in the world are filled with consolation and joy, and deep gratitude toward Jesus Christ, who continues to speak to them through blessed Peter and the either apostles, in their lawful successors, the bishops of the One, Holy, Catholic, Apostolic and Roma n Church.

11. Can Protestant sects claim to be One, Holy, Catholic and Apostolic?

By no means: 1. Because they have no infallible head and teacher, and every Protestant believes what he chooses to believe. 2. Because the

founders of the sects were all wicked men, who taught impious doctrines.
3. Because they sprang up only long after Christ had founded his Church.

At the beginning of the sixteenth century, with the exception of the Greek schismatics, a few Lollards in England, some Waldenses in Piedmont, scattered Albigenses or Manicheans, and a few followers of Huss and Zisca among the Bohemians, all Europe was Roman Catholic. England, Scotland, Ireland. Spain, Portugal, France, Italy, Germany, Switzerland, Hungary, Poland, Holland, Denmark, Norway, and Sweden,—every civilized nation was in the unity of the Catholic faith. Many of these nations were at the height of their power and prosperity. Portugal was pushing her discoveries beyond the Cape of Good Hope and forming Catholic settlements in the East Indies. Christopher Columbus, a Roman Catholic, had discovered America, under the patronage of the Catholic Isabella of Spain. England was in a state of great prosperity. Her two Catholic Universities of Oxford and Cambridge contained, at one time, more than fifty thousand students. The country was covered with noble churches, abbeys, and monasteries, and with hospitals, where the poor were fed, clothed, an d instructed.

However, the progress of civilization tended to foster a spirit of pride and encourage the lust of novelties. The prosperity of the Church led to luxury, and in many cases to a relaxation of discipline. There were, as there always have been, in every period of the Church, the days of the apostles not excepted, bad men in the Church. The wheat and tares grow together until the harvest. The net of the Church encloses good and bad. The writings of Wickliffe, Huss, and their followers, had unsettled the minds of many. Princes were restive under the check held by the Church upon their rapacity and lusts. A Henry VIII, for example, wanted to divorce a wife to whom he had been married twenty years, that he might marry a young and pretty one. He could not do this, so long as he acknowledged the spiritual supremacy of the pope. Philip, Landgrave of Hesse, wanted two wives. No pope would give him a dispensation to marry and live with two women at once. Then there were multitudes of wicked and avaricious nobles, who wanted but an excuse to plunder the churches, abbeys, and monasteries, whose property was held in trust for the education of the people, and the care of the poor, aged, and sick, all-over Europe. Then there were priests and monks eager to embrace a relaxed discipline; and many people who, incited by the cry of liberty, were ready to rush into license, and make war upon every principle of religion and social order, as soon as circumstances would favor the outbreak of this rebel spirit in individuals and masses. Now when God, says St. Gregory, sees in the Church many raveling in their vices, and, as St. Paul observes, believing in God, confessing the truth of his mysteries, but belying their faith by their works, he punishes them by permitting that, after having lost grace, they also lose the holy knowledge which they had of his mysteries, and that, without any other persecution than that of their vices, they deny the faith. It is of these David speaks, when he says: "Destroy Jerusalem to its foundations" (Psalm cxxxvi, 7); leave not a stone upon a stone. When the wicked spirits have ruined in a soul the edifice of virtue, they sap its foundation, which is faith. St. Cyprian, therefore,said: "Let no one think that virtuous men and good Christians ever leave thebosom of the Church; it is not the wheat that the winds lift, but the chaff; trees deeply rooted are not blown down by the breeze, but those which have no roots. It is rotten fruits that fall off the trees, not sound ones; bad Catholics became heretics, as sickness is engendered by bad humors. At first, faith languishes in them, because of their vices; then it becomes sick; next it dies, because, since sin is essentially a blindness of spirit, the more a man sins, the more he is blinded; his faith grows weaker and weaker; the light of this divine torch decreases, and soon the least wind of temptation o r doubt suffices to extinguish it." Witness the great defection from faith in the sixteenth century, when God permitted heresies to arise, in order to exercise his justice against those who were ready to abandon the truth, and his mercy toward those who remained attached to it; to prove, by trials, those who were firm in the faith, and to separate them from those who loved error; to exercise the patience and charity of the Church, and to sanctify the elect; to give occasion for the illustration of religious truth and the holy Scripture; to make pastors more vigilant, and value more the sacred deposit of faith; in fine, to render the authority of tradition more clear and incontestable. Heresy arose in all its strength; Martin Luther was its ring-leader and its spokesman.

Martin Luther, an Augustinian friar, a bold man and a vehement declaimer, having imbibed erroneous sentiments from the heretical writings of John Huss of Bohemia, took occasion, from the publication of indulgences promulgated by Pope Leo X, to break with the Catholic Church, and to propagate his new errors, in 1517, at Wirtemberg, in Saxony. He first inveighed against the abuse of indulgences; then he called in question their efficacy; and at last totally rejected them. He declaimed against the supremacy of the See of Rome, and condemned the whole Church, pretending that Christ had abandoned it, and that it wanted reforming, as well in faith as discipline. Thus this new evangelist commenced that fatal defection from the Ancient faith, which was styled "Reformation." The new doctrines, being calculated to gratify the vicious inclinations of the human heart, spread with the rapidity of an inundation. Frederick, Elector of Saxony, John Frederick, his successor, and Philip, Landgrave of Hesse, became Luther's disciples. Gustavus Ericus, King of Sweden, and Christian III, King of Denmark, also declared in favor of Lutheranism. It secured a footing in Hungary. Poland,

after tasting a great variety of doctrines, left to every individual
the liberty of choosing for himself. Muncer, a disciple of Luther,
set up for doctor himself, and, with Nicholas Stark, gave birth to
the sect of Anabaptists, which was propagated in Suabia, and other
provinces of Germany, in the Low Countries. Calvin, a man of
bold, obstinate spirit, and indefatigable in his labors, in imitation of
Luther, turned Reformer also. He contrived to have his new tenets
received at Geneva, in 1541. After his death, Beza preached the same
doctrine. It insinuated itself into some parts of Germany, Hungary,
and Bohemia, and became the religion of Holland. It was imported by
John Knox, an apostate priest, into Scotland, where, under the name
of Presbyterianism, it took deep root, and spread over the kingdom.
But, among the deluded nations, none drank more deeply of the cup
of error than England. For many centuries this country had been
conspicuous in the Christian world for the orthodoxy of its belief,
as also for the number of its saints. But by a misfortune neve
r to be sufficiently lamented, and by unfathomable judgment from
above, its Church shared a fate which seemed the least to threaten
it. The lust and avarice of one despotic sovereign threw down th
e fair edifice and tore it off from the rock on which it had
hitherto stood. Henry VIII, at first a valiant asserter of the Catholic
faith against Luther, giving way to the violent passions whic
h he had not sufficient courage to curb, renounced the supreme
jurisdiction which the pope had always held in the Church, presumed
to arrogate to himself that power in his own dominions, and thus
gave a deadly blow to religion. He then forced his subjects into the
same fatal defection. Once introduced, it soon overspread the land.
Being, from its nature, limited by no fixed principle, it has sinc
e taken a hundred different shapes, under different names, such as:
the Calvinists, Arminians, Antinomians, Independents, Kilhamites,

Glassites, Haldanites, Bereans, Swedenborgians, New Jerusalemites, Orthodox Quakers, Hicksites, Shakers, Panters, Seekers, Jumpers, Reformed Methodists, German Methodists, Albright Methodists, Episcopal Methodists, Wesleyan Methodists, Methodists North, Methodists South, Protestant Methodists, Episcopalians, High Church Episcopalians, Low Church Episcopalians, Ritualists, Puseyites, Dutch Reformed, Dutch non-Reformed, Christian Israelites, Baptists, Particular Baptists, Seventh-day Baptists, Hardshell Baptists, Softshell Baptists, Forty Gallon Baptists, Sixty Gallon Baptists, African Baptists, Free-will Baptists, Church of God Baptists, Regular Baptists, Anti-mission Baptists, Six Principle Baptists, River Brethren, Winebremarians, Menonites, Second Adventists, Millerites, Christian Baptists, Universalists, Orthodox Congregationalists, Campbellites, Presbyterians, Old School and New School Presbyterians, Cumberland Presbyterians, United Presbyterians, The Only True Church of Christ, 573 Bowery, N. Y., upstairs, 5th story, Latter-day Saints, Restorationists, Schwentfelders, Spiritualists, Mormons, Christian Perfectionists, etc., etc., etc. All these sects called Protestants, because they all unite in protesting are against th eir mother, the Roman Catholic Church.

Sometime after, when the reforming spirit had reached its full growth, Dudithius, a learned Protestant divine, in his epistle to Beza, wrote: "What sort of people are our Protestants, straggling to and fro, and carried about by every wind of doctrine, sometimes to this side, sometimes to that? You may, perhaps, know what their sentiments in matters of religion are today, but you can never tell precisely what they will be tomorrow. In what article of religion do these churches agree which have cast off the Bishop of Rome? Examine all from top to bottom, and you will scarcely find one thing affirmed by one, which was not immediately condemned by another for wicked doctrine." The same confusion of opinions was described by an English Protestant, the learned Dr. Walton, about the middle of the last century, in his preface to his Polyglot, where he says: "Aristarchus heretofore could scarce find seven wise men in Greece; but with us, scarce are to be found so many idiots. For all are doctors, all are divinely learned; there is not so much as the meanest fanatic who does not give you his own dreams for the word of God. The bottomless pit seems to have been opened, from whence a smoke has arisen which has darkened the heaven and the stars, and locusts have come out with stings, a numerous race of sectaries and heretics, who have renewed all the ancient heresies, and invented many monstrous opinions of their own. These have filled our cities, villages, camps, houses, nay, our pulpits, too, and lead the poor deluded people with them to the pit of perdition."

"Yes," writes another author, "every ten years, or nearly so, the Protestant theological literature undergoes a complete revolution. What was admired during the one decennial period is rejected in the next, and the image which they adored is burnt, to make way for new divinities; the dogmas which were held in honor, fall into dis-credit; the classical treatise of morality is banished among the old books out of date; criticism overturns criticism; the commentary of yesterday ridicules that of the previous day, and what was clearly proved in 1840, is not less clearly disproved in 1850. Thetheological systems of Protestantism are as numerous as the political constitutions of France—one revolution only awaits another." (Le Semeur, June, 1850.) It is indeed utterly impossible to keep the various members of one single sect from perpetual disputes, even about the essential truths of revealed religion. And those religious differences exist not only in the same sect, not only in the same country and town, but even in the same family. Nay, the self-same individual, at different periods of his life, is often in flagrant contradiction with himself. Today he avow opinions which yesterday he abhorred, and tomorrow he will exchange these again for new ones. At last, after belonging, successively, to various new-fangled sects, he generally ends by professing unmitigated contempt for them all. By their continual disputes and bickerings, and dividing and subdividing, the various Protestant sects have made themselves the scorn of honest minds, the laughingstock of the pagan and the infidel.

These human sects, the "works of the flesh," as St. Paul calls them, alter their shape, like clouds, but feel no blow, says Mr. Marshall, because they have no substance.

They fight a good deal with one another, but nobody minds it, not even themselves, nor cares what becomes of them. If one human sect perishes, it is always easy to make another, or half a dozen. They have the life of worms and propagate by corruption. Their life is so like death that, except by the putridity which they exhale in both stages, it is impossible to tell which is which, and when they are buried, nobody can find their grave. They have simply disappeared.

The spirit of Protestantism, or the spirit of revolt against God and his Church, sprung up from the Reformers' spirit of incontinency, obstinacy and covetousness. Luther, in despite of the vow he had solemnly made to God of keeping continency, married a nun, equally bound as himself to that sacred religious promise; but, as St. Jerome says, "it is rare to find a heretic that loves chastity?'

Luther's example had indeed been anticipated by Carlostadtius, a priest and ringleader of the Sacramentarians, who had married a little before; and it was followed by most of the heads of the Reformation.

Zwinglius, a priest and chief of the sect that bore his name, took a wife.

Bucer, a member of the order of St. Dominic, became a Lutheran, left his cloister, and married a nun.

Ecolampadius, a Brigittin monk, became a Zwinglian, and also married.

Cranmer, Archbishop of Canterbury, had also his wife.

Peter Martyr, a canon-regular, embraced the doctrine of Calvin, but followed the example of Luther, and married a nun.

Ochin, General of the Capuchins, became a Lutheran, and also married.

Thus, the principal leaders in the Reformation went forth preaching the new gospel, with two marks upon them: apostasy from faith, and open violation of the most sacred vows.

The passion of lust, as has been already said, hurried also Henry VIII of England into a separation from the Catholic Church, and ranked him among the Reformers.

Those wicked men could not be expected to teach a holy doctrine; they preached up a hitherto unheard of "evangelical liberty," as they styled it. They told their fellow men that they were no longer obliged to subject their understanding to the masteries of faith, and to regulate their actions according to the laws of Christian morality; they said that everyone was free to model his belief and practice as it suited his inclinations. In pursuance of this accommodating doctrine, they dissected the Catholic faith till they reduced it to a mere skeleton; they lopped off the reality of the body and blood of Christ, in the Holy Eucharist, the divine Christian sacrifice offered in the Mass, confession of sins, most of the sacraments, penitential exercises, several of the canonical books of Scripture, the invocation of saints, celibacy, most of the General Councils of the Church, and all present Church authority; they perverted the nature of justification, asserting that fait h alone suffices to justify man; they made God the author of sin, and maintained the observance of the commandments to be impossible.

As a few specimens of Luther's doctrine, take the following: "God's commandments are all equally impossible." (De Lib. Christ., t. ii, fol. 4.) "No sins can damn a man, but only unbelief." (De Captio. Bab., t. ii, fol. 171.) "God is just, though by his own will he lays us under the necessity of being damned, and though he damns those who have not deserved it." (Tom. ii, foil. 434, 436.) "God works in us both good and evil." (Tom. ii, fol. 444.) "Christ's body is in every place, no less than the divinity itself." (Tom. iv, fol. 37.) Then for his darling principle of justification by faith, in his eleventh article against Pope Leo, he says: "Believe strongly that you are absolved, and absolved you will be, whether you have contrition or no."

Again, in his sixth article: "The contrition which is acquired by examining, recollecting, and detesting one's sins, whereby a man calls to mind his life past, in the bitterness of his soul, reflecting on the heinousness and multitude of his offences, the loss of eternal bliss, and condemnation to eternal woe,—this contrition, I say, makes a man a hypocrite, nay, even a greater sinner than he was before."

Thus, after the most immoral life, a man has a compendious method of saving himself, by simply believing that his sins are remitted through the merits of Christ.

As Luther foresaw the scandal that would arise from his own and such like sacrilegious marriages, he prepared the world for it, by writing against the celibacy of the clergy and all religious vows; and all the way up, since his time, he has had imitators. He proclaimed that all such vows "were contrary to faith, to the commandments of God, and to evangelical liberty." (DeVotis Monast.) He said again: "God disapproves of such a vow of living in continency, equally as if I should vow to become the mother of God, or to create a new world." (Epist.

ad Wolfgang Reisemb.) And again: "To attempt to live unmarried, is plainly to fight against God."

Now, when men give a loose rein to the depravity of nature, what wonder if the most scandalous practices ensue? Accordingly, a striking instance of this kind appeared in the license granted in 1539 to Philip, Landgrave of Hesse, to have two wives at once, which license was signed by Luther, Melanchthon, Bucer, and five other Protestant divines.

On the other hand, a wide door was laid open to another species of scandal: the doctrine of the Reformation admitted divorces in the marriage state in certain cases, contrary to the doctrine of the Gospel, and even allowed the parties thus separated to marry other wives and other husbands.

To enumerate the errors of all the Reformers would exceed the limits of this work. I shall therefore only add the principal heads of the doctrine of Calvin and the Calvinists: 1, that baptism is not necessary for salvation; 2, good works are not necessary; 3, man has no freewill; 4, Adam could not avoid his fall; 5, a great part of mankind are created to be damned, independently of their demerits: 6, man is justified by faith alone, and that justification, once obtained, cannot be lost, even by the most atrocious crimes; 7, the true faithful are also infallibly certain of their salvation; 8, the Eucharist is no more than a figure of the body and blood of Christ. Thus was the whole system of faith and morality was overturned. Tradition they totally abolished; and, though they could not reject the whole of the Scripture, as being universally acknowledged to be the word of God, they had, however, the presumption to expunge some books of it that did not coincide with their own opinions, and the rest they assumed a right to explain as they saw fit.

To pious souls, they promised a return to the fervor of primitive Christianity: to the proud, the liberty of private judgment; to the enemies of the clergy, they promised the division of their spoils; to priests and monks who were tired of the yoke of continence, the abolition of a law which they said was contrary to nature; to libertines of all classes, the suppression of fasting, abstinence, and confession. They said to kings who wished to place themselves at the head of the Church as well as the State, that they would be freed from the spiritual authority of the Church; to nobles, that they would see a rival order humbled and impoverished; to the middle classes and the vassals of the Church, that they would be emancipated from all dues and forced s ervices.

Several princes of Germany and of the Swiss cantons supported by arms the preachers of the new doctrines. Henry VIII imposed his doctrine on his subjects. The King of Sweden drew his people into apostasy. The Court of Navarre welcomed the Calvinists; the Court of France secretly favored them.

At length Pope Paul III convoked a General Council at Trent, in 1545, to which the heresiarchs had appealed. Not only all the Catholic bishops, but also all Christian princes, even Protestants, were invited to come.

But now the spirit of pride and obstinacy became most apparent. Henry VIII replied to the pope that he would never entrust the work of reforming religion in his kingdom to anyone except to himself. The apostate princes of Germany told the papal legate that they recognized only the emperor as their sovereign; the Viceroy of Naples allowed but four bishops to go to the council; the King of France sent only three prelates, whom he soon after recalled., Charles V created difficulties, and put obstacles in the way. Gustavus Vasa allowed no one to go to the council. The heresiarchs also refused to appear. The council, however, was held, in spite of these difficulties. It lasted over eighteen years, because it was often interrupted by the plague, by war, and by the deaths of those who had to preside over it. The doctrines of the innovators were examined and condemned by the council, at the last session of which there were more than three hundred bishops present; among whom were nine cardinals, three patriarchs, thirty-three archbishops, not to mention sixteen abbots or generals of religious orders, and one hundred and forty-eight theologians. All the decrees published from the commencement were read over and were again approved and subscribed to by the Fathers. Accordingly, Pius IV, in a consistory held on the 26th of January 1564, approved and confirmed the council in a book which was signed by all the cardinals. He drew up, the same year, a profession of faith conformable in all respects with the definitions of the council, in which it is declared that its authority is accepted; and since that time, not only all bishops of the Catholic Church, but all priests who are called to teach the way of salvation even to children, nay, all non-Catholics, on abjuring their errors, and returning to the bosom of the Church, have sworn that they had no other faith than that of this holy council.

The new heresiarchs, however, continued to obscure and disfigure the face of religion. As to Luther's sentiments in regard to the pope, bishops, councils, etc., he says, in the preface to his book, "De Abroganda Missa Privata;" "With how many powerful remedies and most evident Scriptures have I scarce been able to fortify my conscience so as to dare alone to contradict the pope, and to believe him to be Antichrist, the bishops his apostles, and the universities his brothel-houses;" and in his book, "De Judicio Ecclesia de Gravi Doctrina," he says: "Christ takes from the bishops, doctors and councils, both the right and power of judging controversies, and gives them to all Christians in general."

His censure on the Council of Constance, and those that compose it, is as follows: "All John Huss's articles were condemned at Constance by Antichrist and his apostles " (meaning the pope and bishops), "in that synod of Satan, made up of most wicked sophisters; and you, most holy Vicar of Christ, I tell you plainly to your face, that all John Huss's condemned doctrines are evangelical and Christian, but all yours are impious and diabolical. I now declare," says he, speaking to the bishops, "that for the future I will not vouchsafe you so much honor as to submit myself or doctrine to your judgment, or to that of an angel from heaven." (Preface to his book, "Adversus false nominatum ordinem Episcoporum.") Such was his spirit of pride that he made open profession of contempt for the authority of the Church, councils, and Fathers, saying: "All those who will venture their lives, their estates, their honor, and their blood, in so Christian a work as to root out all bishoprics and bishops, who are the ministers of Satan, and to pluck by the roots all them authority and jurisdiction in the world,—these persons are the true children of God, and obey his commandments." ("Contra Staturn Ecclesice et falso nominatum o rdinem Episcoporum").

This spirit of pride and of obstinacy is also most apparent from the fact that Protestantism has never been ashamed to make use of any arguments, though ever so frivolous, inconsistent, or absurd, to defend its errors, and to slander and misrepresent the Catholic religion in every way possible. It shows itself again in the wars which Protestantism has waged to introduce and maintain itself. The apostate princes of Germany entered into a league, offensive and defensive, against the Emperor Charles V, and rose up in arms to establish Protestantism.

Luther had preached licentiousness, and reviled the emperor, the princes, and the bishops. The peasants lost no time in freeing themselves from their masters. They overran the country in lawless bands, burnt down castles and monasteries, and committed the most barbarous cruelties against the nobility and clergy. Germany became at last the scene of desolation and most cruel atrocities during the Thirty Years' War (1618—1648). More than one hundred thousand men fell in battle, seven cities were dismantled, one thousand religious houses were razed to the ground; three hundred churches, and immense treasures of statuary, paintings, books, etc., were destroyed.

But what is more apparent and better known than the spirit of covetousness of Protestantism? Wherever Protestantism secured a footing, it pillaged churches, seized Church property, destroyed monasteries and appropriated to itself their revenues.

In France, the Calvinists destroyed twenty thousand Catholic churches; they murdered, in Dauphiny alone, two hundred and fifty-five priests, one hundred and twelve monks, and burned nine hundred towns and villages. In England, Henry VIII confiscated to the crown, or distributed among his favorites, the property of six hundred and forty-five monasteries and ninety colleges, one hundred and ten hospitals, and two thousand three hundred and seventy-four free-chapels and chantries.

They even dared to profane, with sacrilegious hands, the remains of the martyrs and confessors of God. In many places they forcibly took up the saints' bodies from the repositories where they were kept, burned them, and scattered their ashes abroad. What more atrocious indignity can be conceived? Are parricides or the most flagitious men ever worse treated? Among other instances, in 1562, the Calvinists broke open the shrine of St. Francis of Paula, at Plessis-Lestours; and finding his body uncorrupted fifty-five years after his death, they dragged it about the streets, and burned it in a fire which they had made with the wood of a large crucifix, as Billet and other historians relate.

Thus at Lyons, in the same year, the Calvinists seized upon the shrine of St. Bonaventure, stripped it of its riches, burned the saint's relics in the market-place, and threw his ashes into the river Saone, as is related by the learned Possevinus, who was in Lyons at the time.

The bodies, also, of St. Irenaeus, St. Hilary, and St. Martin, as Surius asserts, were treated in the same ignominious manner. Such, also, was the treatment offered to the remains of St. Thomas, Archbishop of Canterbury, whose rich shrine, according to the words of Stowe, in his Annals, "was taken to the king's use, and the bones of St. Thomas, by the command of Lord Cromwell, were burnt to ashes in September, 15 38."

The Catholic religion has covered the world with its superb monuments. Protestantism has now lasted three hundred years; it was powerful in England, in Germany, in America. What has it raised? It will show us the ruins which it has made, amidst which it has planted some gardens, or established some factories. The Catholic religion is essentially a creative power, built up, not to destroy, because it is under the immediate influence of that Holy Spirit which the Church invokes as the creative Spirit, "Creator Spiritus." The Protestant, or modern philosophical spirit, is a principle of destruction, of perpetual decomposition and disunion. Under the dominion of English Protestant power, for four hundred years, Ireland was rapidly becoming as naked and void of ancient memorials as the wilds of Af rica.

The Reformers themselves were so ashamed of the progress of immorality among their proselytes that they could not help complaining against it. Thus spoke Luther: "Men are now more revengeful, covetous, and licentious, than they were ever in the Papacy." (Postil, super Evang. Dom. i, Advent.) Then again: "Heretofore, when we were seduced by the pope, every man willingly performed good works, but now no man says or knows anything else than how to get all to himself by exactions, pillage, theft, lying, usury." (Postil, super Evang. Dom. xxvi, p. Trinit.)

Calvin wrote in the same strain: "Of so many thousands," said he, "who, renouncing Popery, seemed eagerly to embrace the Gospel, how few have amended their lives! Nay, what else did the greater part pretend to, than, by shaking off the yoke of superstition, to give themselves more liberty to follow all kinds of licentiousness?" ("Liber de Scandalis.") Dr. Heylin, in his History of the Reformation, complains also of "the great increase, of viciousness" in England, in the reforming reign of Edward VI.

Erasmus says: "Take a view of this evangelical people, the Protestants. Perhaps 'tis my misfortune, but I never yet met with one who does not appear changed for the worse." (Epist. ad Vultur. Neoc.) And again: "Some persons," says he, "whom I knew formerly innocent, harmless, and without deceit, no sooner have I seen them joined to that sect (the Protestants), than they began to talk of wenches, to play at dice, to leave off prayers, being grown extremely worldly, most impatient, revengeful, vain, like vipers, tearing one another. I speak by experience." ("Ep. ad Fraires Infer. Germanite."

M. Scherer, the principal of a Protestant school in France, wrote, in 1844, that he beholds in his reformed church "the ruin of all truth, the weakness of infinite division, the scattering of flocks, ecclesiastical anarchy, Socinianism ashamed of itself, Rationalism coated like a pill, without doctrine, without consistency. This Church, deprived alike of its corporate and its dogmatic character, of its form and of its doctrine, deprived of all that constituted it a Christian church, has in truth ceased to exist in the ranks of religious communities. Its name continues, but it represents only a corpse, a phantom, or, if you will, a memory or a hope. For want of dogmatic authority, unbelief has made its way into three-fourths of our pupils." ("L'Etai Actual de l'Eglise Reformee en France, 1844.)

Such has been Protestantism from the beginning. It is written in blood and fire upon the pages of history. Whether it takes the form of Lutheranism in Germany, Denmark, and Sweden; Anglicanism in Great Britain, or Calvinism and Presbyterianism in Switzerland, France, Holland, Scotland, and America, —it has been everywhere the same. It has risen by tumult and violence; propagated itself by force and persecution; enriched itself by plunder, and has never ceased, by open force, persecuting laws or slander, its attempt to exterminate the Catholic faith, and destroy the Church of Christ, which the fathers of Protestantism left from the spirit of lust, pride, and covetousness,—a spirit which induced so many of their countrymen to follow their wicked example; a spirit, on account of which they would have been lost anyhow, even if they had not left their mother, the One Holy Roman Catholic and Apostolic Church. Having seen the total absence of unity in Protestantism, total absence of holiness in its authors and their principles, total absence of catholicity, for want of truth, which alone can rule and enforce obedience everywhere throughout the world; and total absence of apostolicity, because it arose only three hundred years ago,—and no honest man will say that the apostles were Protestants,—it is easy to answer the question :

12. If, then, only the Roman Church is one, holy, Catholic and Apostolic, what follows?

It follows that the Roman Catholic Church alone is the one true Church of Christ.

There are men foolish enough to talk of Protestantism as if it were a name for some religious faith, system, or organization! They even speak of the Protestant religion, or the Protestant Church! There is nothing ofthe kind. There is, and there can be, but one true religion. The word "religion," says St. Augustine, is derived from the Latin word re-eligendo (to reelect), because, after having lost our Lord by sin, we ought to reelect, or choose him again, as our true and Only Lord and sovereign Master. But, according to the same saint, the word "religion" is derived from religando (to reunite), because, it reunites man with God, with whom he was primitively united, but from whom he voluntarily separated by sin. Hence, according to St. Thomas Aquinas, religion is a virtue which teaches us to live in union with God. Now, to live in union with God is to keep our will united to his; in other words, it is to do the will of God. Religion, therefore, is the knowing and doing of God's will. He alone who knows and does the will of God has religion—is a truly religious man. Hence religion has always been one and the same: 1, in its Author, who is God, who taught man his will, either in person or through those to whom he made his will known; 2, in its doctrine.

As God has always taught man the same truths concerning himself, man, the world, morality, divine worship, grace, the object of religion, and the means to preserve and spread it, it is clear that religion must always have been one and the same from the beginning of the world.

As to himself God has always taught, from the beginning of the world, that he alone is the only one God, infinitely perfect, the Creator and Redeemer of all things; that the Redeemer would save the world, and that we would be sanctified by his Spirit. These truths, however, are more fully known to Christians than they were to the Jews.

Concerning man, God has always taught that he created him to his likeness, being composed of a body, and a soul which is spiritual, free, and immortal; that man fell through his own fault; that all men are born in a state of sin and degradation; that they will all rise at the last day, and that there will be eternal rewards for the just, and eternal punishment for the wicked.

With regard to the world, God has always taught that he created it out of nothing; that, by his infinite power and wisdom, he governed and preserved it; that he will purify it by fire, and that there will be a new heaven and a new earth.

As to morality, God has always taught the same laws, the same distinction between good and evil; always commended the same virtues and condemned the same vices.

As to his worship, God has always taught the same two essential acts of worship, viz.: prayer and sacrifice.

As to grace, God has always taught that it was necessary for every man to be saved; that he would give it, on account of the Redeemer, to all those who would use those means through which he wished to bestow it.

As to the object of religion, God has always taught that it was to destroy sin, and to lead men to true happiness.

As to the means of preserving and spreading it, God has always used the same means, choosing certain men, and investing them with his own authority, to teach his religion authoritatively, and with divine certainty. So that to hear and believe the infallible teachers chosen and sent by God, is to hear and to believe God himself. Such infallible teachers were, as we have seen, the patriarchs and Moses and the prophets, before the coming of the Redeemer; and Jesus Christ, the Son of God, and his teaching Church,—St. Peter and the other apostles, and their lawful successors, in the New Law. As religion has always been one and the same from the beginning of the world, because the same God has always taught one and the same religion, in like manner the teaching authority has always been the same, which is God's own infallible authority, invested in those of whom he said: "He who heareth you heareth me." There has, therefore, always been but one and the same religion, but one and the same Church. As man, by passing through the different stages of life, does not cease to be the same man, so religion has never ceased to be the same, though it has not at all times been taught as fully as it is at the present day; and the Christian religion, as taught by Christ in the Roman Catholic Church, is far more perfect, and is far richer in graces, than it was before the coming of the Redeemer.

It is, therefore, quite absurd to speak of Protestantism as of a religion or church; the truth is one, errors are many; the Church, the pillar and ground of truth, is one; sects are many that deny the truth and the Church's infallible authority to teach truth. Every sensible man, then, seeing a class of men drawn into a whirlpool of endless religious variations and dissensions, is forced to say: "This is only an ephemeral sect, without substance and without any divine authority; it is a plant not planted by the hand of Almighty God, and therefore it will be rooted up; it is a kingdom divided against itself, and therefore it will be made desolate; it is a house built on sand, and therefore it cannot stand; it is a cloud without water, which is carried about by the winds; a tree of autumn, unfruitful, twice dead, by the want of faith and morality, and therefore it will be plucked up by the roots; a raging wave of the sea, foaming out its own confusion; a wandering star, to which the storm and darkness are reserved forever; a withered branch, cut off from the body of Christ, the One Holy Roman Catholic and Apostolic Church, which alone is established by Christ on earth as his 'pillar and ground of truth,' in one fold, watched over by his one chief shepherd, ever immovable amid the storms of hell; with unshaken faith, amid the variations of philosophical systems, the infernal persecutions of the wicked, the revolutions of empires, the attacks of interest, of prejudice, of passion, the dissolving labors of criticism, the progress of physical, historical, and other sciences, the unrestrained love of novelty, the abuses which sooner or later undermine the most firmly established human institutions. The faith of this Church alone is divine, because she alone teaches with divine aut hority."

This is clear to every unprejudiced and well-reflected mind. Mr. T. W. M. Marshall relates the following, in one of his lectures:

"A young English lady, with whom I became subsequently acquainted, and from whose lips I heard the tale, informed her parents that she felt constrained to embrace the Catholic faith. Hereupon arose much agitation in the parental councils, and a reluctant promise was extorted from the daughter that she would not communicate with any Catholic priest till she had first listened to the convincing arguments with which certain clerical friends of the family would easily dissipate her unreasonable doubts. These ministers were three in number, and we will call them Messrs. A, B and C. The appointed day arrived for the solemn discussion, which one of the ministers was about to commence, when the young lady opened it abruptly with the following remark: "I am too young and uninstructed to dispute with gentlemen of your age and experience, but perhaps you will allow me to ask you a few questions?" Anticipating an easy triumph over the poor girl, the three ministers acceded with encouraging smiles to her request. 'Then I will ask you,' she said to Mr. A, 'whether regeneration always accompanies the sacrament of baptism?' 'Undoubtedly,' was the prompt reply; 'that is the plain doctrine of our Church.' 'And you, Mr. B,' she continued,—'do you teach that doctrine?' 'God forbid, my young friend,' was his indignant answer, 'that I should teach such soul destroying error! Baptism is a formal rite, which,' etc., etc. 'And you, Mr. C,' she asked the third, 'what is your opinion?' 'I regret,' he replied with a bland voice, for he began to suspect they were making a mess of it, 'that my reverend friends should have expressed themselves a little incautiously. The true doctrine lies between these extremes'—and he was going to develop it, when the young lady, rising from her chair, said: 'I thank you, gentlemen; you have taught me all that I expected to learn from you. You are all ministers of the same church, yet you each contradict the other, even upon a doctrine which St. Paul calls one of the foundations of Christianity. You have only confirmed me in my resolution to enter a Church whose ministers all teach the same thing.' And then they went out of the room, one by one, and probably continued their battle in the street. But the parents of the young lady turned her out of doors the next day, to get her bread as she could. They sometimes do that sort of thing in England.

"Another friend of mine, also a lady, and one of the most intelligent of her sex, was for several years the disciple of the distinguished minister who has given a name to a certain religious school in England. Becoming disaffected toward the Episcopalian Church, which appeared to her more redolent of earth, in proportion as she aspired more ardently toward heaven, she was persuaded to assist at a certain Ritualistic festival, which it wa shoped would have a soothing effect upon her mind. A new church was to be opened, and the ceremonies were to be prolonged through an entire week. All the Ritualistic celebrities of the day were expected to be present. Her lodging was judiciously provided in a house in which were five of the most transcendental members of the High Church party. It was hoped that they would speedily convince her of their apostolic unity, but, unfortunately, they only succeeded in proving to her that no two of them were of the same mind. One recommended her privately to pray to the Blessed Virgin, which another condemned as, at best, a poetical superstition. One told her that the pope was, by divine appointment, the head of the Universal Church; another, that he was a usurper

and a schismatic. One maintained that the 'Reformers' were profane
scoundrels and apostates; another, that they had at all events good
intentions. But I need not trouble you with an account of their various
creeds. Painfully affected by this diversity, where she had been taught
to expect complete uniformity, her doubts were naturally confirmed.
During the week she was invited to take a walk with the eminent
person whom she had hitherto regarded as a trustworthy teacher. To
him she revealed her growing disquietude and presumed to lament
the conflict of opinions which she had lately witnessed, but only to
be rewarded by a stern rebuke; for it is a singular fact that men who
are prepared at any moment to judge all the saints and doctors, will
not tolerate any judgment which reflects upon themselves. It was
midwinter, and the lady's companion, pointing to the leafless trees by
the roadside, said, with appropriate solemnity of voice and manner:
'They are stripped of their foliage now, but wait for the spring, and
you will see them once more wake to life. So shall it be with the Church
of England, which now seems to you dead? 'It may be so,' she replied,
'but what sort of a spring can we expect after a winter which has lasted
three hundred years?' You will not be surprised to hear that this lady
soon after became a member of a Church which knows nothing of
winter, but within whose peaceful borders reigns eternal spring."

And why do we see an eternal spring within the peaceful borders
of the Catholic Church? The reason is contained in the answer to the
question:

13. Is the faith of the Roman Catholic divine or human?

*The faith of the Roman Catholic is divine, for, to believe the Catholic
Church is to believe God himself.*

The Roman Catholic Church is the heir to the rights of Jesus Christ. She is the faithful depositary of the spiritual treasures of Jesus Christ. She is the infallible teacher of the doctrines of Jesus Christ. She wields the authority of Jesus Christ. She lives by the life and spirit of Jesus Christ. She enjoys the guidance and help of Jesus Christ. She speaks, orders, commands, concedes, prohibits, defines, looses and binds, in the name of Jesus Christ. The Catholic believes in this divine authority of the Church, and therefore believes and obeys her; and in believing and obeying her, he believes and obeys Almighty God himself, who said to the apostles and their lawful successors in the Catholic Church: "He that heareth you heareth me, and he that despises you despises me." (Luke x, 16). His faith, therefore, is divine, because it is based on divine authority; it gives peace to his soul, and contentment to his heart; it is for him, as it were, a perpetual spring of happiness and joy.

14. Do Protestant sects teach divine faith on divine authority?

No; the faith of Protestants is based upon human authority, because their founders were not sent by God, nor did they receive any mission from his Church.

The aim of Protestantism was to declare every man independent of the divine authority of the Catholic Church, and to substitute for this divine authority that of the Bible, as interpreted by himself. Protestants, therefore, hold that man is himself his own teacher and his own lawgiver; that it is each one's business to find out his own religion, that is to say, that everyone must judge for himself what doctrines are most consistent with reason and the holy Scriptures; or that he must follow the teaching of the clergyman whose views best commend themselves to his judgment. He does not acknowledge that God has a right to teach him: or, if he acknowledges this right, he does not feel himself bound to believe all that God teaches him through those whom God appointed to teach mankind. He says to God: If thou teach me, I reserve to myself the right to examine thy words, to explain them as I choose, and admit only what appears to me true, consistent, and useful. Hence, St. Augustine says: "You who believe what you please, and reject what you please, believe yourselves or your own fancy, rather than the Gospel." The faith of the Protestant, then, is based upon his private judgment alone; it is human. As his judgment is alterable, he naturally holds that his faith and doctrine is alterable at will and is therefore continually changing it. Evidently, then, he does not hold it to be the truth; for truth never changes. Nor does he hold it to be the law of God, which he is bound to obey; for, if the law of God be alterable at all, it can only be altered by God himself, never by man, any body of men, or any creature of God.

But some Protestants, for instance, the Anglicans, think that they approach very near to the Catholic Church. They will tell you that their prayers and ceremonies are like many prayers and ceremonies of the Catholic Church, that their creed is the Apostles' Creed. But, in principle, they are all equally far off. Thus they profess to believe in one Church, which has, unfortunately, became half a dozen; in unity, which ceased to exist long ago, for want of a center; in authority, which nobody needs obey, because it has lost the power to teach; in God's presence with the Church, which does not keep her from stupid errors; in divine promises, which were only made to be broken; in a divine constitution, which needs to be periodically reformed; in a mission to teach all nations, while she is unable to teach even herself; in saints, to whom Anglicans would be objects of horror and aversion; and in the sanctity of truths which their own sect has always defiled, and which are profanely mocked at this hour by its bishops, clergy, and people, all around them. The world has had occasion to admire, in various ages, many curious products of human imbecility, but at no time, and among no people, has it seen anything which could be matched with this. Compared with Anglicanism and its myriad contradictions, the wildest phantom which ever mocked the credulity of distempered fanaticism was a form of truth and beauty, a model of exact reasoning and logical symmetry.

Even an untutored Indian chief, by the aid of his rude commonsense, and the mere intuition of natural truth, does not fail to see the folly of Protestant belief, and confounds and ridicules it before those Protestant missionaries who come to convert his tribe to Protestantism. Elder Alexander Campbell, in a lecture before the American Christian Missionary Association, relates the following: "Sectarian missionaries had gone among the Indians to disseminate religious sentiments. A council was called, and the missionaries explained the object of their visit. 'Is not all the religion of a white man in a book?' quoth a chief. 'Yes,' replied the missionaries. 'Do not all white men read the book?' continued the chief. Another affirmative response. 'Do they all agree upon what it says?' inquired the chief, categorically. There was a dead silence for some moments. At last, one of the missionaries replied: 'Not exactly, they differ upon some doctrinal points.' 'Go home, white man,' said the chief, 'call a council, and, when the white men all agree, then come teach the red men!'"

The absurdity of Protestantism being so easily perceived by the rude child of the forest, Protestantism has never been able to convert a heathen nation, although it has every human means in its power. It has a vast number of ministers, plenty of ships to carry these ministers to every country, boundless wealth, and great armies and navies to terrify the heathen, also its merchants scattered through every quarter of the globe; with all this, Protestantism has not converted a nation, nor even a city or tribe, of heathens to Christianity, after three hundred years' existence. It has been ascertained that, during the last fifty years, Protestantism, in Europe and America, has collected and spent over one hundred and twenty-five millions of dollars, for the purpose of converting the heathens. One hundred millions of Bibles, Testaments, and tracts, have been printed in various languages and scattered throughout the world for the same purpose. Five thousand missionaries, with large salaries, varying from a hundred to five hundred pounds each, and also an additional allowance for their wives and families, are kept annually employed in the work, and yet all to no purpose. No result whatever can be shown.

During every month of May, the various sects of Protestants hold their anniversary meetings in London and New York. At these gatherings speeches are made and reports read, in which the people are told of the wonderful conversions that are just going to take place; of a great door opened for the Gospel; of fields white for the harvest; of bright anticipations; of missionaries who now enjoy the confidence of the natives; of Pagans stretching, or who are about to stretch, forth their hands to God immediately; of printing-presses which are in constant operation; of schools to be opened; of sums spent in Bibles; of Bibles, Testaments, and tracts distributed. Every promise is made for the future, but nothing whatever is shown for the past. The meetings are ended, votes of thanks are given to the various chairmen, prayers said, subscriptions received, and the huge delusion lives on from year to year.

Some of the missionaries give up the work in despair, others in disgust. Some run away from the first appearance of danger; others fly from persecution, being terrified at the very idea of martyrdom. One missionary comes back to his native country, because of the sudden death of his wife; another, to bury his youngest daughter in her mother's grave; another leaves the field of his missionary labors, to console his dear mother on her death-bed; another comes home to look after some small property left him by his father, who recently died; one comes home to preserve the life of a delicate child, who did not seem to thrive in the place where he was stationed; another left to attend to the education of his children, whom he could not feel in his heart to rear up amongst Pagans; another comes home, because his wife has quarreled with the wives of some of the other missionaries; another, to be present at his eldest daughter's marriage. Many Protestant missionaries give up the work of saving souls for more lucrative pursuits, such as, good commercial or government situations, or to become merchants on their own account; whilst a few, possessed of sufficient ability, have become newspaper correspondents; and more than one, instead of converting the Pagans, have themselves become converts to the Jewish and Mahometan religions, having got rich wives of these persuasions.

Protestant travelers and writers who have visited the fields of Protestant missionary labor, have themselves furnished the world with these details. They tell of a few converts here and there, who relapse into paganism whenever the missionaries withdraw. They tell us that the missionaries become tyrants and persecute the people when they get the chance; that they drive the natives into the Protestant meeting-houses by force, and make them more brutal, profligate, crafty, treacherous, impure, and disgusting, than they were before. One writer states how he found, in the Sandwich Islands, that the Protestant missionaries had civilized the people into draught-horses, and evangelized them into beasts of burden; that they were literally broken into the traces, and harnessed to the vehicles of their spiritual instructors, like so many beasts of burden. The poor natives are compelled to draw their pastors, as well as their wives and daughters, to church, to market, or for pleasure, and are whipped like horses. The same writer says, the missionaries destroy heathenism, and the heathens also; that they extirpate Paganism and the people at the same time; that the natives are robbed of their land, in the name of religion, and that disease, vice, and premature death, make their appearance together with Protestantism. The missionaries are dwelling in picturesque and prettily furnished coral-rock villas, while the miserable natives are committing all sorts of crime and immorality around them. The depopulated land is recruited from the rapacious hordes of enlightened individuals who settle within its borders, and clamorously announce the progress of the truth. Neat villas, trim gardens, shaven lawns, spires, and cupolas arise, while the poor savage soon finds himself an interloper in the country of his fathers, and that, too, on the very site of the hut where he was born.

When will Protestants learn wisdom from the rude child of the forest? When will they see the absurdity of their teaching? It is strange how men will put their reason in their pocket, and prefer darkness to light, error to truth, folly to wisdom.

That man might know what to believe, Christ, who alone could tell him, founded the Roman Catholic Church, to be forever "the pillar and ground of truth?" Whoever declines to follow this guide, must live without any sure guide. There is no other, because God has given no other. Hence Pius IX spoke lately of Protestantism, in all its forms, as "revolt against God," it being an attempt to substitute a human for a divine authority, and a declaration of the creature's independence of the Creator. The creed of the apostate has only one article. If God, it proclaims, chose to found a church without consulting man, it is quite open to man to abolish the church without consulting God.

A body which has lost the principle of its animation becomes dust. Hence it is an axiom that the change or perversion of the principles by which anything was produced, is the destruction of that very thing: if you can change or pervert the principles from which anything springs, you destroy it. For instance, one single foreign element introduced into the blood produces death; one false assumption admitted into science destroys its certainty; one false principle admitted into faith and morals is fatal. The Reformers started wrong. They would reform the Church, by placing her under human control. Their successors have, in each generation, found they did not go far enough, and have, each in turn, struggled to push it further and further, till they find themselves without any church life, without faith, without religion, and beginning to doubt if there be even a God.

It is a well-known fact that, before the Reformation, infidels were scarcely known in the Christian world. Since that event they have come forth in swarms. It is from the writings of Herbert, Hobbes, Bloum, Shaftesbury, Bolingbroke, and Boyle, that Voltaire and his party drew the objections and errors which they have brought so generally into fashion in the world. According to Diderot and d'Alembert, the first step that the untractable Catholic takes is to adopt the Protestant principle of private judgment. He establishes himself judge of his religion—leaves and joins the reform. Dissatisfied with the incoherent doctrines he there discovers, he passes over to the Socinians, whose inconsequence soon drive him into Deism. Still pursued by unexpected difficulties, he finds refuge in universal doubt; but still haunted by uneasiness, he at length resolves to take the last step, and proceeds to terminate the long chain of his errors in infidelity. Let us not forget that the first link of this chain is attached to the fundamental maxim of private judgment. They judged of religion as they did of their breakfast and dinner. A religion was good or bad, true or false, just as it suited their tastes, their likings; their religious devotion varied like the weather; they must feel it as they felt the heat and cold.

New fashions of belief sprang up, and changed, and disappeared, as rapidly as the new fashions of dress. Men judged not only of every revealed doctrine, but they also judged of the Bible itself. Protestantism, having no authority, could not check this headlong tendency to unbelief. Its ministers dare no longer preach or teach any doctrine which is displeasing to the people. Every Protestant preacher who wishes to be heard, and to retain his salary, must first feel the pulse of his hearers; he must make himself the slave of their opinions and li kings.

It is, therefore, historically correct that the same principle that created Protestantism three centuries ago has never ceased, since that time, to spin it out into a thousand different sects, and has concluded by covering Europe and America with that multitude of free-thinkers and infidels who place these countries on the verge of ruin.

What is the spiritual life of Protestants? They seem to have lost all spiritual conceptions, and no longer to possess any spiritual aspiration. Lacking, as they do, the light, the warmth, arid the life-giving power of the sun of the Catholic Church, they seem to have become, or to be near becoming, what our world would be if there were no sun in the h eavens.

For this reason, it is that Protestants are so completely absorbed in temporal interests, in the things that fall under their senses, that their whole life is only materialism put in action. Lucre is the sole object on which their eyes are constantly fixed. A burning thirst to realize some profit, great or small, absorbs all their faculties, the whole energy of their being. They never pursue anything with ardor but riches and enjoyments. God, the soul, a future life, —they believe in none of them; or rather, they never think about them at all. If they ever take up a moral or a religious book, or go to a meeting house, it is only by way of amusement—to pass the time away. It is a less serious occupation than smoking a pipe or drinking a cup of tea. If you speak to them about the foundations of faith, of the principles of Christianity, of the importance of salvation, the certainty of a life beyond the grave, —all these truths which so powerfully impress a mind susceptible of religious feeling, —they listen with a certain pleasure; for it amuses them and piques their curiosity. In their opinion all this is "true, fine, grand." They deplore the blindness of men who attach themselves to the perishable goods of this world; perhaps they will even give utterance to some fine sentences on the happiness of knowing the true God, of serving him, and of meriting by this means the reward of eternal life. They simply never think of religion at all, they like very well to talk about it, but it is as of a thing not made for them, —a thing with which, personally, they have nothing to do. This indifference they carry so far,—religious sensibility is so entirely withered or dead within them,—that they care not a straw whether a doctrine is true or false, good or bad. Religion is to them simply a fashion, which those may follow who have a taste for it. "By and by, all in good time," they say; "one should never be precipitate; it is not good to be too enthusiastic. No doubt the Catholic religion is beautiful and sublime; its doctrine explains, with method and clearness, all that is necessary for man to know. Whoever has any sense will see that and will adopt it in his heart in all sincerity; but after all, one must not think too much of these things, and increase the cares of life. Now, just consider we have a body: how much care it demands! It must be clothed, fed, and sheltered from the injuries of the weather; its infirmities are great, and its maladies are numerous. It is agreed on all hands that heal this our most precious good. This body that we see, that we touch, must be taken care of every day, and every moment of the day. Is not this enough, without troubling ourselves about a soul that we never see? The life of man is short and full of misery; it is made up of a succession of important concerns, that follow one another without interruption . Our hearts and our minds are scarcely sufficient for the solicitudes of the present life: is it wise, then, to torment oneself about the future? Is it not far better to live in blessed ignorance?"

Ask them, what would you think of a traveler who, on finding himself at a dilapidated inn, open to all the winds, and deficient in the necessaries of life, should spend all his time in trying how he could make himself most comfortable in it, without ever thinking of preparing himself for his departure, and his return into the bosom of his Family? Would this traveler be acting in a wise and reasonable manner? "No," they will reply; "one must not travel in that way. But man, nevertheless, must confine himself within proper limits. How can he provide for two lives at the same time? I take care of this life, and the care of the other I leave to God. If a traveler ought not regularly to take up his abode at an inn, neither ought he to travel on two roads at the same time. When one wishes to cross a river, it will not do to have two boats, and set a foot in each: such a proceeding would involve the risk of a tumble into the water, and drowning oneself." Such is the deep abyss of religious indifferentism into which so many Protestants of our day have fallen, and from which they naturally fall into one deeper still: infidelity.

15. Will such human faith save them?

No; for St. Paul says: "It is impossible to please God without faith."
(Hebrews xi, 6.)

To be saved, we must do the will of God: "Not everyone that says to me Lord, Lord, shall enter into the kingdom of heaven; but he that does the will of my Father who is in heaven, he shall enter into the kingdom of heaven." (Matthew vii, 21.) The will of God the Father is that men hear and believe his Son, Jesus Christ: "This is my well-beloved Son. Him you shall hear." Now, Jesus Christ said to his apostles and their lawful successors: "He that hears you hears me, and he that despises you despises me; and he that despises me despises him that sent me,"—the heavenly Father. Now, Protestants despise God the Father, because they do not listen to his Son speaking to them through Peter and the apostles, in their lawful successors. Turning, as they do, their back upon them most contemptuously, they follow their own will in all religious matters. Assuredly no Protestant would engage and pay a servant who would tell him, "I will serve you according to my will, not according to yours." How, then, could God the Father admit one into his kingdom who has always refused to do his will,—who, instead of learning the will of God, the full doctrine of Christ, through the Catholic Church, was himself his own teacher, his own lawgiver, his own judge, in religious matters? Everyone who is not a Catholic should remember that there never was a time, from the beginning of the world, when God left men free to fashion their own religion, to invent their own creed and their own form of worship. Christ never designed that the sacred truths of his religion should be submitted to the people by the apostles and their successors for discussion, for criticism, and for private interpretation, with liberty to alter and amend, or reject them, as ignorance, prejudice, or caprice might dictate. He never submitted his doctrines to the opinions or criticisms of the Scribes, Pharisees, or Sadducees of Jerusalem, or the learned Pagan philosophers; he never sanctioned what is termed, in modern times, "freedom of conscience" and "private interpretation;"

on the contrary, from the beginning of the world, God established on earth a visible teaching authority, to which it was the bounden duty of every man to submit, if he would be saved. If one, then, who is not a Catholic, seriously considers the question, "Is it God that speaks through the Catholic Church?" he fulfils a most sacred duty, and acts according to reason. Far from offending God, he honors him by using his reason to distinguish the voice of God from that of man—the supreme, divine authority from mere human authority.

But as soon as he is convinced that the authority of the Church is from God, he is bound to believe most firmly all that he is told on this authority. Common-sense tells him that, when he hears God speak, he hears nothing but truth; no matter whether or not he understands it, he is obliged to say, Amen, it is so. "Without such faith" says St. Paul, "it is impossible to please God".

Take the case of one who is not a Catholic, but who has studied all the doctrines of the Church. He makes up his mind that all that the Church teaches is reasonable and consistent with holy Scripture, and so he believes, and becomes a Catholic. Is his faith divine? Does he become a Catholic in the right way? No, his faith is based, as yet, on individual reason alone.

There is another. He considers the antiquity of the Roman Catholic Church; her unity in faith; the purity and holiness of her doctrine: her establishment by poor fishermen all over the world, in spite of all kinds of opposition; her invariable duration from the time of the apostles; the miracles which are wrought in her; the holiness of all those who live according to her laws; the deep science of her doctors; the almost infinite number of her martyrs; the peace of mind and happiness of soul experienced by those who have entered her bosom; the fact that all Protestants admit that a faithful Catholic will be saved in his religion; the frightful punishment inflicted by

God upon all the persecutors of the Catholic Church; the melancholy death of the authors of heresies; the constant fulfilment of the words of our Lord, that his Church would always be persecuted. He seriously considers all this; he is enlightened by God's grace to see that the Roman Catholic Church alone is the true Church of Jesus Christ; he is convinced that her authority is from God, and that to hear and obey her authority is to hear and obey God himself: and so he accepts and believes all that she teaches, because it comes to him on the authority of God, and therefore must be true; not because he himself sees how or why it is true. This is true divine faith—this is the right way to become a Catholic. Such faith is absolutely necessary. It is necessary by necessity of precept. Our blessed Lord says: "He that believeth and is baptized shall be saved. He that believeth not shall be condemned." This precept is affirmative; in as far as it obliges us to believe all that God has revealed: it is negative, in as far as it forbids us to hold any opinions contrary to the revealed truth.

Such faith is necessary by necessity of medium, for, "without faith, it is impossible to please God," (Hebrews xi, 6.) "If you believe not, you shall die in your sins." (John v, 38; viii, 27.)

16. Must, then, all who wish to be saved die united to the Catholic Church?

Yes, for out of the Catholic Church there is no salvation: 1, because she alone teaches the true faith; 2, because in her alone are found the means of grace and salvation.

Our divine Savior says: "No one can come to the Father except through me." If we then wish to enter heaven, we must be united to Christ,—to his body, which is the Church, as St. Paul says. We must then be united to his Church. Therefore, out of that Church there is no salvation.

Again, Jesus Christ says: Whoever will not hear the Church, look upon him as a heathen and a great sinner. Therefore, out of the Church there is no salvation.

Holy Scripture says (Acts ii, 47): "The Lord added daily to the Church such as should be saved." Therefore, the apostles believed, and the holy Scriptures teach, that there is no salvation out of the Church.

Hence the Fathers of the Church never hesitated to pronounce all those forever lost who die out of the Roman Catholic Church: "He who has not the Church for his mother," says St. Cyprian, "cannot have God for his Father;" and with him the Fathers in general say that, "as all who were not in the ark of Noe perished in the waters of the Deluge, so shall all perish who are out of the true Church." St. Augustine and the other bishops of Africa, at the Council of Zirta, A. D. 412, say: "Whosoever is separated from the Catholic Church, however commendable in his own opinion his life may be, he shall, for the very reason that he is separated from the union of Christ, not see life, but the wrath of God abideth on him." Therefore, says St. Augustine, "a Christian ought to fear nothing so much as to be separated from the body of Christ (the Church). For, if he be separated from the body of Christ, he is not a member of Christ; if not a member of Christ, he is not quickened by his Spirit." (Tract, xxvii, in Joan., n. 6, col. 1992, tom. iii.)

"In our times," says Pius IX, "many of the enemies of the Catholic faith direct their efforts toward placing every monstrous opinion on the same level with the doctrine of Christ, or confounding it therewith; and so they try more and more to propagate that impious system of the indifference of religions. But quite of late, we shudder to say it, certain men have not hesitated to slander us by saying that we share in their folly, favor that most wicked system, and think so benevolently of every class of mankind as to suppose that not only the sons of the Church, but that the rest also, however alienated from Catholic unity they may remain, are alike in the way of salvation, and may arrive at everlasting life. We are at a loss, from horror, to find words to express our detestation of this new and atrocious injustice that is done us. We love, indeed, all mankind with the inmost affection of our hearts, yet not otherwise than in the love of God and our Lord Jesus Christ, who came to seek and to save that which had perished, who died for all, who wills all men to be saved, and to come to the knowledge of the truth; who, therefore, sent his disciples into the whole world to preach the Gospel to every creature, proclaiming that those who should believe and be baptized should be saved, but that those who should not believe should be condemned. Let those, therefore, who wish to be saved, come to the pillar and the ground of faith, which is the Church; let them come to the true Church of Christ, which, in her bishops and in the Roman Pontiff, the chief head of all, has the succession of apostolical authority which has never been interrupted, which has never counted anything of greater importance than to preach, and by all means to keep and defend the doctrine proclaimed by the apostles at Christ's command. This apostolical authority of the Church has, from the apostles' time, ever increase d in the midst of difficulties of every kind; it has become illustrious throughout the whole world, by the splendor of miracles and by the blood of martyrs; it has been exalted by the virtues of confessors and virgins; it has been strengthened by the most wise testimonies and writings of the Fathers; it has flourished, and does flourish, in all the regions of the earth, and shines refulgent in the perfect unity of faith, of sacraments, and of holy discipline. We who, though unworthy, hold this supreme See of the Apostle Peter, wherein Christ has laid the foundation of the same Church of his, shall never at any time abstain from any cares or labors that, by the grace of Christ himself, we may bring those who are ignorant, and who are going astray, to this only road of truth and salvation. But let all those who oppose themselves, remember that heaven and earth shall indeed pass away, but that nothing can ever pass away of the words of Christ, nor change be made in the doctrine which the Catholic Church has received from Christ, to be kept, defended, and preached." (Allocution to the Cardinals, held on the 17th Dec., 1847.)

17. Who are not members of the Roman Catholic Church?

All unbaptized persons, unbelievers, apostates, heretics, and all excommunicated persons.

But how do we know that unbaptized persons are not saved? We know it, because Jesus Christ has said: "Unless a man be born again of water and the Holy Ghost, he cannot enter into the kingdom of God." (John iii, 5.)

Heaven is the union of Almighty God with the elect,— those who are quite pure, without the least stain of sin. But God, who is holiness itself, cannot unite himself to a soul that is in sin. Now, as those who die without baptism remain forever stained with original sin, they can never be united to Almighty God in heaven.

And why are unbelievers and apostates lost? Unbelievers and apostates are lost, because it is said that, "without faith, it is impossible to please God." In our day and country, it is become fashionable for a large number of men to have no religion, and even to boast of having none. To have no religion is a great crime; but to boast of having none is the height of folly.

The man without religion is a slave to the most degrading superstition. Instead of worshipping the true, free, living God, who governs all things by his providence, he bows before the horrid phantom of blind chance or inexorable destiny. He is a man who obstinately refuses to believe the most solidly established facts in favor of religion, and yet, with blind credulity, greedily swallows the most absurd falsehoods uttered against religion. He is a man whose reason has fled, and whose passions speak, object, and decide in the name of reason. He is sunk in the grossest ignorance regarding religion. He blasphemes what he does not understand. He rails at the doctrines of the Church, without knowing really what her doctrines are. He sneers at the doctrines and practices of religion, because he cannot refute them. He speaks with the utmost gravity of the fine arts, the fashions, and matters the most trivial, while he turns the most sacred subjects into ridicule. In the midst of his own circle of fops and silly women, he utters his shallow conceits with all the pompous assurance of a pedant.

But why is it that he makes his impious doctrines the subject of conversation on every occasion? It is, of course, first to communicate his devilish principles to others, and make them as bad as he himself is but this is not the only reason. The good Catholic seldom speaks of his religion; he feels assured, by the grace of God, that his religion is the only true one, and that he will be saved if he lives up to it. Such is not the case with the infidel; he is constantly tormented in his soul: "There is no peace, no happiness for the impious," says the holy Scripture. He tries to quiet the fears of his soul, the remorse of his conscience; so he communicates to others, on every occasion, his perverse principles, hoping to meet with some of his fellowmen who may approve of his impious views, that he thus may find some relief for his interior torments. He resembles a timid man, who is obliged to travel during a dark night, and who begins to sing and cry out, to keep away fear. The infidel is a sort of night-traveler; he travels in the horrible darkness of his impiety. His interior conviction tells him that there is a God who will certainly punish him in the most awful manner. This fills him with great fear, and makes him extremely unhappy every moment of his life; he cannot bear the sight of a Catholic church, of a Catholic procession, of an image of our Lord, of a picture of a saint, of a prayer-book, of a good Catholic, of a priest; in a word, he cannot bear anything that reminds him of God, of religion, of his own guilt and impiety: so, on every occasion, he cries out against faith in God, in all that God has revealed and proposes to us for our belief by the holy Catholic Church. What is the object of his impious cries? It is to deafen, to keep down, in some measure, the clamors of his conscience. Our hand will involuntarily touch that part of the body where we feel pain; in like manner, the tongue of the infidel touches, on all occasions, involuntarily as it were, upon all those truths of our holy religion which inspire him with fear of the judgments of Almighty God. He feels but too keenly that he cannot do away with God and his sacred religion, by denying his existence.

The days of the infidel are counted. What a fearful thing it is for him to fall into the hands of God in the hour of death! He knows this truth, and because he knows it, he dies in the fury of despair, and, as it were, in the anticipated torments of the suffering that awaits him in hell. Witness Voltaire, the famous infidel of France! He wished to make his confession at his last hour. But the priest of St. Sulpice was not able to go to his bedside, because the chamber-door was shut upon him. So Voltaire died without confession. He died in such a terrible paroxysm of fury and rage, that the marshal of Richelieu, who was present at his horrible agony, exclaimed: "Really, this sight is sickening; it is insupportable!" M. Tronchin, Voltaire's physician, says: "Figure to yourself the rage and fury of Orestes, and you'll still have but a feeble image of the fury of Voltaire in his last agony. It would be well if all the infidels of Paris were present. Oh, the fine spectacle that would have met their eyes!". Thus is fulfilled in infidels what God says in holy Scripture: "I will laugh at the destruction of those who laughed at me during their life."

Witness Tom Paine! A short time before he died, he sent for the Rev. Father Fenwick. Father Fenwick went, in company of Father Kohlman, to see the infidel in his wretched condition. When they arrived at Paine's house, at Greenwich, his housekeeper came to the door and inquired whether they were the Catholic priests: "For," said she, "Mr. Paine has been so annoyed of late by ministers of different other denominations calling upon him, that he has left express orders with me to admit no one today but clergymen of the Catholic Church." Upon assuring her that they were Catholic clergymen, she opened the door, and invited them to sit down in the parlor. "Gentlemen," said she, "I really wish you may succeed with Mr. Paine; for he is laboring under great distress of mind ever since he was informed by his physicians that he cannot possibly live and must die shortly. He sent for you today, because he was told that if anyone could do him good, you might. He is truly to be pitied. His cries, when he is left alone, are truly heart-rending. 'O Lord! help me!' he will exclaim during his paroxysms of distress. 'God, help, Jesus Christ, help me!' repeating the same expressions without any the least variation, in a tone of voice that would alarm the house. Sometimes he will say, 'O God! what have I done to suffer so much?' Then shortly after: 'If there is a God, what will become of me?' Thus he will continue for some time, when on a sudden he will scream as if in terror and agony, and call out for me by name. On one of these occasions, which are very frequent, I went to him and inquired what he wanted. 'Stay with me,' he replied, 'for God's sake; for I cannot bear to be left alone.' I then observed that I could not always be with him, as I had much to attend to in the house. 'Then,' said he, 'send even a child to stay with me; for it is a hell to be alone.' I never saw," she concluded, "a more unhappy, a more forsaken man. It seems he cannot reconcile himself to die."

The fathers did all in their power to make Paine enter into himself and ask God's pardon. But all their endeavors were in vain. He ordered them out of his room, in the highest pitch of his voice, and seemed a very maniac with rage and madness. "Let us go," said Father Fenwick to Father Kohlman. "We have nothing more to do here. He seems to be entirely abandoned by God. Further words are lost upon him. I never before or since beheld a more hardened wretch." ("Lives of the Catholic Bishops of America," p. 379, etc.)

To the infidel and evil doer these examples present matter worthy of serious reflection, while the believer will recognize in them the special judgment of God, which is too clearly indicated to be doubted by any honest mind. Let the unbeliever remember that the hour will come when he shall open his eyes to see the wisdom of those who have believed; when he also shall see, to his confusion, his own madness in refusing to believe. "Oh, that he would be wise, and would understand that there is none that can deliver out of the hand of the Lord!" (Deuteronomy xxxii, 39.)

18. Why are those persons lost who have been justly excommunicated, and who are unwilling to do what is required of them before they are absolved?

Because the sin of great scandal, for which they, as dead members, were expelled from the communion of the Church, excludes them from the kingdom of heaven.

Such excommunicated persons are, for instance, all members of secret societies. The aim of secret societies is to abolish the Christian religion and the Church of Christ; nay, to banish the law of God, and the very idea of his overruling providence; to overturn every legitimate secular authority; to destroy the present basis of society, and to construct a new one, wherein all may be free to follow their passions. The members of these societies have been excommunicated by several popes: by Clement IX, Benedict XIV, Leo XII, and Pius IX.

Our Lord gave to his Church the power of separating men from the "onefold," and making them "heathens and publicans. The purpose and effect of communication are to cut culprits off from the body of Christ; to cast them out of his Church, as unworthy of the Christian name, and as deprived of rights which were acquired by baptism. The excommunicated, then, are shut out from those avenues of grace which have been provided in the Church; they cannot receive the sacraments; the holy sacrifice of the Mass is not daily offered forthem; and if death surprises them while they still obstinately defy the Church, the separation from the Church, which they have willfully chosen to maintain on earth, will be maintained also in the other world—they will remain separated forever from the communion of the saints in heaven?' (See Part I, Secret Societies, § 15.)

Why are heretics lost? Heretics, that is to say, baptized persons who choose such doctrines of the Roman Catholic Church as please them, and reject the rest, are lost for the reason given by St. Paul the Apostle, who says: "A man that is a heretic, after the first and second admonition, avoid; knowing that he who is such an one is subverted, and sinneth, being condemned by his own judgment" (Titus iii, 10, 11 .)

The word of God, in the first commandment, is: "I am the Lord thy God." By this commandment all men are obliged to believe

in God as the Infinite Being, who is essentially good and just,
the sovereign Author and Lord of all things, who has an absolute
authority over all, —an authority which he can exercise either directly
by himself, or through an angel, a prophet, or one or more of his
reasonable creatures. God, therefore, has a right to command the
human understanding to admit certain truths, the human will to
perform certain duties, the senses to make certain sacrifices. Nothing
can be more reasonable than to submit to such a command of God.
This submission is called faith, which, as St. Paul says, "bringeth
into captivity every understanding to the obedience of Christ." (2
Corinthians X, 5.) As soon, then, as man hears the voice of his Maker,
he is bound to say, "Amen: it is so." I believe it, no matter whether I unde
rstand it or not.

But Protestants have no regard for God when he says, "I am the
Lord thy God. I have a right to tell you what you must believe and
do, to be saved, and you are bound to submit to my will, and practice
the religion which I have established." The Protestant answers: "Of
course, I believe that thou art the Lord of heaven and earth, but I
believe only what I choose to believe;" thus defying the Almighty to
prescribe a religion for him. Protestants, therefore, live constantly in
violation of the first commandment.

They also transgress the second commandment of God, which says:
"Thou shalt not take the name of the Lord thy God in vain." By
this commandment God forbids all men to blaspheme him or any of
his saints, or to ridicule religion. Yet what is more common among
Protestants than to blaspheme Jesus Christ in his Mother and other
saints; what more common than to ridicule the religion of Christ
and its holy practices? Are not Protestant books, sermons, tracts,
and conversations, filled with abusive language, invectives, mockeries
against Christ, his religion and his saints?

Protestants also transgress the third commandment of God, which says: "Remember thou keep holy the Sabbath day." By this commandment God commands all men to worship him in the manner which he has prescribed. From the beginning of the world, God wished to be worshipped by the offering of sacrifices; but Protestants have done away with the worship of the sacrifice of the Mass, which Christ commanded to be offered up by his priests and all Christians. They refuse to give God the honor of adoration; that is, to honor him as the sovereign Lord of all creatures, and to acknowledge their entire dependence on him, by offering the sacrifice of the body and blood of his divine Son, Jesus Christ, in holy Mass. Instead of thus honoring and worshipping him, they blaspheme Christ by calling this holy sacrifice a superstitious ceremony or abominable idolatry, whilst their own worship is a false worship, which is an abomination in the sight of God.

Protestants transgress the fourth commandment, by refusing obedience to the lawful ecclesiastical superiors. They transgress the fifth commandment, by refusing to make use of the means of grace, —the sacraments,—to obtain God's grace, and preserve themselves in his holy friendship. They transgress the sixth and the ninth commandments, which forbid adultery, and even the desire to commit it. Jesus Christ says: "I say to you, that whosoever shall put away his wife, and shall marry another, committeth adultery; and he that shall marry her that is put away, committeth adultery." (Matthew xix, 9.) "No," says Protestantism to a married man, "you may put away your wife, get a divorce, and marry another."

God says to every man: "Thou shalt not steal." "No," said Luther to secular princes, "I give you the right to appropriate to yourselves the property of the Roman Catholic Church." And the princes, from that day to this, have been only too happy to profit by this pleasing advice.

Jesus Christ says: "Hear the Church." "No," says Protestantism, "do not hear the Church; protest against her with all your might." Jesus Christ says: "If anyone will not hear the Church, look upon him as a heathen and publican." "No," says Protestantism, "if anyone does not hear the Church, look upon him as an apostle, as an ambassador of God." Jesus Christ says: "The gates of hell shall not prevail against my Church." "No," says Protestantism, "'tis false: the gates of hell have prevailed against the Church for a thousand years and more." Jesus Christ has declared St. Peter, and every successor to St. Peter, —the pope, —to be his Vicar on earth. "No," says Protestantism, "the pope is Antichrist." Jesus Christ says: "My yoke is sweet, and my burden is light." (Matthew xi, 30.) "No," said Luther and Calvin, "it is impossible to keep the commandments." Jesus Christ says: "If thou wilt enter into life, keep the commandments." (Matthew xix, 17.) "No," said Luther and Calvin, "faith alone, without good works , is sufficient to enter into life everlasting." Jesus Christ says: "Unless you do penance, you shall all likewise perish." (Luke iii, 3.) "No," says Protestantism, "fasting and other works of penance are not necessary, in satisfaction for sin." Jesus Christ says: "This is my body." "No," said Calvin, "this is only the figure of Christ's body; it will become his body as soon as you receive it." ,

The Holy Ghost says in holy Scripture: "Man knoweth not whether he be worthy of love or hatred." (Eccl. ix, 1.) "Who can say, My heart is clean, I am pure from sin?" (Proverbs xx, 9); and "work out your salvation with fear and trembling." (Philippians ii, 12.) "No," said Luther and Calvin, "but whosoever believes in Jesus Christ is in the state of grace."

St. Paul says: "If I should have faith, so that I could remove mountains, and have not charity, I am nothing." (1 Corinthians xiii, 2.) "No," said Luther and Calvin, "faith alone is sufficient to save us."

St. Peter says that in the Epistles of St. Paul there are many things "hard to be understood, which the unlearned and unstable wrest, as also the other Scriptures, to their own perdition." (2 Epistle iii, 16.) "No," says Protestantism, "the Scriptures are very plain, and easy to be understood."

St. James says: "Is any man sick among you? Let him bring in the priests of the Church, and let them pray over him, anointing him with oil, in the name of the Lord." (Chapter v, 14.) "No," says Protestantism, "this is a vain and useless ceremony."

Protestants being thus impious enough to make liars of Jesus Christ, of the Holy Ghost, and of the apostles, need we wonder if they continually slander Catholics, telling and believing worse absurdities about them than the heathens did? What is more absurd than to preach that Catholics worship stocks and stones for gods; set up pictures of Jesus Christ, of the Blessed Virgin Mary, and Other saints, to pray to them, and put their confidence in them; that they adore a god of bread and wine; that their sins are forgiven by the priest, without repentance and amendment of life; that the pope or any other person can give leave to commit sin, or that for a sum of money the forgiveness of sins can be obtained? To these and similar absurdities and slanders, we simply answer: "Cursed is he who believes in such absurdities and falsehoods, with which Protestants impiously charge the children of the Catholic Church. All those grievous transgressions are another source of their reprobation."

But there are other reasons still, why Protestants cannot be saved. Jesus Christ says: "Except you eat the flesh of the Son of man, and drink his blood, you shall not have life in you." (John vi, 54.) Now,

Protestants do not receive the body and blood of our Lord, because their ministers are not priests, and consequently have no power from Jesus Christ to say Mass, in which, by the words of consecration, bread and wine are changed into the body and blood of Christ. It follows, then, clearly that they will not enter into life everlasting, and deservedly so, because they abolished the holy sacrifice of the Mass: and by abolishing that great sacrifice they robbed God the Father of the infinite honor which Jesus Christ renders him therein, and themselves of all the blessings which Jesus Christ bestows upon those who assist at this holy sacrifice with faith and devotion: "Wherefore the sin of the young men (the sons of Heli) was exceeding great before the Lord, because they withdrew men from the sacrifice of the Lord." (1 Kings ii, 17.) Now, God the Father cannot admit into heaven these robbers of his infinite honor; because, if those are damned who steal the temporal goods of their neighbor, how much more will those be damned who deprive God of his infinite honor, and their fellow men of the infinite spiritual blessings of the Mass!

Again, no man is saved who dies in the state of mortal sin, because God cannot unite himself to a soul in heaven who by mortal sin is his enemy. But Protestants are enemies of God, committing, as they do, other mortal sins besides those already mentioned; for, if it is a mortal sin for a Roman Catholic willfully to doubt only one article of his faith, it is also, most assuredly, a mortal sin for Protestants willfully to deny not only one truth, but almost all the truths revealed by Jesus Christ. On account of the sins of apostasy, blasphemy, slander, etc., they remain enemies of God, as long as they do not repent, and receive absolution of these sins. Jesus Christ assures us that those sins which are not forgiven by the absolution of his apostles or their successors, will not be forgiven: "Whose sins you retain, they are retained." (John xx, 22, 23.) But Protestants are unwilling to confess their sins to a Catholic bishop or a priest, who alone has power from Christ to forgive sins: "Whose sins you shall forgive, they are forgiven them." They generally have an utter aversion to confession; they die in their sins, and are lost; for sins, unrepented and unatoned for, stand t hrough all eternity.

Again, no grown person can enter the kingdom of heaven without good works. On the great day of judgment Jesus Christ will say to the wicked: "Depart from me, ye cursed, into everlasting fire. For I was hungry, and you gave me not to eat; I was thirsty, and you gave me not to drink," etc.(Matthew xxv, 41, 42.) It is true that many regular, naturally good Protestants practice good works, make long prayers, fast, give alms, and perform other works of natural virtue, all of which are, indeed, laudable actions. But all these works are destitute of one essential thing, viz., docility to faith, without which there is neither merit nor recompense. For merely natural virtues there are natural rewards. But works, to be meritorious of heaven, must be performed in the state of grace; they must proceed from, and be vivified by, divine faith, to deserve an eternal reward; for then it is that they proceed, as it were, from God himself, and from his divine Spirit, who lives in us, and urges us on to the performance of good works.

Hence, as faith without works is dead, so also works without faith are dead and cannot save the doer from destruction. Splendid, but barren works! apparently delicious fruit, but rotten within! In vain, then, shall they glory in these works. The Gospel will always tell them that he "who does not believe, is already judged." (John iii, 18.) The apostle will ever declare to them that "without faith it is impossible to please God." (Hebrews xi, 6.) Jesus Christ himself will ever command us to look upon "him as the heathen and the publican, who will not hear the Church" (Matthew xviii, 17), though otherwise he should be as severe in his life as an anchoret, as enlightened in his understanding as an angel. "In the Catholic Church," says St. Augustine, "there are both good and bad. But they who are separated from her, as long as they remain in their opinion against her, cannot be good; for, although a kind of laudable conversation seems to show forth some of them as good, the separation itself makes them bad, the Lord saying: 'He who is not with me is against me: and he who gathereth not with me, scattereth.'" (Ep. ccviii, n. 6, col. 1177.) What, then, will be the astonishment, sorrow, and despair of those who, void of faith, and separated from the Church, will one day present themselves before God, and, imagining to have heaped up treasures of merits, will appear in his sight with their hands empty?

In the history of the foundation of the Society of Jesus, in the Kingdom of Naples, is related the following story of a noble youth of Scotland, named William Ephinstone: He was a relative of the Scottish king. Born a heretic, he followed the false sect to which he belonged; but enlightened by divine grace, which showed him his errors, he went to France, where, with the assistance of a good Jesuit Father, who was also a Scotchman, he at length saw the truth, abjured heresy, and became a Catholic. He went afterward to Rome, joined the Society of Jesus, in which he died a happy death. When at Rome, a friend of his found him one day very much afflicted, and weeping. He asked him the cause, and the young man answered that in the night his mother had appeared to him, and said: "My son, it is well for thee that thou hast entered the true Church; I am already lost, because I died in heresy." (St. Liguori, "Glories of Mary.")

We read, in the Life of St. Rose of Viterbo, that she was inflamed with great zeal for the salvation of souls. She felt a most tender compassion for those who were living in heresy. To convince a certain lady, who was a heretic, that she could not be saved in her sect, and that it was necessary for salvation to die a true member of the Catholic

Church, she made a large fire, threw herself into it, and remained in it for three hours, without being hurt. This lady, together with many others, on witnessing the miracle, abjured their heresy, and became Cat holics.

When the Emperor Valens ordered that St. Basil the Great should go into banishment, God, in the high court of heaven, passed, at the same time, sentence against the emperor's only son, named Valentinian Galatus, a child then about six years old. That very night the royal infant was seized with a violent fever, from which the physicians were unable to give him the least relief; and the Empress Dominica told the emperor that this calamity was a just punishment of heaven for his banishing the bishop, on which account she had been disquieted by terrible dreams. Thereupon Valens sent for the saint, who was about to go into exile. No sooner had the holy bishop entered the palace, than the fever of the child began to abate. St. Basil assured the parents of the absolute recovery of their son, on condition that they would order him to be instructed in the Catholic faith. The emperor accepted the condition, St. Basil prayed, and the young prince was cured. But Valens, unfaithful to his promise, afterward allowed an Arian bishop to baptize the child. The young prince immediately relapsed and died. (Butler's "Lives of the Saints," June 14th.) By this miraculous cure of the child, God made manifest the truth of our religion; and by the sudden death of the child, which followed upon the heretical baptism, God showed in what abomination he holds those who profess heresy.

But is it not a very uncharitable doctrine to say that out of the Church there is no salvation? If we desire that all those who are not members of the Catholic Church should cease to deceive themselves as to the true character of their belief and propose to them considerations which may contribute to that result, it is certainly not from enmity to their persons, nor indifference to their welfare. As long as they remain victims of a delusion as gross as that which makes the Jew still cling to his abolished synagogue, and which only a miracle of grace can dispel, they will probably resent the counsels of their truest friends: but why do they take us for enemies? "The Christian," as Tertullian said, "is the enemy of no one," not even of his persecutors. He hates heresy because God hates it, but he has only compassion for those who are caught in its snare. Whether he exhorts or reproves them, he displays not malice, but charity. He knows that they are, of all men, the most helpless; and when his voice of warning is most vehement, he is only doing what the Church has done from the beginning. His voice is but the echo of hers. We are told that, before the Council of Nice, she had already condemned thirty-eight different heresies; and in every case she pronounced anathema upon those who held them. And she was as truly the mouthpiece of God in her judicial as in her teaching office.

The Church is, indeed, uncompromising in matters of truth. Truth is the honor of the Church. The Church is the most honorable of all societies. She is the highest standard of honor, because she judges all things in the light of God, who is the source of all honor. A man who has no love for the truth, a man who tells a willful lie or takes a false oath, is considered dishonored. No one cares for him; and it would be unreasonable to accuse one of intolerance or bigotry because he refuses to associate with a man who has no love for the truth. It would be just as unreasonable to accuse the Catholic Church of intolerance, or bigotry, or want of charity, because she excludes from her society, and pronounces anathema upon, those who have no regard for the truth, and remain willfully out of her communion.

If the Church believed that men could be saved in any religion whatever, or without any at all, it would be uncharitable in her to announce to the world that out of her there is no salvation. But, as she knows and maintains that there is but one faith, as there is but one God and Lord of all, and that she is in possession of that one faith, and that without that faith it is impossible to please God and be saved, it would be very uncharitable in her, and in all her children, to hide Christ's doctrine from the world. To warn our neighbor when he is in imminent danger of falling into a deep abyss, is considered an act of great charity. It is a greater act of charity to warn non-Catholics of the certain danger in which they are of falling into the abyss of hell, since Jesus Christ, and the apostles themselves, and all their successors, have always most emphatically asserted that out of the Church there is no s alvation.

Here it may be asked: Are all those who are out of the Church equally guilty in the sight of God? We answer: No; some are more guilty than others. It cannot be considered the personal fault, however great and terrible the misfortune, of any individual of the children of Adam, that our first parents sinned. So it is not the fault of those who were born and educated in any of the errors or negations of Protestantism, in its hundred various forms. Involuntary error is a misfortune to be pitied, a calamity to be deplored. Only when entered into, or persisted in, against light and knowledge, can it be considered a sin, or other than a sin of ignorance. There are persons who sometimes commit actions which, in themselves, are very wrong, but are not punishable in the sight of God, because they do not proceed from willful malice, as those who commit them are not aware in the least that by such actions God is offended. So there may be persons who live in infidelity or heresy without being in the least aware of it. Now such inculpable ignorance will, of course, not save them; but, if they fear God, and live up to their conscience, God, in his infinite mercy, will furnish them with the necessary means of salvation, even so as to send, if needed, an angel to instruct them in the Catholic faith, rather than let them perish through inculpable ignorance.

But there are others who are guilty in the sight of God. They are those who know the Catholic Church to be the only true Church, but do not embrace her faith, as also those who could know her, if they would candidlysearch, but who, through indifference, and other culpable motives, neglect to do so.

19. Would it be right to say that one who was not received into the Church before his death is damned?

No; because, in his last hour, such a one may receive the grace to die united to the Catholic Church.

It is not our business to say whether this or that one who was not received into the Church before his death is damned. What we condemn is the Protestant and the heathen system of religion, because they are utterly false; but we do not condemn any person—God alone is the judge of all. It is quite certain, however, that, if any of those who are not received into the Church before their death, enter heaven, —a lot which we earnestly desire and beg God to grant them,—they can only do so after undergoing a radical and fundamental change before death launches them into eternity. This is quite certain, for the reason, among others, that they are not one; and nothing is more indisputably certain than this, that there can be no division in heaven: "God is not the God of dissension," says St. Paul, "but of peace." He has never suffered the least interruption of union, even in the Church Militant no earth; most assuredly he will not tolerate it in the Church Triumphant. God most certainly will remain what he is. Non-Catholics, therefore, in order to enter heaven, must cease to be what they are, and become something which now they are not.

God, in his infinite mercy, may enlighten, at the hour of death, one who is not yet a Catholic, so that he may know and believe the necessary truths of salvation, be truly sorry for his sins, and die in such disposition of soul as is necessary to be saved. Such a one, by an extraordinary grace of God, ceases to be what he was; he dies united, at least, to the soul of the Church, as theologians call it.

With regard to Catholics, the case is quite different. No change need come upon them, except that which is implied in passing from the state of grace to the state of glory.

They will be one there, as they have been one here. For them the miracle of supernatural unity is already worked. That mark of God's hand is already upon them. That sign of God's election is already gravened upon their foreheads. Faith, indeed, will be replaced by sight, but this will be no real change, because what they see in the next world will be what they have believed in this. The same sacramental King (to borrow an expression of Father Faber), whom here they have worshipped upon the altar, will there be their everlasting portion. The same gracious Madonna who has so often consoled them in the trials of this life, will introduce her own children to the glories of the next. They will not, in that hour, have to "buy oil" for their lamps, for they are already kindled at the lamp of the sanctuary. No wedding-robe will have to be provided for them, for they received it long ago at the baptismal font and have washed away its stains in the tribunal of penance. The faces of the saints and angels will not be strange to them, for have they not been familiar with them from infancy as friends, companions, and benefactors? And being thus, even in this world, of the household of faith, and the family of God, not only no shadow of change need pass upon them, but to vary in one iota from what they now believe and practice, would simply cut them off from the communion of saints, and be the most overwhelming disaster which co uld befall them.

We have seen that there is no salvation possible out of the Roman Catholic Church. It is therefore very impious for one to think and to say that "every religion is good." To say every religion is good, is as much as to say: The devil is as good as God. Hell is as good as heaven. Falsehood is as good as truth. Sin is as good as virtue. It is impious to say, "I respect every religion." This is as much as to say: I respect the devil as much as God, vice as much as virtue, falsehood as much as truth, dishonesty as much as honesty, hell as much as heaven. It is impious to say, "It matters very little what a man believes, provided he be an honest man. Let such a one be asked whether or no the believes that his honesty and justice are as great as the honesty and justice of the Scribes and Pharisees. These were constant in prayer, they paid tithes according to the law, gave great alms, fasted twice in every week, and compassed sea and land to make a convert, and bring him to the knowledge of the true God. Now, what did Jesus Christ say of this justice of the Pharisees? "Unless," he says, "your justice shall exceed that of the Scribes and Pharisees, you shall not enter into the kingdom of heaven." (Matthew v, 20.) The righteousness of the Pharisees, then, must have been very defective in the sight of God. It was, indeed, nothing but an outward show and ostentation. They did good only to be praised and admired by men; but, within, their souls were full of impurity and malice. They were lewd hypocrites, who concealed great vices under the beautiful appearance of love for God, charity to the poor, and severity to themselves. Their devotion consisted in exterior acts, and they despised all who did not live as they did; they were strict in the religious observances of human traditions but scrupled not to violate the commandments of God. No wonder, then, that this Pharisaic honesty and justice were condemned by our Lord. To those, therefore, who say, "It matters little what a man believes, provided he be honest," we answer: "Your outward honesty, like that of the Pharisees , may be sufficient to keep you out of prison, but not out of hell. It should be remembered that there is a dishonesty to God, to one's own soul and conscience, as well as to one's neighbor."

You say, it is enough to be an honest man. What do you mean by an honest man? The term, honest man, is rather a little too general. Go, for instance, to that young man whose shameful secret sins are written on his hollow cheeks, in his dull, lack-luster eye: ask him if one can be an honest man who gratifies all his brutal, shameful passions. What will be his answer? "Why," he will say, "these natural follies and weaknesses do not hinder a man from being honest. To tell the truth, for instance, I am somewhat inclined that way myself, and yet I would like to see the man that would doubt my honesty."

Go to that covetous shopkeeper, who sells his goods as if they were of the finest quality; go to that tradesman, that mason, that bricklayer, or carpenter, who does not work even half as diligently when he is paid by the day as when he is paid by the job; go to these men that have grown rich by fraudulent speculation, by cheating the public or government; go to the employers that cheat the servant and the poor laborer: ask them if what they do, prevents them from being honest people, and they will answer you coldly that they are merely tricks of trade, shrewdness in business; that they do not by any means hinder one from being an honest man.

Go, ask that habitual drunkard, ask that man who has grown rich by selling liquor to drunkards: ask them whether these sins do not hinder them from being honest, and they will tell you, "By no means. They are honest men, very honest men."

Go, ask that man or that woman who sins against the most sacred laws of nature; go, ask that doctor who murders the poor helpless babe before it can see the blessed light of day: ask them if those who are guilty of such foul deeds are honest gentlemen, and they will tell you, with the utmost assurance, that such trifles do not hinder one from being a gentleman—from being a respectable lady!

True faith requires obedience, humility, and childlike simplicity; it excludes pride, self-will, clinging to our own ideas, and that unwillingness to obey which hurled the angels from heaven, and cast our first parents out of paradise. Faith is a duty which God requires of us, and unless we fulfil this duty sincerely, we can never enter the kingdom of heaven. One may say: "To submit to the yoke of faith is to submit to a spiritual and moral tyranny; it is to lose one's liberty." There is liberty, and there is license. To be the slave of vile passions, and seek to satisfy them always, and at any cost, is not true liberty. Surely God is free. But God cannot sin. It is, therefore, no mark of liberty to be under the power of sin; on the contrary, it is the very brand of slavery. The power of sin implies the possibility of becoming a slave of sin and the devil. Those, then, who are greatly under the power of sin, and so go to hell, cannot truly be called free men. They are blinded and brutalized by satisfying the promptings of their brute nature, and thus renounce their glorious freedom, to sell it for a bestial gratification. He only is truly free who wills and does what God wishes him to do for his everlasting happiness. Now, as we have seen, God wishes that all should be saved in the Roman Catholic Church. Those, therefore, who believe and do what the Church teaches do not lose their liberty; on the contrary, they enjoy true liberty, and make the proper use of it. Hence, the greater our power of will is, and the less difficulty we experience in following the teaching of the Church, the greater is our liberty. Accordingly, Catholics, who, live up to the teaching of the Church, enjoy greater liberty, and peace, and happiness, than Protestants and unbelievers, because they are the children of the light of truth, that leads them to heaven; whilst those who live out of the Church are the children of the darkness of error, which leads them, finally, into the abyss of hell.

If no one, then, can be saved except in the Roman Catholic Church, all those who are out of it are bound to become members of the Church. This is what common sense tells every non-Catholic. In worldly affairs, Protestants never presume to act without good advice. They never compromise their pecuniary interests or their lives, by becoming their own private interpreters and practitioners of law or medicine. Both the legal and the medical books are before them, written by modern authors, in clear and explicit language, but they have too much practical common-sense to attempt their interpretation. They prefer always to employ expert lawyers and physicians, and accept their interpretations, and act according to their advice. Now, every non-Catholic believes that every practical member of the Catholic Church will be saved. Hence, when there is question about eternal salvation and eternal damnation, a sensible man will take the surest way to heaven. It was this that decided Henry IV of France to abjure his errors. A historian relates that this king, having called before him a conference of the doctors of either Church, and seeing that the Protestant ministers agreed, with one accord, that salvation was attainable in the Catholic religion, immediately addressed a Protestant minister in the following manner: "Now, sir, is it true that people can be saved in the Catholic religion?" "Most assuredly it is, sire, provided they live up to it." "If that be so," said the monarch, "prudence demands that I should be of the Catholic religion, not of yours, seeing that in the Catholic Church I may be saved, a seven you admit; whereas, if I remain in yours, Catholics maintain that I cannot be saved. Both prudence and good sense tell me that I should follow the surest way, and so I propose doing." Some days after, the king made his abjuration at St. Denis. (Guillois, ii, 67.)

Christ assures us that the way to everlasting life is narrow and trodden by few. The Catholic religion is that narrow road to heaven. Protestantism, on the contrary, is that broad way to perdition trodden by so many. He who is content to follow the crowd, condemns himself by taking the broad way. A man says: "I would like to believe, but I cannot." You say you "cannot believe." But what have you done, what means have you employed, in order to acquire the gift of faith? If you have neglected the means, you show clearly that you do not desire the end.

God bestowed great praise upon his servant Job. He said of him that "he was a simple and upright man, fearing God and avoiding evil." (Job. i, 8.) There is nothing that renders a soul more acceptable to God than simplicity and sincerity of heart in seeking him. There is, on the other hand, nothing more detestable to him than a double-minded man, who does not walk sincerely with his God: "Woe to them that are of a double heart, . . . and to the sinner that goeth on the earth two ways." (Ecclus. ii, 14.) Such a man should not expect that the Lord will enlighten and direct him. Our Savior assures us that Ins heavenly Father makes himself known to the little ones, that is, to those who have recourse to him with a simple and sincere heart.

This sincerity and uprightness of heart with God are especially necessary for him who is in search of the true religion. We see around us numberless jarring sects, contradicting one another; we see the one condemning what the other approves, and approving what others condemn; we see some embracing certain divine truths, and others rejecting those truths with horror, as the doctrine of devils. Now common-sense tells everyone that both parties cannot be right; that the true religion cannot be on either side. Among such confusion of opinions, the mind is naturally at a loss how to discover that one true Church in whose bosom the truth is to be found.

In the search for truth, one must find immense difficulties. There is prejudice. It is the effect of early training, of life-long teaching, of reading, and of living in the world. It is the result of almost imperceptible impressions, and yet its force, as an obstacle, is such as in many cases to defy human efforts to remove it. It is like the snow which begins to fall, as the darkness sets in, on roof and road, in little flakes that come down silently all the night, and in the morning the branches bend, and the doors are blocked, and the traffic on road and rail is brought to a stand still.

There, again, is the favor of friends, the fear of what the world will say, worldly interest, and the like. All these will be set to work by the enemy of souls to blind the understanding, that it may not see the truth and to avert the will from embracing it. Nothing but a particular grace from heaven can enlighten the mind to perceive the light of truth through such clouds of darkness, and to strengthen the will with courage to embrace it, in spite of all these difficulties. It is, without doubt, the will of God, that "all men should be saved, and come to the knowledge of the truth" (1 Timothy ii, 4); but it is also the will of God that, in order to come to this knowledge, men must seek it with a sincere and upright heart, and this sincerity of heart must show itself in their earnest desire to know the truth: "Blessed are they that hunger and thirst after justice, for they shall be filled." Hence, they must labor diligently to find out the truth, using every means in their power for that purpose. Negligence of inquiry, and the evidence of our faith, are great, and therefore the ignorance of many must needs be highly sinful. Man's understanding was given to him, to enable him to embrace holy and salutary truths. Negligence in this is worthy of damnation; and as everything tends easily to its natural end, so our natural, intellectual virtue is nearer finding God than it is finding his contrary, for God is always ready to aid those who seek him with a good and honest heart: and thus we find that to Cornelius, a Pagan, yet living religiously, and fearing God, St. Peter was sent to convert him and all his family. God, says St. Thomas Aquinas, will send an angel to a man ignorant of the Christian law, but living up to his conscience, to instruct him in the Christian religion, rather then let him perish through inculpable ignorance.

There are laws to regulate man's will and affections, and so there are also laws to fix limits to his understanding— to determine what he should believe, and what he should not believe; and therefore, ignorance is damnable, for men ought to believe what they do not; and they ought curiously to inquire what are these laws. Whereas, the multitude run, with all their strength, to sin and death as their end, and it is not strange that they should find it.

The first and great cause of all these errors is negligence of inquiry; and the second is, aversion to believe what ought to be believed of God, and a hatred for the things that would enlighten and convert the soul. If men will not heed either holy words or miracles, it is not strange that they remain in error. They must study religion, with a sincere desire to find out the truth. If they wish to find out the truth, they must not appeal to the enemies of truth. They must consult those who are well instructed in their religion, and who practice it. They must consult the priest. He will explain to them the true doctrine of the Catholic Church. Moreover, sincerity of heart must show itself in a firm resolution to embrace the truth whenever it shall be found, and whatever it may cost the seeker. He must prefer it before every worldly consideration, and be ready to forfeit everything in this life: the affections of his friends, a comfortable home, temporal goods, and prospects in business, rather than deprive his soul of so great a treasure.

The New York Freeman's Journal, Sept. 2d, 1854, contains the following notice on the late General Thomas F. Carpenter. The words of this notice are written by ex-Governor Laurence. The general, when about to become a Catholic, made known his intention to a friend. The friend, of course, was surprised. He instanced the fearful results consequent upon a proceeding so unpopular, the loss of professional practice, the alienation of friends, the scoffs of the crowd, etc. "All such blessings," replied General Carpenter, "I can dispense with, all such insults I can despise, but I cannot afford to lose my immortal soul." The general spoke thus, because he knew, and firmly believed, what Jesus Christ has solemnly declared, to wit: "He who loveth father or mother more than me, is not worthy of me; and he that loveth son or daughter more than me, is not worthy of me" (Matthew x, 37); and as to the loss of temporal gain, he has answered: "What will it profit a man if he gain the whole world, and suffer the loss of his soul?" (Mark viii, 36.)

But would it not be enough for such a one to be a Catholic in heart only, without professing his religion publicly? No; for Jesus Christ has solemnly declared that "he who shall be ashamed of me and of my words, of him the Son of man shall be ashamed when he shall come in his majesty, and that of his Father, and of the holy angels." (Luke ix, 2 6.)

But might not such a one safely put off being received into the Church till the hour of death?

This would be to abuse the mercy of God, and, in punishment for this sin, to lose the light and grace of faith, and die a reprobate. In order to obtain heaven, we must be ready to sacrifice all, even our lives: "Fear ye not them," says Christ, "that kill the body, and are not able to kill the soul; but rather fear him that can destroy both soul and body in hell." (Matthew x, 28.)

How often do we meet with men who tell us that they would gladly become Catholics, but it is too hard to live up to the laws and maxims of the Church! They know very well that, if they become Catholics, they must lead honest and sober lives, they must be pure, they must respect the holy sacrament of marriage, they must check their sinful passions; and this they are unwilling to do: "Men love darkness rather than light," says Jesus Christ, "because their deeds are evil." Remember the well-known proverb: "There are none so deaf as those that will not hear."

They are kept back from embracing the faith, because they know that the truths of our religion are at war with their sinful inclinations. It is not surprising that these inclinations should revolt against immolation. The prudence of the flesh understands and feels that it loses all, if the truths of faith are listened to and taken for the rule of conduct; that it must renounce the unlawful enjoyments of life, must die to the world and to itself, and bear the mortification of Jesus Christ in its body.

At the mere thought of this crucifixion of the flesh and its concupiscence, imposed on everyone who would belong to the Savior, the whole animal man is troubled. Selflove suggests a thousand reasons to delay at least the sacrifices that affright them. The prudence of the flesh, having the ascendency, obscures the simplest truths, attracts and flatters the powers of the soul; and when, afterward, faith endeavors to interpose its authority, it finds the understanding prejudiced, the will overcome or weakened, the heart all earthly-minded ; and hard, indeed, is it for faith to reduce the soul to its dominion. Those who listen to the prudence of the flesh will never become Catholics.

Finally, those who seek the truth must show their sincerity of heart in fervently and frequently praying to God that they may find the truth, and the right way that leads to it. Faith is not a mere natural gift; it is not an acquired virtue or habit; it is something altogether supernatural. The right use of the natural faculties can, indeed, prepare one to receive faith; but true faith,—that is, to believe, with an unwavering conviction, in the existence of all those things which God has made known,— is a supernatural gift,—a gift which no one can have of himself; it is the free gift of God: "For by grace you are saved, through faith, and that not of yourselves, for it is the gift of God." (Ephesians ii, 8.) God is so great and good, that we cannot merit and possess this good by anything we may do. Now, it is by the gift of faith that we have in some measure a glimpse of all that God is, and that consequently we attach ourselves to this supreme good and behold, we are saved! We can say with David, in the truest sense, that in enlightening us the Lord saves us: "The Lord is my light, and my salvation." (Psalm xxvi, 1.) Hence it is evident that this gift is a free gift of God, without the least merit on our part. When this light or grace shines upon the understanding, it enlightens the understanding, so as to render it most certain of the truths which are proposed to it. But this mere knowledge of the truth is not as yet the full gift of faith. St. Paul says (Romans i, 2) that the heathens knew God, but they would not obey him, and consequently their knowledge did not save them. You may convince a man that the Catholic Church is the true Church, but he will not, on that account, become a Catholic. Our Savior himself was known by many, and yet he was followed only by few. Faith, then, is something more than knowledge. Knowledge is the submission of the understanding to truth; but faith implies also the submission of the will to the truth. It is for this reason that the light or grace of faith must also move the will, because a good will also belongs to faith, since no one can believe unless he is willing to believe. It is for this reason that faith is also rewarded by God, and infidelity punished: "He that believeth and is baptized shall be saved; but he that believeth not shall be condemned." (Mark xvi, 16.) God will never refuse to bestow this gift of faith upon those who seek the truth with a sincere heart, use their best endeavors to find it, and sincerely pray for it with confidence and perseverance. Witness Clovis, the heathen King of the Franks. When he, together with his whole army, was in the greatest danger of being defeated by the Alemanni, he prayed as follows: "Jesus Christ, thou of whom Clotilde (the king's Christian wife) has often told me that thou art the Son of the living God, and that thou gives aid to the hard-pressed, and victory to those who trust in thee! I humbly crave thy powerful assistance. If thou grant me the victory over my enemies I will believe in thee, and be baptized in thy name; for I have called upon my gods in vain. They must be impotent, as they cannot help those who serve them. Now I invoke thee, desiring to believe in thee; do, then, deliver me from the hands of my adversaries!"

No sooner had he uttered this prayer than the Alemanni were panic-stricken, took to flight, and soon after, seeing their king slain, sued for peace. Thereupon Clovis blended both nations, the Franks and the Alemanni, together, returned home, and became a Christian.

Witness F. Thayer, an Anglican minister. When as yet in great doubt and uncertainty about the truth of his religion, he began to pray as follows:

"God of all goodness, almighty and eternal Father of mercies, and Savior of mankind! I implore thee, by thy sovereign goodness, to enlighten my mind, and to touch my heart, that, by means of true faith, hope, and charity, I may live and die in the true religion of Jesus Christ. I confidently believe that, as there is but one God, there can be but one faith, one religion, one only path to salvation; and that every other path opposed thereto can lead but to perdition. This path, O my God! I anxiously seek after, that I may follow it, and be saved. Therefore, I protest, before thy divine majesty, and I swear by all thy divine attributes, that I will follow the religion which thou shalt reveal to me as the true one, and will abandon, at whatever cost, that wherein I shall have discovered errors and falsehood. I confess that I do not deserve this favor for the greatness of my sins, for which I am truly penitent, seeing they offend a God who is so good, so holy, and so worthy of love; but what I deserve not, I hope to obtain from thine infinite mercy; and I beseech thee to grant it unto me through the merits of that precious blood which was shed for us sinners by thine only Son, Jesus Christ our Lord, who liveth and reigneth, etc. Amen."

God was not slow to hear so sincere and fervent a prayer, and Thayer became a Catholic. Let anyone who is as yet groping in the darkness of infidelity and error, pray in the same manner, and the God of all light and truth will bestow upon him the gift of faith in a high degree. It is human to fall into error, devilish to remain in it, and angelical to rise from it, by embracing the truth which leads to God, by whom it has been revealed and is preserved in his Church.

20. Will all Catholics be saved?

No: those Catholics only will be saved who believe and practice what the Church teaches.

We teach, indeed, and we firmly believe, that there is no salvation out of the Catholic Church; yet we do not teach that all who are members of the Catholic Church will be saved. Certainly in our cities and large towns, nay, even in small villages of our great country, may be found many so-called liberal or nominal Catholics, who are no credit to their religion, to their spiritual mother, the Church. Subjected as they were, in the land of their birth, to the restraints imposed by Protestant or quasi-Protestant governments, they feel, on coming here, that they are loosed from all restraint; and forgetting the obedience that they owe to their pastors, to the prelates whom the Holy Ghost has placed over them, they become insubordinate, and live more like non-Catholics than Catholics. The children of these are, to a great extent, shamefully neglected, and suffered to grow up without sufficient moral and religious instruction, and to become the recruits of our vicious population. This is certainly to be deplored, but can easily be explained without prejudice to the truth and holiness of the Catholic religion, by adverting to the condition to which those individuals were reduced before coming to this country; to their disappointments in a strange land; to their exposure to new and unlooked-for temptations; to the fact that they were by no means the best of Catholics, even in their native countries; to their poverty, destitution, ignorance, insufficient culture, and a certain natural shiftlessness and recklessness, as well as to the great lack of Catholic schools, churches, and fervent priests. As low and degraded as this class of the Catholic population may be, they are not so low as the corresponding class of non-Catholics in every nation; at the worst, there is always some germ that, with proper care, may be nursed into life, that may blossom and bear fruit. Their mother, the Church, never ceases to warn them to repent, and be cleansed from their sins by the sacrament of penance. If they do not heed the voice of their mother, but continue to live in sin to the end of their lives, their condemnation will be greater than that of those who were born to an inheritance of error, and whose minds have never been penetrated by the light of truth: "That servant," says Jesus Christ, "who knew the will of his Lord, and did not according to his will, shall be beaten with many stripes. But he that knew not, and did things worthy of stripes, shall be beaten with few stripes. And unto whomsoever much is given, of him much shall be required; and to whom they have committed much, of him they will demand the more." (Luke xii, 47, 48.) "Woe to thee, Corozain, woe to thee, Bethsaida; for if in Tyre and Sidon had been wrought the mighty works that have been wrought in you, they would have done penance long ago, sitting in sackcloth and ashes. But it will be more tolerable for Tyre and Sidon at the judgment than for you; and thou, Capharnaum, which art exalted unto heaven, thou shalt be thrust down to hell." (Luke x, 13-15.) To know, then, and to believe the Catholic doctrine, —the will of God, —is one thing, and to live up to it is another. Hence, "Not the hearers of the law are just before God, but the doers of the law shall be justified." (Romans ii, 13.) Holy Scripture compares the true faith, sometimes to a buckler, and sometimes to a sword. The buckler protects him only who covers himself with it: and a sword, to be useful to repel an enemy, must be drawn from the scabbard. So it is not mere faith, but its practice, which constitutes its merit, and strength, and reward. The Gospel brought light and death: light to those who practice it, and death to those who neglect its practice. "From the days of John the Baptist until now," says our Lord, "the kingdom of heaven suffereth violence, and the violent bear it away." (Matthew xi, 12.) The difference between the practical and the lukewarm Christian is simply this: the latter regards faith as a matter of fact, but without its consequences, or practical part. He remembers, it is true, from time to time, the great truths of religion: death, judgment, heaven and hell; but he remembers these and othe r truths, and his duties, only in a superficial manner; he never reflects seriously on them, and for this reason he is never touched by them. No wonder if he continues to walk on the broad road to hell and is lost. But the practical Christian always tries to walk on the narrow road to heaven. He constantly meditates upon the sacred truths of his religion. Everywhere he carries with him their wholesome impression. The truths of faith animate him in all the details of life. He has for his principle of action the Holy Ghost, —the Spirit of Jesus Christ. It is no more he who lives; it is Jesus Christ who lives in him. Accordingly, he judges of the things of this world in the knowledge which Jesus Christ has given us in their regard; that is, he judges of them even as Jesus Christ himself judges of them. Hence it is that he fears only that which faith teaches him to fear. He desires only those things which faith tells him to wish for; he hopes only for that which faith teaches him to hope for. He loves, or he hates, or he despises, all that faith teaches him to love, or to hate, or to despise. What does he say of the riches of this world? He says, with Jesus Christ: "Blessed are the poor in spirit, for theirs is the kingdom of heaven" (Matthew v, 3); and, "Woe to you that are rich, for you have your consolation." (Luke vi, 24.)

What does he say of the honors of this world? He says, with Jesus Christ: "Woe to you when men shall bless you." (Luke vi, 26.)

What does he say of the wisdom of this world? He says, with St. Paul: "The wisdom of this world is foolishness with God." (1 Corinthians iii, 19.) And with Jesus Christ, he says: "Unless you become as little children, you shall not enter the kingdom of heaven."

What judgment does he pass upon the pleasures of this world? He says, with Jesus Christ: "Woe to you that now laugh, for you shall mourn and weep." (Luke vi, 25.) "Watch ye, therefore, because you know not at what hour the Lord will come." (Matthew xxiv, 42.)

What judgment does he pass upon old age! With the Holy Ghost, he says: "Venerable old age is not that of long time, nor counted by the number of years, but a spotless life is old age." (Wisdom iv, 8.)

What does he say of the trials, persecutions, and injustices of this world? He says, with Jesus Christ: "Blessed shall ye be when men shall hate you, and when they shall separate you, and shall reproach you, and cast out your name as evil, for the Son of man's sake. Be glad in that day and rejoice, for behold your reward is great in heaven." (Luke vi, 22.)

He watches and prays. He watches over his soul, that no sinful thought may enter there; and should it enter unawares, he casts it out instantly. He watches over his heart, that no sinful affection may possess it. He watches over his eyes, that they may not gaze on any pictures, books or other objects, that could soil the purity of his soul. He watches over his ears, that they may not listen to any immodest words, or words of double meaning. He watches over his tongue and remembers that his tongue has been sanctified in holy communion, by touching the virginal flesh and blood of Jesus Christ. He watches over his whole body; for he knows that the body of the good Christian is the temple of the Holy Ghost, consecrated in baptism, and that he who desecrates a holy temple is accursed of God. He is watchful day and night, and avoids the occasions of sin, —those persons and places which might be to him an occasion of sin.

He also prays often to Jesus. He knows that Jesus is a jealous God, who commands us to call upon him, especially in the hour of temptation, and to receive him often in holy communion. He prays to Mary, the mother of faith, the lovely standard-bearer of all the elect. The very name of Mary is sweet balm to him, which heals and fortifies the soul. The very thought of Mary's purity is a check upon his passions—a fragrant rose that puts to flight the foul spirit of uncleanness.

Thus he thinks, judges, and acts according to the truths of the Gospel, or the principles of Jesus Christ; and it is thus that he lives by faith, as St. Paul says. Faith is the life of the just man. It is the life of his intellect, by the truths which enlighten him; it is the life of his heart, by the sentiments of justice and holiness which it imparts; it is the life of his works, which it renders meritorious for all eternity; and this happy life is obtained and enjoyed in the Church Militant of Christ alone—in the One Holy Roman Catholic and Apostolic

Church, "which Christ so took unto himself, as to make it a partaker of his own divinity. He, therefore, who confesses in God this holy Church is so united to Christ, as to be translated into the whole glory of his divinity—the body being united to its head; the Bride (Church) to her Bridegroom, Jesus Christ." (St. Peter Chrysologus, Serm. 57, 58 a nd 60.)

21. What do we believe when we say, I believe the holy Catholic Church?

We believe: 1, that the holy Catholic Church alone is the true Church of Christ; 2, that she is infallible in her teaching, and endless in her duration; 3, that out of the Catholic Church there is no salvation.

It is now nearly nineteen centuries since the Roman Catholic Church was established by Christ. Ever since that time she has been like a "city set upon a hill, which cannot be hid." She can be seen by all. She can be known to all by the marks of unity, holiness, Catholicity and Apostolicity, which are indelibly stamped upon her. She is "one body," living under one Head; she is "one sheepfold under one Shepherd;" she is a kingdom under one King; she is an ark or ship commanded by one Captain; she is built on an immovable rock, which is Peter: she is possessed of the rights of Jesus Christ; she is the infallible teacher of the doctrines of Jesus Christ; she exercises the authority of Jesus Christ; she is the faithful guardian of the spiritual treasures of Jesus Christ: she lives by the life and spirit of Jesus Christ; she is guided and protected by Jesus Christ; she speaks, she gives orders and commands, she makes concessions, prohibitions, and definitions, she looses and binds, in the name of Jesus Christ.

The Church is the salt of the earth, which preserves the world from corruption; she is the guide of men, to prevent them from falling into the pitfalls of Satan; she is the light of the world, to reveal to mankind the false maxims which are gnawing at their lives, and the fallacies which are undermining their happiness; she is the remedy for all ills, and the fountain of all blessings; she can never give up the work for which Jesus Christ has established her; she has Christ's promises: "I will give you the spirit of faith;" "I will be with you always;" "The gates of hell shall not prevail against thee;" "Whatsoever you shall bind on earth shall be bound in heaven, and whatsoever you shall loose on earth shall be loosed in heaven;" "He that heareth you heareth me;" "If any man will not hear the Church, let him be as the pagan and a publican;" "The Church is the pillar and foundation of the truth."

From the time of the apostles the true followers of Christ have been called Catholics. The meaning of this appellation has always been that they belonged to the One Holy Catholic Apostolic and Roman Church. The term "Catholic" has always distinguished them from every heretical sect. They were known by this term in every part of the world. Within the few last years, however, certain persons have arisen who are not satisfied with the name of Catholic. Hence they call themselves "Liberal Catholics." If asked in what they differ from Catholics, they answer: "Our motto is: Catholic with the pope, but liberal with the government."

Liberal Catholics falsely assert "that it is a mistake to protect and foster religion; because religion," they say, "will flourish much better if left alone; that the world has entered a new phase, and has begun to run a new course, and consequently the Church should accommodate herself to the spirit of the age; that religion has nothing to do with politics; that it has to do only with the private lives of men; that religion must keep inside the Church—that it is meant for Sundays alone; that we must be generous in our religious feelings toward non-Catholics; that a Catechism, therefore, in which every truth taught by the Church is set forth in its full bearing, is not fit to be put in the hands of our children, because it is calculated to repel the children of non-Catholics, and alienate their feelings, and to make religious fanatics of our good children," and the like. A Liberal Catholic, therefore, is a compound of true and false principles. He has two consciences: one for his public, and another for his private life. The motto, "Catholic with the pope, but liberal with the government," has for its basis the infidel doctrine of the separation of the Church from the State; of the spiritual from the temporal,—a doctrine condemned by Pius IX, in the fifty-fifth proposition of the Syllabus. This doctrine tends to put the State above the Church, as if the State were the omnipotent ruler of all things, the teacher of truth, the fountain of right, the source of law, and the interpreter of faith. In the eightieth proposition of the Syllabus, all the false principles of Liberalism, of progress, and of modern civilization, are declared to be irreconcilable with the Catholic faith.

On the 18th of June 1871, Pope Pius IX, in replying to a French deputation headed by the Bishop of Nevers, spoke as follows: "My children, my words must express to you what I have in my heart. That which afflicts your country, and prevents it from meriting the blessings of God, is the mixture of principles: I will speak out, and not hold my peace. That which I fear is not the Commune of Paris, those miserable men, those real demons of hell, roaming upon the face of the earth—no, not the Commune of Paris; that which I fear is Liberal Catholicism. ... I have said so more than forty times, and I repeat it to you now, through the love that I bear you. The real scourge of France is Liberal Catholicism, which endeavors to unite two principles, as repugnant to each Other as fire and water. My children, I conjure you to abstain from those doctrines which are destroying you. ... If this error be not stopped, it will lead to the ruin of religion and of

France." In a brief, dated July 9, 1871, to Mgr. Segur, the Holy Father says: "It is not only the infidel sects who are conspiring against the Church and society that the Holy See has often reproved, but also those men who, granting that they act in good faith, and with upright intentions, yet err in caressing liberal doctrines." On July 28, 1873, his Holiness thus expressed himself: "The members of the Catholic Society of Quimper certainly run no risk of being turned away from their obedience to the Apostolic See by the writings and efforts of the declared enemies of the Church; but they may glide down the incline of those so-called liberal opinions which have been adopted by many Catholics, otherwise honest and pious, who, by the influence of their religious character, may easily exercise a powerful ascendency over men, and lead them to very pernicious opinions. Tell, therefore, the members of the Catholic Society that, on the numerous occasions on which we have censured those who hold literal opinions, we did not mean those who hate the Church, whom it would have been useless to reprove, but those whom we have just described. Those men preserve and foster the hidden poison of liberal principles, which they sucked as the milk of their education, pretending that those principles are not infected with malice, and cannot interfere with religion; so they instill this poison into men's minds, and propagate the germs of those perturbations by which the world has for a long time been vexed."

A Liberal Catholic, then, is no true Catholic. The word Catholic is no vain and empty word. To be a true Catholic means to hold most firmly all those truths which Christ and his apostles have taught, which the Catholic Church has always proclaimed, which the saints have professed, which the popes and councils have defined, and which the Fathers and Doctors of the Church have defended. He who denies but one of those truths, or hesitates to receive one of them, is not a Catholic. He claims to exercise the right of private judgment in regard to the doctrine of Christ, and therefore he is a heretic. The true Catholic knows and believes that there can be no compromise between God and the devil, between truth and error, between orthodox faith and heresy. St. Stephen, the first martyr, was no compromiser. When accused of being a follower of Jesus of Nazareth, he, in his turn, accused his enemies of being the murderers of Christ. All the holy martyrs of the Church were no compromisers. Being charged by the heathens with the folly of worshipping and following a crucified God, they, in their turn, charged the heathens with the impiety of worshipping creatures, and following the devil. Why is our Holy Father, Pope Pius IX, a prisoner? It is because he is not, and cannot be, a compromiser. Why are, at this time, so many bishops and priests exiled or in prison? It is because they are no compromisers. Why is the Catholic Church persecuted in Germany and other parts of the world? It is because God, by means of persecution, purifies his Church from liberal or compromising Catholics. And as there are so many liberal Catholics in this country, persecution must come to separate them from the Church.

The good Catholic knows and understands that the Catholic Church never has required, nor will require, a particular form of civil government; for she has lived with the Venetian aristocracy, with the Swiss democracy, with the mixed aristocracy and democracy of Genoa, with the British and the united States constitutions, and with many absolute monarchies. But he knows, at the same time, that no form of government, no times and circumstances, can change the doctrine and constitution of the Church, because they are divine, immutable, and everlasting. The good Catholic, therefore, is always in readiness to obey, in all things, the true Spouse of Christ our Lord, the holy Roman Catholic Church. The well-instructed Catholic knows that between Jesus Christ and his Spouse, the Church, there is but one and the same

Spirit, who governs and directs us all to our salvation,— that same Spirit and Lord who one day gave the law on Mount Sinai, and who now rules and governs the holy Church. This firm adhesion to every truth of the Church distinguishes the true Catholic from the Liberal Catholic, as well as from all Protestants, from all schismatics, from all heretics. When Protestants abandoned the Church, the guardian of divine truth, they gave themselves up to hundreds of errors. Good Catholics, on the contrary, keeping, as they do, in the footsteps of the Church, and humbly submitting to all her doctrines, retain within themselves the principle of truth and of divine certainty. They feel assured that what the Church orders, is ordered by Jesus Christ; and that what the Church forbids, is also forbidden by Jesus Christ.

The principle of heresy is the principle of rebellion against the Church, and against every lawful authority on earth. The principle of the Church, on the contrary, is to be submissive to every lawful authority. The essential principle of politics and of life is ardently to love the Church, profoundly to revere the Church, unhesitatingly to submit to the Church, and to be most closely united with the Church. Our Lord asks of us no other submission; he requires of us no other faith than that which the Church teaches. His will and his truth are made known in the Church. As he and his Father are one, so also he and his Church are one. No one can, in truth, call God his Father, who does not look upon the Church as his mother.

In the Church alone there are certainty and security against error. Around this Rock we behold nothing but raging tempests, nothing but disastrous shipwrecks, indifference to religion, negation of all worship, the abomination of atheism and immorality, derision of holy things, a fanatic pietism, a delirious religiousness, rationalism, or the denial of all revelation and of everything supernatural. Every non-Catholic who earnestly seeks to learn what he is to believe, everyone who yearns to obtain certainty in religious matters, must sooner or later turn to the Church as the only source of certainty, the only guardian of the true religion, the only fountain of true peace and happiness in life and in death.

There are many noble-hearted souls created by God for a high purpose—to shine amid the angels throughout all eternity. Their sensibilities are so keen that they seem born only to suffer and weep. Their path to heaven is, indeed, a path of thorns. Their griefs and yearnings are such that, but few can understand them. God help these noble souls if they are deprived of the strength and consolation of the Catholic Church! Out of the Church they must bear their anguish alone. In the hour of happiness they were told that religion would console them in the hour of sorrow. And now the hour of sorrow has come, whither shall they turn for strength and consolation? To books—to the Bible? Books are cold and wearisome; their words are dead. Oh, how they envy the penitent Magdalen, who could sit at the feet of Jesus, and hear from his blessed lips the sweet words of pardon and peace! They turn to God in prayer, but God answers them not by the Urim and Thummim; and, in their doubt and loneliness, they envy even the Jews of old. In vain do they listen to the voice of God, because God has appointed a voice to speak and answer in his name; but that voice is only within the shepherd's fold, the Roman Catholic Church; and they are kept without the fold by cruel enemies, where the voice of the shepherd cannot reach them.

How different it is with the faithful Catholic soul! Try to call to mind some virtuous friend of yours; try to imagine one who is learned and pious, devoting his whole life, not to the care of a family, but solely to the service of God; imagine such a one ever ready to aid you in your necessities, spiritual and even temporal, ever wise in giving counsel, gentle in reproving, clear in teaching, and powerful in word and deed; imagine that such a one were your friend,—your intimate friend,—how great would be your happiness!

Imagine, moreover, that this kind, trustworthy friend is appointed by God himself to be your constant guide and director; imagine him bound by the most sacred oath never to reveal, even by word or look, any secret you may confide to him; imagine, moreover, that this friend has received from God the power to forgive every sin that you confess to him with true contrition,— imagine all this, and you will have what every Catholic has in the priest of his Church. The priest, invested as he is by the Church with her divine powers, stands conspicuous in the midst of his people. He has, however, not received his extraordinary powers for himself, he has received them for the benefit of the people; he is to live, not for himself, no, he is to live for the people; he is the companion of their hardships; he is the soother of their afflictions, the guardian of their interests; he is the trustee of their hearts, the sentinel of their death-beds. Hence the good Catholic is accustomed, even from his childhood, to communicate to his confessor every trial and temptation that disturbs his peace of heart. He goes to his confessor for consolation in the hour of darkness and sorrow; he asks his advice when in doubt; he consults him in every important undertaking. Our Lord Jesus Christ promised his beloved disciples that, though he would quit the earth, yet he would not leave them "orphans"—he would send them the Spirit of Truth to be their comforter. Now this divine promise was ratified, and even in a great measure fulfilled, when, on Easter Sunday night, Jesus appeared to his apostles, and gave them the Holy Ghost, saying: "Receive ye the Holy Ghost. Whosesoever sins you forgive, they are forgiven them; and whosesoever sins you retain, they are retained." At that solemn moment Jesus constituted his priests fathers of the faithful, from whom they were to receive the spirit of grace and consolation, even to the end of time.

The same divine hand which poured such wonderful affection into the heart of the mother, fills the heart of the good priest with divine charity, and teaches him to adapt his treatment to the spiritual wants of his penitent. The priest feels for his penitent as an earthly father feels for his child; and as a spiritual father, he judges and decides according as he thinks it is best for the eternal welfare of the penitent.

To the faithful Catholic soul, the portals of the Catholic Church, his most tender mother, stand ever open. Hither she may come as to a healing fountain, whose waters ever flow. Here she may lave her burning brow; here she may drink of the cooling stream and allay the feverish anguish of her soul. Here Jesus himself, the dearest of friends, speaks to her by the mouth of him to whom he has given the Holy Ghost, —the spirit of consolation.

Mrs. Moore, a very intelligent lady of Edinton, North Carolina, and a convert to our holy faith, said to her Protestant children on her death-bed: "O my children, there is such hope, such comfort in our holy religion! When I was so near death, and believed I should never see you again, my soul was filled with anguish. When I thought I was so soon to, meet my God, I feared; but when I had made my confession to his own commissioned minister, and received absolution in the name of the Holy Trinity, death was divested of every sting. Each day I thank God more and more that he has given me grace to break the ties that kept me from the Church. I have never looked back with regret, and, in fact, I wonder why I could ever have been anything but a Catholic."

Go to the sick-bed; draw near the bedside of that poor wretch whom everyone has forsaken; ask him who is the consoling angel that pours upon his weary heart the balm of hope and consolation, and he will tell you it is the Roman Catholic priest. About twenty years ago, when the French troops were encamped around Gallipolis, the cholera burst suddenly upon them. They were unprepared for that terrible visitor. Father Gidriot, S. J., was alone in an army of ten thousand men. "I was obliged," says he, "to hear their confessions on my knees, and stooping by their couches. Indeed, I learned then that, to save souls for Jesus Christ, it is necessary to undergo, with him, the double agony of mind and body. Yet my greatest trial was my loneliness. I was alone; I had not had the consolation of confession for six weeks past; everybody died around me, and, should I be taken sick, there was none to assist me in my dying hour. But God, in his mercy, preserved me, that I might attend to the wants of souls so well prepared. The trials were certainly great, but great were also the consolations. Whenever I entered those places of desolation, I was hailed from all parts—'Chaplain, here! come here to me! Make haste to reconcile me to God! I have only a few moments to live!' Some would press my hand to their hearts, and say, with grateful feelings: 'How lucky for us that you are here! Were you not with us, who would console us in our last moments?'"

Enter the dark and moldy dungeon where the unhappy prisoner pines away in weary captivity; ask him who it is that lightens his chains, and makes his prison walls look less dreary, and he will tell you it is the priest of the Catholic Church.

Go upon the scaffold where the wretched criminal is about to expiate his crime. Who is it that stands at his side, and strips death of its terrors? It is again the priest. With one hand the priest shows the dying man the cross, the hope of the repentant sinner, and with the other he points to heaven, that blessed home where the weary find rest.

In 1851, a murder was committed near Paris, in France. A captain of the carabineers, an excellent officer, beloved by all, going, as usual, the rounds of the stables, had reprimanded one of the troopers whose conduct had not been very regular. The latter made no reply, but turned away with apparently a calm countenance, and went up to the messroom. There he loaded one of his horse-pistols, and, going back to the stable, approached his captain, and, with a deadly aim, discharged the arm against the loins of the officer.

The unfortunate man fell, weltering in blood. They took him up, carried him to his room, and the surgeons pronounced the wound mortal. In fact, the poor captain breathed his last a few hours after, in the arms of his old mother, in the midst of horrible sufferings, endured heroically, and with sentiments of faith and charity truly admirable. He had made his confession with great piety, had received the blessed sacrament, and in imitation of his divine Master praying on the cross for his crucifiers, had pardoned his murderer, and begged for his pardon with the most touching and pressing appeal.

The murderer had been arrested on the spot, and transferred to the prison in Paris. There he was abandoned by all, except by the priest. Two or three days after the deed had been committed, the priest went to see the trooper for the first time, in the cell of the military prison. He encouraged him to hope in the mercy of God, and to prepare himself for a good confession, and to accept death in expiation for his crime. The poor criminal was touched by the words of the priest and said: "I have been the victim of a moment of fury and insanity. It was a punishment from God, whom I had abandoned. Had I always prayed as I do now, I should not have come to this pass. My father said to me often: 'Fear God, and pray to him; he alone is good, all the rest are nothing!' But it is so hard to do so at the regiment; we are always surrounded by young men who say nothing but what is bad." When he heard that he was sentenced to death, he exclaimed: "The sentence is just; to appeal would be going against the goodness of God. They would show me a mercy that I do not wish for, because the punishment must be undergone. I must atone for what I have done. My hopes are no longer here below; I have only God now to look to.

He is now everything to me; in him alone do I trust; I feel quite calm; I feel no rebellion in my heart; I am perfectly resigned to the will of God."

Now, what brought about that calmness, that happiness, in this poor prisoner? It was his sincere confession, which the priest was kind enough to hear; it was holy communion, which the priest brought to him several times; in a word, it was the charity of the priest, who often went to see him in his prison, in order to console him, and to inspire him with great confidence in the mercy of God.

During the three hours and a half of the drive to the place of execution, he never lost his calmness; God was with him in the person of the priest, who accompanied him to the Savory Plains, where he was to be shot. What a touching spectacle, to behold, on a wagon, a tall man, the culprit, followed by the priest of God; to see how the priest was even paler than the culprit; and to see them walking side by side, you would think that he was the one to be shot!

The expression of the culprit's countenance was great calmness and resignation: his eyes betrayed at once sorrow and hope. He seemed to pray with fervor. There was no sadness in his looks; there could even be seen the reflection of a certain inward joy. He listened, with love and deep attention, to the words addressed to him by the minister of Jesus Christ. When the priest said to him, "Our Lord is between us two; my poor child, we are always well when the good Savior is with us," he replied: "Oh, yes, my heart is perfectly happy! I did not think I should tell you, but I feel as if I was going to a wedding. God has permitted all this for my good, to save my soul. I feel so much consoled, thinking that my poor captain died a good Christian! I am going to see him: he is praying for me now. My God has saved me; I feel that he will have mercy on me. He ascended Calvary, carrying his cross; I accompany him. I shall not resist whatever they wish to do with me—tie me or bandage my eyes. Ah, the poor soldiers are lost because they do not listen to you priests. Without you, without religion, the whole world would be lost!"

When they drove by the barracks, where he had committed the murder, he offered a prayer for his captain. "I can't conceive how I could have done it! I had no ill-will against him! Could the commission of a sin save me from being shot, I would not do it: I think so now. I have nothing to keep me here; I am going to see God!"

When they had arrived at the place of execution, the priest and the culprit alighted. An officer read the sentence. The culprit replied: "I acknowledge the justice of my punishment, I am sorry for what I have done, I beg of God to pardon me; I love him with all my heart!" Then he knelt, the priest gave him the crucifix to kiss, for the last time. "My father," he said, with feeding expression, — "my father, I place my soul within your hands: I unite my death with that of my Savior, Jesus. Farewell! farewell!" The priest embraced him once more. Then, with his arms extended in the form of a cross, the culprit inclined his head, and awaited his death. The priest retired to pray at some distance. One minute after, human justice had been satisfied, and the soul of the unfortunate soldier, purified and transformed by religion, had fled to the bosom of Him who pardons all to those who repent. The priest resumed his place by him, and, with tears in his eyes, prayed, on his knees, for the departed soul of the unfortunate carabineer.

Go where you will, through all the miseries of this life, and you will find that everywhere the consoling angel of God, the father of the poor and friendless, is the priest of the Catholic Church. He labors day and night, without boasting, without praise, and often without any other reward, in this life, than contempt and ingratitude. If a dangerous disease breaks out in the parish, the priest does not abandon the post of danger. The Catholic priest is no coward, the Catholic priest is no hireling. Devoted and fearless, he remains to encourage his flock, to give them the last sacraments, and, if need be, even to die wit h them.

A poor man is dying in his wretched hovel. In the midst of the winter's night the priest hears a knock at his door; he is told that one of his flocks requires his assistance. The bleak winter wind howls around him, the chilling rain beats pitilessly in his face, yet he hurries on; there is a soul to save, there is a soul to aid in its fearful death-struggle: that makes him forget everything else. At last, he enters the house of death; he enters the sick man's room, though he knows that the very air of that room is loaded with pestilence. He receives the last whisper of the dying man; he breathes into his ear the sweet words of pardon and of peace. He bends diver the sick man's infected body and breathes the tainted breath from his imprisoned lips. The priest is willing to risk his own life, provided he can save the soul of his fellowman.

During the Crimean War, the cholera raged in the division of Herbillon. The soldiers became restless; they looked gloomy, and spoke despondingly, because the victims were many, and it was not the kind of death a soldier likes. What troubled the soldiers most, was the prevailing thought tha tthe plague was communicated by contact: and there was great dejection in camp. "What shall we do, Monsieur l'Abbe?" said the general to Father Parabere. "Those boys look as if they were frightened." "Oh, it is necessary to let that fear know that it has to attack Frenchmen and Christians! Leave it to me, general." And the dauntless priest walked straight to the very quarters where the pest raged most furiously. A poor soldier was in the last convulsions, and in the throes of his agony. The heroic priest had still time left to console and to absolve him, and then he closed his eyes. Then he called all the comrades of the dead man around his couch, and endeavored to persuade them that the scourge was not contagious; but as some of them shook their heads, he added, "You will not believe me today, you shall tomorrow." And just think of it, the brave priest lies down on the same couch with the man dead of cholera and prepares himself to pass the night with that novel bedfellow! Many hours passed away, and Pere Parabere, who certainly had worked enough during the day to need rest, did not quit his post until he was called to prepare another man for death. On the morrow, the whole camp had heard of it, and the soldiers, recovering from their fear, said to one another, "There's a man who has no fear!"

It is only a few years ago that a young Irish priest, then in the first year of his mission in this country, received what to him was literally the death-summons. He was lying ill in bed when the "sick call" reached his house, the pastor of the district being absent. The poor young priest did not hesitate a moment: no matter what the consequence to himself might be, the Catholic should not be without the consolations of religion. To the dismay of those who knew of his intention, and who remonstrated in vain against what to them appeared to be an act of madness, he started on his journey, a distance of thirty-six miles, which he accomplished on foot, in the midst of incessant rain. Ah, who can tell how often he paused involuntarily on that terrible march, or how he reeled and staggered as he approached its termination? Scarcely had he reached the sick man's bed, and performed the functions of the ministry, when he was conscious of his own approaching death; and there being no brother priest to minister to him in his last hour, he administered the viaticum to himself, and instantly sank on the floor, a corpse.

How often does not the priest risk his health, his honor, his life, and even his immortal soul, to help a poor dying sinner! How often is not the priest found on the battlefield, whilst the bullets are whistling, and the shells are shrieking around him! How often is he not found on his knees beside the dying soldier, hearing his last confession, and whispering into his ear the sweet words of pardon and peace! How often must not the priest visit the plague-stricken in the hospitals, and in the wretched hovels of the poor! How often must he not remain, even for hours, in a closed room, beside those infected with the most loathsome diseases! When all else, when friends and relatives, when the nearest and dearest have abandoned the poor dying wretch, then it is that only the priest of God can be found to assist him in his last and fearful struggle.

Whilst St. Charles Borromeo was Bishop of Milan, there broke out a fierce plague in that city. The priests of the city generously offered their services. They entered the houses of the plague-stricken, they heard their confessions, and administered to them the last sacraments. Neither the loathsome disease, nor the fear of certain death, could appall them, and they all soon fell victims to their zeal. Death swept them away, but their places were filled by other generous priests, who hastened from the neighboring towns, and, in a short time, one thousand eight hundred priests fell victims to their charity.

And not in Italy alone, in every clime beneath the sun, the Catholic priest has proved the earnestness of his charity, by the generous sacrifice of his life. I need only mention the sufferings and heroism of the Catholic priests of Ireland, during the long and bloody persecutions that have afflicted that ill-fated country. The Catholic priests of Ireland were outlawed; they were commanded to quit the country; they were hunted down like wolves. But, for all that, they did not abandon their poor suffering children. They laid aside their rich vestments, they laid aside their priestly dress, and disguised themselves in the poorest and most humble attire. Their churches were burned down and desecrated; but then the cabins of their persecuted countrymen were opened to them. And the Catholic priest shared in the poverty and the sorrows of his poor children. He followed them into the forest; he descended with them into the caves. Often in some lonely hut, in the midst of a dreary bog, or amid the wild fastnesses of the rugged mountains, the priest could be found kneeling at the bedside of a poor dying father or mother, whilst pale and starving children were weeping around. There you could find the Catholic priest hearing the last confession of that poor soul, aiding her in her death-struggle, and reciting the touching prayers of the Church, by the dim flickering of a poor rushlight. The Catholic priest did not abandon his poor, persecuted flock, even though he knew that a price was set on his head, though he knew that spies and informers were in search of him, though he knew that well-trained bloodhounds were sent out to track him. The Catholic priest did not forsake his children, though he knew that if he were taken the rack and the gibbet awaited him. He suffered not only poverty and sorrows with his poor flock, but he often underwent the cruelest death; for, whenever a priest was found in the country, the tender mercy of the tyrant had decreed that he was to be hanged, drawn and quartered.

Would to God I could take you to the Martyr's Room in Paris, where priests, loving their God and their neighbors, are incessantly preparing themselves to go to preach the Gospel, suffer and die for the faith, among the Pagans! Would to God you could see there that sacred army, filled with generous soldiers of Jesus Christ, who aspire to the pacific conquest of infidel realms: who burn with the hopes of shedding their blood on the battlefields of faith, sacrifice, and martyrdom; who very often attain, after a life of labors, toils, and torments, the ensanguined crown, which has been the goal of their life-long aspirations!

When they have attained it, when their heads have fallen under a Pagan's sword, their vestments, their hallowed bones, the instruments of their martyrdom, are reverently gathered by the Christians of the lands where they have been martyred and sent to Paris; and the hall where all these precious relics are gathered is called the Martyr's Room. The sight alone of this sanctuary, fresh with the blood of those lovers of Jesus Christ, is the most eloquent of sermons on the priest's charity toward the people. Bones and skeletons, and skulls of martyred priests, enclosed in glass cases; instruments of martyrdom; paintings representing insufferable torments; iron chains which tortured the limbs of the confessors of faith; ropes which strangled them; crucifixes crimsoned with the blood of those who impressed on them their last kiss of love; garments, ensanguined linen:—oh! what a sight! Great God, what a lesson!

Here a huge cangue, which rested for six long months on the shoulders of Bishop Borie; there a mat clogged with the blood of John Baptist Cornay, who upon it was beheaded and quartered, like the animal that is butchered. Nearby, a painting describing the horrible torment of the blessed Marchant, whom the executioners chopped all alive, from head to foot, until he died of suffering and exhaustion; everywhere, in every corner, the image of the good priest dying for the love of God and of his brethren, and of the fiend in human shape crucifying, with an indefatigable hatred, our Lord Jesus Christ in the person of his priests.

If you wish to know what the Catholic priest has done, go ask the winds, that have heard his sighs and his prayers; ask the earth, that has drunk in his tears and his blood; go ask the ocean, that has witnessed his death struggle, whilst speeding on an errand of mercy! Go to the dreary shores of the icy North, go to the burning sands of the distant South, and the bleached and scattered bones of the Catholic priest will tell you how earnestly he has labored for the welfare of his fellowmen.

If the many happy souls that have died in the arms, died with the blessing, of the priest, could appear before you at this moment, they would describe to you, in glowing language, the great benefits they have derived from the Catholic priest. They would say to you: "We were weak and helpless, but the consoling words of the priest gave us strength. We trembled at the thought of God's judgments, but the blessing and absolution of the priest gave us a supernatural courage. We were tormented by the assaults of the devil, but the power of the priest put the Evil One to flight. We were heartbroken at the thought of bidding a long farewell to wife and children, to the nearest and dearest, but the priest turned our weeping eyes toward a happier home, where there is no parting, no weeping, no mourning, anymore! And even when our soul had left the body, when our friends were shedding fruitless tears over the cold corpse, even then the priest of God still followed us with his prayers; he commended us to the mercy of God; he called upon the angels and saints to come to our aid, to present us before the throne of God. Ah, now we understand, indeed, that whosesoever sins the priest forgives on earth, they are truly forgiven them in heaven."

The priest has enemies. He knows it, but he does not complain. The world, too, hated and persecuted his divine Master. But the priest opens his lips only to pray for them; he raises his hand only to bless them. He remembers the words of Jesus: "I say to you, love your enemies, do good to those that hate you, bless those that curse you, and pray for those that persecute and calumniate you;" and, like his divine Master, the priest says: "Father, forgive them."

During the French Revolution, a wicked minister who had often dyed his hands in the blood of priests, fell dangerously ill. He had sworn that no priest should ever set his foot in his house, and that, if any dared to enter, he should never leave it alive. A priest heard of his illness; he heard, too, of the impious vow he had made. But he heeded it not. The good shepherd must be ready to lay down his life for his sheep. As soon as this wicked monster saw the priest standing before him, he flew into a rage: "What!" cried he, "a priest in my house! Bring me my pistols." Then the dying ruffian raised his brawny arm, and shook it threateningly at the priest. "See!" he cried, with a horrible oath, "this arm has murdered twelve of such as you."

"Not so, my good friend," answered the priest, calmly, "you murdered only eleven. The twelfth now stands before you." Then baring his breast, he said: "See here, on my breast, the marks of your fury! See here the scars that your hand has made! God has preserved my life, that I might save your soul." With these words the priest threw his arms around the neck of the dying murderer, and, with tears in his eyes, conjured him, by the precious blood of Jesus Christ, to have pity on his poor soul, and make his peace with God.

Such is the Catholic priest. I tell the truth when I say that he is indeed an angel of God, with the heart of a man; and this angel of the Lord is found in the Roman Catholic Church alone.

O glorious Church of Rome! whence Peter will forever strengthen his brethren! In thee there is neither Greek, nor Barbarian, nor Scythian, nor Jew, nor Gentile; in thy bosom all are as one people. Thou art the mighty tree which has been planted by the hand of Jesus Christ. Every branch which is separated from that tree fades, withers, dies, and is thrown into the fire. Thou art a most tender mother. Whence is it that thy divine authority should give such vain offence to so many unnatural children, make them rise up against thee, and see in thee but a step-mother? Thou art the great city of refuge. In thee alone are found true comfort, strength, and peace of heart. Out of thee there is nothing but anguish and black despair.

In this Church, where dwells the hidden God of love,
The good, and pure, and true die never;
On high they reign with God forever!

God speed the day when all division in religion shall end! God speed the hour when all men shall be united in this one, true, enduring fold; when the scepter of the Roman Catholic Church shall be extended benignly over an obedient and rejoicing world; and when all, upon being asked, "What do we believe when we say, I believe the holy Catholic Church?" will unanimously answer: "We believe that the holy Catholic Church alone is the true Church of Christ; that she is infallible in her teaching, and endless in her duration; and that out of the Catholic Church there is no salvation"!

A WORD TO EVERY CATHOLIC

HOLY Scripture tells us that, when the holy man Tobias considered the great benefits which God had bestowed upon his family through the angel Raphael, he was seized with fear: he was at a loss how to express his gratitude; he and his family fell prostrate upon their faces for three hours, thanking and blessing the Lord. He called his son Tobias, and said to him: "What can we give to this holy man that is come with thee?" And the young Tobias said to his father: "Father, what wages shall we give him, or what can be worthy of his benefits? He conducted me, and brought me safe again; he received the money of Gabelus, he caused me to have my wife, and he chased from her the evil spirit; he gave joy to her parents, myself he delivered from being devoured by the fish; thee also he hath made to see the light of heaven, and we are filled with all good things through him. What can we give him sufficient for these things? But I beseech thee, my father, to desire him that he would vouchsafe to accept of half of all the things that have been brought." (Tobias, xii.) It is thus that this holy family showed themselves thankful to God and his holy angel for the divine blessings.

Now you have seen that the priest is, for you, the true angel of God; you have seen that his dignity is far more sublime than that of the

angel Raphael; you have seen that the priest's powers far surpass those
of all the angels of heaven; that his offices are of greater importance
to you than those of the angels: that the benefits which God bestows
upon you, through the hands of the priest, far surpass those which
he bestows through his holy angels; you have seen that the Catholic
priest lives not for himself, but exclusively for you; that he is invested
with the most extraordinary powers, not for his benefit, but for yours;
in a word, you have seen that God has given you, in the priest, all
the goods and blessings of heaven and earth. What fitting thanks
can you, then, offer to the Almighty? Ah, if the Lord had only once
shown you but one single mark of affection, even then you would be
under infinite obligations to him, and he would deserve an infinite
thanksgiving from you inasmuch as that affection is the gift and favor
of an infinite God. But since you daily receive, through the priest,
blessings of God, infinite in number and greatness, what should then
be your thanksgivings to God and his angel, the priest? With Tobias
you should say: "What shall we give to this holy man? What can be
worthy of his benefits?" Were you, in imitation of Tobias, to offer
to God and his priest one-half of all your goods, it would be a poor
return for the divine blessings. Believe me, you will never be able, in
this world, fully to understand what God has given to you in the priest,
and what you should be to the priest; you will understand it only in
the world to come. But let me beseech you to believe, at least, what you
cannot understand. And if you live up to this belief, you will listen to
our Lord when he speaks of the priest, and says: "He that receiveth you
receiveth me; and he that receiveth me receiveth him that sent me."
(Matthew x, 41.) Our divine Savior spoke these words to his apostles,
and to all his priests in general, to encourage them in establishing on
earth his kingdom, the Catholic Church. You know very well that,
to establish, and keep established, the holy Church, the priests must

announce the Gospel truths; they have to administer the sacraments. But this is not enough: they have also to build churches, or keep the old ones, and everything that belongs to them, in good condition and repair; they must erect and to support Catholic schools, hospitals, and orphan asylums. They are the ministers of God, and, as such, they are charged with the honor of his worship, and the care of his sacred temples. They are, moreover, the almoners of the poor, and the fathers of the needy. How, think you, can poor priests meet all the expenses that they must necessarily incur in the exercise of the sacred ministry? Only put yourselves a day or two in the place of your priests; take care of all the poor of the place; assist all the needy that come to your door, or that modestly hide their poverty from everyone but the priest of God. Try to support Catholic schools, colleges, hospitals, orphan asylums. Build new churches or keep old ones in good condition. Do all this, and more, and you will find out what the difficulties and crosses, the troubles and hardships, of the priests are in this country. You will find out that it requires heroic virtue, angelic patience, and superhuman courage in the priests, to comply with their duties toward God and men.

Jesus Christ knew full well all the difficulties which his poor priests had to encounter. But he encourages them; he says to them: "He that receiveth you receiveth me; and he that receiveth me receiveth him that sent me. He that receiveth a prophet" (a priest) "shall receive the reward of a prophet" (of a priest). Jesus Christ made the salvation of the people dependent on the priest, and he made, also, the priest dependent on the people for his support, and other expenses which he must incur in the exercise of the sacred ministry. It is by this mutual dependence that our divine Savior keeps the priests united with the people. The devil, the cursed spirit of discord, has often tried to break up this sacred union between Catholic nations and their clergy. He has succeeded in many countries by means of Protestant governments, but he never could succeed in one country, —in the country of the glorious St. Patrick, in Ireland. There the government of England offered, some years ago, to support the Catholic clergy. Had this offer been accepted, the Catholic priests of Ireland would have become dependent on the English government; and that close union and warm love, that deep-rooted respect and esteem, which, for so many centuries, have existed between the Irish Catholics and their priests, would soon have fallen a prey to the devilish trick of the government. But, thanks be to God, and to the foresight and wisdom of the Irish clergy! the devil and his colleague, the English government, met, in this instance, as in many others, with a cold reception— with a flat refusal.

Jesus Christ has given to his priests ever so many reasons to keep up mutual love between themselves and the people. Priests, no doubt, will do all in their power to establish and to preserve this love. But Jesus Christ wishes also that the people should preserve this mutual love between themselves and the clergy. To obtain this object, they are commanded to support and assist the clergy; but in order to make them observe this commandment joyfully, Jesus Christ holds out to the people a most powerful inducement. He says to every Catholic: "If you receive my priest, you receive me; and by receiving me, you receive my heavenly Father?' In other words, Jesus Christ says that, by supporting and assisting the priests, you support and assist your divine Savior himself, who looks upon all the difficulties of his priests as his own, because they are his representatives on earth.

Moreover, to make Catholics cling to their priests, and keep them closely united with them, Jesus Christ promises them an immense reward. He says: "He that receiveth a prophet" (a priest) "shall receive the reward of a prophet." Our divine Savior has attached great blessings to the charity which is shown to the least of his brethren on earth: "Amen I say to you, as long as you did it to one of these, my least brethren, you did it to me." (Matthew xxv, 40.) By saying, "To the least of these, my brethren," Jesus Christ gives us to understand that there is another class of his brethren who are great in his sight, and whom he loves most tenderly. Now, if God bestows such great blessings upon those who are charitable to the least of the brethren of Jesus Christ, how much more abundantly will he not bestow his blessings upon those who are charitable to his great friends! The Holy Ghost calls our particular attention to this great truth when he says, in holy Scripture: "If thou do good, know to whom thou does it, and there shall be much thanks for thy good deeds. Do good to the just, and thou shalt find great recompense; and if not of him, assuredly of the Lord." (Ecclus. xii, 1, 2.) To the just, especially to those who are eminently just, may be applied what the angel of the Lord said of John the Baptist, namely, that "he was great before God." (Luke i, 15.) The reason of this is, because Jesus Christ lives in the just by his grace: "I live, now not I," says St. Paul, "but Christ lives in me." (Galatians ii, 20.) Hence, whatever is given to a just man, is given to Christ himself in a more special manner. To show this in reality, Christ has often appeared in the form and clothing of a poor man, and as such begged and received alms. This happened to John the Deacon, as is related in his life by St. Gregory. The same saint relates also (Homily 39, in Evang.) that Jesus Christ, in the form of a leper, appeared to a certain charitable monk, named Martyrius, who carried him on his shoulders. The same happened to St. Christopher, and also to St. Martin, Bishop of Tours. When St. Martin was still a soldier, and receiving instruction for admission into the Catholic Church, he gave one-half of his mantle to a poor man; the following night Jesus Christ appeared to him, wearing this mantle, and said to the angels who surrounded him: "Behold! this is Martin who gave me this mantle!"

Once St. Catharine of Sienna gave to a poor beggar the silver cross she wore, having nothing else about her to give. During the night Christ appeared to her, and said that, on the day of judgment, he would show that cross to the whole world in proof of her charity. God, then, rewards liberally those who are charitable to the least of his brethren; but he rewards far more liberally all those who are charitable to his friends,—to the just: "He that receives a just man," says Jesus Christ, "in the name of a just man (that is, because he is a just man, a friend of God), shall receive the reward of a just man."

But what will be the reward of all those who liberally and joyfully support and aid the priests, —the ministers and true representatives of God, —through whose ministry men are made just and holy? To understand this, I must make here a very important remark, to which I call your special attention, namely: that there are degrees in this welldoing. The more just a man is, both for himself and others; the more souls he leads to justice, to holiness of life, the greater will be his reward, and consequently the greater, also, will be the reward of him who assists such a just man: "They that instruct many to justice, shall shine as stars for all eternity?7 (Daniel xii, 3.) To whom can these words of holy Scripture be applied more truly than to fervent pastors of souls and missionary priests? They devote their whole life to the salvation of souls. Now, there is nothing more pleasing in the sight of God than laboring for the salvation of souls: "We cannot offer any sacrifice to God," says St. Gregory, "which is equal to that of the zeal for the salvation of souls." "This zeal and labor for the salvation of men," says St. John Chrysostom, "is of so great a merit before God, that to give up all our goods to the poor, or to spend our whole life in the exercise of all sorts of austerities, cannot equal the merit of this labor. This merit of laboring in the vineyard of the Lord is something far greater than the working of miracles. To be employed in this blessed labor is even more pleasing to the Divine Majesty than to suffer martyrdom." If, then, in the opinion of the Fathers of the Church, and of all the saints, there can be no greater honor and no greater merit than that of working for the salvation of souls, we must also say that there can be no work of corporal mercy more honorable and more meritorious than that of giving charitable aid to the pastors of souls, to missionary priests, and to persons consecrated to God. To such as give this aid may be applied the words of the prophet: "They shall shine as stars for all eternity." "The charity which you bestow," says Aristotle (Ethic., lib. i, c. 3), "will be so much the more divine, the more it tends to the common welfare." But what kind of charity is tending more to the common welfare than that which is bestowed upon such apostolic laborers as spend their life exclusively in laboring for the salvation of souls? Now this charity is divine in a most eminent degree, and consequently it makes all those divine who bestow it. They shall, without doubt, shine as the stars, nay, even as the sun, throughout all eternity: "Then the just shall shine as the sun in the kingdom of their Father" (Matthew xiii, 43); and this glory and happiness of theirs in heaven will be in proportion to the zeal and fervor with which they have continued to furnish charitable aid to Jesus Christ in the persons of the ministers of the holy Catholic Church: "He that receives a prophet, shall have the reward of a prophet." He who receives a prophet, says our Lord, that is, he who gives charitable aid to a priest, will receive the reward of a priest. The reason of this is, because, by his charitable aid, he contributes toward the spreading of the Gospel; and therefore, as he thus shares in the labor and in the merits of the Gospel, he must also share in the reward promised to the true minister of God. Should you aid a man in performing sinful actions, you would become accessory to his sins. So, in like manner, by assisting the priests of God in performing good works for the salvation and sanctification of souls, you share in all their good works —in their merits and in their rewards. "A willow-tree," says St. Gregory, "bears no fruit; but supporting, as it does, the vine together with its grapes, it makes these its own, by sustaining what is not its own." (Homily 20, in Evang.) In like manner, he who supports the priest makes his own all those good works which are performed by the priest; that is to say, he preaches through the priest, he hears confessions through him, he converts sinners through him, he consoles the sick through him, he encourages the desperate through him, he confirms the just in their good resolutions through him; in a word, he sanctifies the world through the priest, and is, through him, the cause that the most precious blood of Jesus Christ is not shed in vain; and he gladdens, through him, the angels and saints in heaven, and especially the Sacred Hearts of Jesus Christ and the Blessed Virgin Mary.

On this account, St. Ignatius, in his Epistle to the Smyrnians, rightly concludes, from the above sentence of Christ on the last day, that he who honors a prisoner of Christ will receive the reward of the martyrs; because by honoring such a prisoner, he encourages him to suffer martyrdom. For this reason, many Christians formerly merited the grace of martyrdom, because they encouraged, fed, served, and buried the martyrs. In like manner, we lawfully infer, from the above sentence of Christ, that those who receive and aid the priests of the Church, the pastors of souls, will receive the reward of pastors of souls, on condition, however, that the assistance which they give is offered with a cheerful heart. When God, in his bounty, vouchsafes to call you to cooperate in any of his works, he does not employ soldiers, or tax gatherers, or constables, to collect the impost—he accepts from you only a voluntary assistance. The Master of the universe repudiates constraint, for he is the God of free souls; he does not consent to receive anything which is not spontaneous and offered with a cheerful heart.

To conclude. The Catholic priest is the priest of the Lord of heaven and earth: it is impossible for you to conceive a higher dignity. The Catholic priest is the plenipotentiary of God: it is impossible for you to conceive a greater power. The Catholic priest is the minister of God: it is impossible for you to conceive an office more sublime and more important. The Catholic priest is the representative of God: it is impossible for you to conceive a higher commission. The Catholic priest is the vicegerent of God: it is impossible for you to conceive a higher merit. The Catholic priest is the treasurer of God: it is impossible for you to conceive a greater benefactor of mankind, a man worthier of your love and veneration, of your charity and liberality.

May you, therefore, always receive the priest as the Galatians received St. Paul the Apostle: "You despised me not," writes this great apostle to the Galatians, "you did not reject me, but you received me as an angel of God, even as Christ Jesus. I bear you witness that, if it could be done, you would have plucked out your own eyes, and would have given them to me." (Galatians iv, 14, 15.)